LAW&COVENANT

LAW&COVENANT

RONALD L. DART

Wasteland Press
Shelbyville, KY USA
www.wastelandpress.net

Law & Covenant
By Ronald L. Dart

First Printing – June 2007
ISBN13: 978-1-60047-104-9
ISBN10: 1-60047-104-8

Unless otherwise indicated, All Scripture citations are the King James
Version, paraphrased, others as indicated in the text:

NASB: Scripture quotations taken from the New American Standard
Bible®, Copyright © 1960, 1962, 1963, 1968, 1971, 1972, 1973,
1975, 1977, 1995 by The Lockman Foundation. Used by permission.
(www.Lockman.org)

NIV: Scripture taken from the HOLY BIBLE, NEW
INTERNATIONAL VERSION®. Copyright © 1973, 1978, 1984
International Bible Society. Used by permission of Zondervan. All
rights reserved.

Printed in the U.S.A.

Table of Contents

Prologue

"Let not the wise man boast of his wisdom
or the strong man boast of his strength
or the rich man boast of his riches,
but let him who boasts boast about this:
that he understands and knows me,
that I am the LORD, *who exercises kindness,*
justice and righteousness on earth,
for in these I delight," declares the LORD
(Jeremiah 9:23-24 NIV).

This is the third book I have opened with that Scripture.[1] I didn't start out with it in mind, but it seems to have made itself my ongoing theme through all three books. It calls on me to understand that the Creator is not only intelligent and powerful (as a deist might believe), but that he also possesses a character that can be known and understood. Moreover, he has a name. He is to be known as Jehovah, "who exercises lovingkindness, judgment and righteousness here on earth" (Jeremiah 9:24 KJV).

This intensely personal God declares that the pursuit of understanding him, of knowing him, is a glorious pursuit, a rewarding pursuit: "For he that comes to God must believe that he is, and that he rewards them that diligently seek him" (Hebrews 11:6).

I started this book with the simple idea of right and wrong. The Hebrew word for righteousness is *tsedaqah,* and is derived from a verb that means, simply, to be right or to do right. Thus it is a glory

---

1. The first book was *The Lonely God,* and the second was *The Thread, God's Appointments with History.*

1

for a man to come to understand that God is right and that what he does is right. The inevitable question that arises next is, "What is right?" What makes one action right and another wrong? Elsewhere, a psalmist answers the question: "May my tongue sing of your word, for all your commands are righteous" (Psalm 119:172 NIV). It is thus the Law of God that defines right and wrong for man.

But it seems to me that man has made a fundamental error in understanding that law. We tend to think of laws as regulatory and absolute because that is the way we encounter law in our world. Not so long ago, in a previous energy crisis, speed limits across the the United States were arbitrarily reduced from 70 to 55 miles per hour. The rationale was that gas goes further at 55 MPH than it does at 70. It also goes further at 40 MPH, but no one believed the public would live with that. No one liked 55 very much either, because it increased time on the road. So the law was repealed. Every law that Congress passes is arbitrary and can be repealed.

This is what we are used to, so it is only natural to assume that the Law of God is likewise regulatory and at least somewhat arbitrary. One assumes that the sovereign God said, "Let's consider what laws we can hand down for man." Then he proceeded to give a set of laws to Moses. This is what I call "the arbitrary God theory." And it follows as day follows night if you accept the idea that the Old Testament Law was abolished in Christ. If the law could be abolished, then it might not have been necessary in the first place. Where Congress is concerned, they are human. They make mistakes. They try to regulate things that can't be regulated and end up having to repeal some of the laws they pass. When Congress repeals a law, it is a tacit admission that the law was a mistake.[1]

But God does not make mistakes. Thus the law cannot be arbitrary. And on the heels of this comes a realization: If the law is not arbitrary, then perhaps it is not entirely regulatory either. This is not to say that the law cannot be used to regulate. It is merely to say that there is an underlying reality of the law that must be grasped before attempting to regulate man's behavior.

Here is a short, contrasting idea about the law that we can lay out on the examining table: The law is not regulatory, it is

---

1. The constitutional amendment prohibiting alcohol comes to mind.

revelatory. It is a revelation of the way things are. The law does not create right and wrong. It reveals what is right and what is wrong. The law says, "You shall not steal." Stealing did not become wrong when the Ten Commandments were written on stone by the finger of God. Stealing was wrong from the day when there was a man who could take things that were not his to take. The law is what it is because to be otherwise would be wrong. And for God to know that it is wrong and to fail to tell us would be, well, wrong.[1]

Now, what lies beyond understanding and knowing God? There we find a relationship with God, a covenant. The archetype of all covenants in the Bible is the covenant God made with a man named Abraham. Later, God would make a covenant with a nation of people, Israel. Still later, Jesus would make a New Covenant with his disciples.[2]

You will not be reading dogma here. The subject is far too important for that. When you are trying to know and understand God, you can't afford to be locked into one way of looking at things. God has taken pains to reveal himself in so many ways. Our problem is that we are too often inattentive to what he has had to say.

Years ago, in a moment of personal crisis, something truly profound dawned on me. I realized that I had absolutely nothing to fear from the truth. Truth is glorious. It is exciting. And it can set you free. It would be a shame to let fear keep us from pursuing truth wherever it leads.

In the pages that follow, we will follow these ideas and see where they take us. We may not follow a straight line, because that is not always the way understanding comes. Abraham did not know what Moses came to know. And neither of them knew what Jesus revealed to his disciples.[3] And then there was Paul.

Take your time while you read this book. There will be times when you need to lay it down and stare into space for a while. Some ideas will require that you sleep on them. It is not my purpose to tell you what to believe. Rather, I want to walk alongside you and talk about things I am coming to see.

---

1. That there would later come a regulatory law was inevitable. The need for that came as soon as a community was created. More on that later.

2. See Luke 22:20.

3. 1 Peter 1:10-12.

I will delight myself in thy statutes:
I will not forget thy word.
Deal bountifully with thy servant,
that I may live, and keep thy word.
Open my eyes, that I may behold
wondrous things out of thy law
(Psalm 119:16-18).

Some notes: The chapters of this book are derived, in some measure, from sermons, radio programs, and essays. Consequently, there may be some repetition of themes. Also, from long habit, I read the King James Version, but paraphrase it as I go, changing "thee" to "you," etc. I have frequently followed that practice in this book. Other translations are designated by abbreviations as noted on the copyright page. I encourage you to keep your own Bible handy so you can read the context of citations.

On the matter of the divine name, *YHWH*, in Hebrew is usually rendered in small caps, LORD, in most English versions. Written Hebrew has no vowels, thus it is not certain how the name should be pronounced. The consensus is *Yahweh*, but I lean toward the older *Jehovah*, because of long familiarity. In most cases, "LORD" is clear enough, but there are instances where the passage makes much more sense if we recognize that our LORD has a name. In Hebrew, names have meaning, and the translation of *Jehovah* is "I am."

My thanks to Mickie Ranaldo and Allie Dart for their indispensable assistance in editing and manuscript preparation.

1

The Jigsaw Principle

Open my eyes that I may see wonderful things in your law.
I am a stranger on earth; do not hide your commands from me.
My soul is consumed with longing for your laws at all times.[1]

Few things are more chaotic, more confused, than a 1000 piece jigsaw puzzle coming out of the box. The pieces lie there in a heap with no apparent relationship between them. Some pieces are upside down, others are right side up, their colors and designs vary; and they are all cut out of the picture with shapes that look like they might fit together. No two pieces are exactly the same. If you have a good puzzle and you have the patience, you can put it together with the picture face down.

Most of us adopt a system to approach a puzzle like that. First, we get all the pieces right side up. Then we sort them roughly by colors. While we are doing that, we look for edges and corners. The corners and edges help us get the scope of the puzzle and establish boundaries. After that, we look for patterns and shapes, and we begin to piece the puzzle together.

Why do we do it this way? Well, it's logical. But what does it mean to say that a system is logical? Consider this. Every human child born into the world arrives with a built-in system of logic. We don't have to be taught it, because it is hardwired into us. The brain itself is "wired" according to a logical system, and the mind operates on that system. So we start out in life with a mind that is

---

1. Psalm 119:18-20 NIV.

5

logical. It is untrained, but the logical system gives it enormous potential for development.

The Apostle Paul didn't use the language of logic, but he came to the same conclusion. Speaking of a man's ability to know right from wrong, he said:

> Indeed, when Gentiles, who do not have the law, do by nature things required by the law, they are a law for themselves, even though they do not have the law, since they show that the requirements of the law are written on their hearts, their consciences also bearing witness, and their thoughts now accusing, now even defending them (Romans 2:14-15 NIV).

I think this is Paul's way of saying that the Gentiles were born hardwired to the logic of the law. C. S. Lewis came to a similar conclusion in what he called the Law of Nature. By that, he did not mean laws like gravity or thermodynamics, but rather the Law of *Human* Nature. Unlike physical laws, this is a law we can break, and do. This is from his classic, *Mere Christianity*:

> I do not succeed in keeping the Law of Nature very well, and the moment anyone tells me I'm not keeping it, there starts up in my mind a string of excuses as long as your arm. The question at the moment is not whether they are good excuses. The point is that they are one more proof of how deeply, whether we like it or not, we believe in the Law of Nature. If we do not believe in decent behavior, why should we be so anxious to make excuses for not having behaved decently? [1]

I'm not sure whether Lewis drew his idea from Paul or came up with it independently. I think it may have arisen from the logical structure of the argument he was advancing, because he doesn't approach Christianity, per se, until later in the book. His point, though, is clear. The human mind does operate according to a system of internal logic.[2]

---

1. C. S. Lewis, *Mere Christianity*, (MacMillan, 1952), 20.
2. Here is a question for the philosophers among us to ponder. Was this system a manifestation

God gave man a system of logic out of which language grows, so he could communicate with man and be understood. It is this underlying principle which makes translation possible, and which has enabled the translations of ancient documents even though they are written in languages no longer in use.

It is remarkable that man, in the absence of revelation, can come to a pretty good estimation of right and wrong. But the mind alone won't get you all the way. Everyone knows there is a difference between right and wrong, but they often fall down sorting out which is which. Everyone knows that a child needs exercise. Fortunately, children are hardwired at birth with a desire to play, and that desire gets them out of doors, up trees, exploring caves and streams. (Someone felt sure that kids all have guardian angels, for if they didn't, none of them would ever reach adulthood.) It is not so certain that everyone understands that a child's mind and spirit need exercise as well as his body. The author of Hebrews drew an analogy to this:

> For when for the time you ought to be teachers, you have need that one teach you again the first principles of the oracles of God; and are become such as have need of milk, and not of strong meat. For every one that uses milk is unskillful in the word of righteousness: for he is a babe. But strong meat belongs to them who are of full age, even those who by reason of use *have their senses exercised to discern both good and evil* (Hebrews 5:12-14).

Discerning good and evil is made possible by the logical design of the human mind. But if the senses aren't exercised, the mind, like the body, grows flabby and indolent.

Also wired into the human mind is an insatiable thirst for meaning, so I often find myself looking up the meaning of the Greek and Hebrew words of the Bible. In my search, I often gain insight, and sometimes amusement. The Greek word for senses in the passage above, *aistheterion* (from which we derive the word "aesthetic"), denotes the organs of perception—all of them. But the

---

of the Law of God, or was the system created logically and then the law written to reveal the system?

word for "exercise," *gumnazo*,[1] means "to practice naked." The Greeks always exercised and competed in the nude. But the author is talking about mental pushups, spiritual weight lifting, and for all we know, he may have had in mind an oblique reference to being naked before God.

So, I take it that, just as we are born with bones, nerves, muscle and tissue, and just as we have to exercise to build them up to peak performance, so also we are born with a mind that must be exercised for peak performance. So much more is known today about the way a child develops. We've known for a long time that there is a connection between the attention a child gets in the earliest years and the overall development of intelligence. What we are only now learning is how it works, and what we are learning is fascinating. I came upon this item recently:

> To understand the link between early emotional bonding and brain development, it helps to know what's going on in your baby's brain. You've heard that a baby's brain grows most rapidly during the first three years of life. During the first year, brain cells are busy making millions of connections. The connections peak at about one year and, in a process called "pruning," they are eliminated if they are not used. The connections that you regularly use are the ones that you keep.[2]

That last should make every parent sit bolt upright. We have heard forever, "Use it or lose it." It is as true of the brain as it is of the body, and there sits your child with a developing brain, learning stuff at a phenomenal rate. Or not. It really depends on you.

Peter, in his first letter adopted the same analogy as Paul: "As newborn babes, desire the sincere milk of the word, that ye may grow thereby" (1 Peter 2:2). What is of special interest in this passage is that, in speaking of "the word," Peter uses the Greek, *logikos*, from which the English word "logic" is derived. It is the "pure milk" of divine logic we are after. What I take Peter and Paul

---

1. The Greek, *gumnazo*, is the root of the English "gymnasium." There is no "y" in Greek, but the pronunciation of the Greek letter, upsilon, approximates the letter "y" in English.

2. Caroline Knorr and Deirdre Wilson, "Your Child's Growing Brain," *United Parenting Publications*, February 2003.

to be saying is that we are born with a system of logic that has to be informed, developed, and trained to a higher system—a higher system that is, nevertheless, built on the same base.

So, from a biblical perspective, what do we need to do to develop that higher logic? A psalmist one day sat down to write a treatise on the subject. He organized his work alphabetically in segments to aid memorization, each section beginning with the next letter of the Hebrew alphabet. Some versions of the Bible include these titles, and that makes it easier to note the eight verse stanzas.

In this Psalm, we find all the synonyms for law, seven or eight of them in the first two sections. It is almost as though he is calling our attention to the fact that the various categories and descriptions of the law are all part of a single system. He speaks of the Law of the LORD, the Way, Testimonies, Precepts, Decrees, Statutes, Commandments, Judgments, and the Word, all in the first ten verses. And he tends, as the Psalm progresses, to use each of these words as a synonym for the whole of Divine Law. Having laid out the use of the words in the first section of the Psalm, he proceeds with the gymnastics of the mind and spirit that he uses to make his life work.

> How can a young man keep his way pure? By living according to your word. I seek you with all my heart; do not let me stray from your commands. I have hidden your word in my heart that I might not sin against you. Praise be to you, O LORD; teach me your decrees. With my lips I recount all the laws that come from your mouth. I rejoice in following your statutes as one rejoices in great riches. I meditate on your precepts and consider your ways. I delight in your decrees; I will not neglect your word (Psalm 119:9-16 NIV).

His mental pushups included concentration, attentiveness, memorization, and meditation. To hide words in the heart is to internalize. Memorization is accomplished by oral recitation, "With my lips I recount all the laws." Without internalizing the precepts, the last item becomes very hard; how can a man meditate on what he cannot remember? We have an enormous advantage in that we have the Scriptures in books we can carry with us. In those days, a shepherd camped out with his sheep had only his memory for meditation. And meditation is crucial, as we will see.

Years ago, in a series of workshops on management, the instructor challenged us to keep a time log of everything we did for one week in ten minute increments. The following week, he relaxed the requirement to 15 minute intervals, but a new wrinkle was added. He required us to spend a total of one hour in that week doing absolutely nothing but thinking. We couldn't think at the keyboard or while driving a car. At most, we were allowed to tap a pencil on the table.

That week was a turning point for me. I came to realize that, while we do think during every waking hour, we manage to keep ourselves distracted from the really important things. Sitting quietly in a chair, eyes closed, doing nothing at all, was a strange experience. But during that one hour, I mentally worked my way through the most serious problem facing me on my job and found a solution that worked. *In one hour.*

When you apply this principle to the law, some very interesting things happen. In the first place, the temptation to legalism is foreclosed. Legalism is a perspective that sees the law as an absolute requirement from God. The law is there; we have to do it. Thinking is not required or even encouraged. Who are we to second-guess God? The letter of the law controls.

But when you stop to meditate on the law, something else begins to happen. The law begins to shine a new light on your problems, your headaches, your challenges. Decisions become easier, because you now have a logical framework into which they can be placed and by which they can be judged.

If all this logic sounds too pat, too unemotional, you haven't thought about it long enough. Legalism is unemotional, pat, locked in place. Meditation opens the way to understanding. Emotions and feelings are not enough. You have to do something about those feelings, and the logic of the law keeps you from doing stupid, hurtful things. Our psalmist continues.

Do good to your servant, and I will live; I will obey your word. Open my eyes that I may see wonderful things in your law. I am a stranger on earth; do not hide your commands from me. My soul is consumed with longing for

10

your laws at all times (vv. 17-20 NIV).

The law is so much higher than most people think. It is not just so much pharisaical legalism. It is not a matter of a heavy burden to be borne. It is a matter of a man in business facing a decision that requires sound judgment and discernment. "Open my eyes that I can see this clearly," he prays. "I am consumed with longing for your law." Why? Because it is in that system of logic that the solution to his problem lies.

If the law looks like a yoke of bondage to you, then you need to look again. It makes all the difference how you *think* about it. What the psalmist sees in the law is a Divine Logic that transcends what he can see by himself. He wants to see more.

Remove from me *the way of lying*: and grant me thy law graciously. I have chosen *the way of truth*: thy judgments have I laid before me. I have stuck unto thy testimonies: O LORD, put me not to shame. I will run the way of thy commandments, when thou shalt enlarge my heart (vv. 29-32 KJV).

All this is related to the statement: "Remove from me the way of lying." Two roads lie before you. This is not a choice to be made once and then laid aside, but a road you choose to walk. One is the way of lying; the other is the way of truth. Nothing can do more damage to your judgment than walking in the way of lying.

Every child is born into the world with a built-in lie detector. It has to be trained, but the circuits are all there. As we grow up, sometimes it seems to work and sometimes it doesn't. Why is that? What makes the difference?

Well, in the first place, if you lie, you degrade your own lie detector. We also degrade our lie detectors by not listening to them. Why would anyone do such a foolish thing? To answer that question, we have to lay the Psalm aside for a moment and read something from Paul's letter to the Thessalonians. Warning about the nature of "the lawless one," he wrote this:

The coming of the lawless one will be in accordance with the work of Satan displayed in all kinds of counterfeit miracles, signs and wonders, and in every sort of evil that deceives those who are perishing. They perish because they refused to love the truth and so be saved. For this reason God sends them a powerful delusion so that they will believe the lie and so that all will be condemned who have not believed the truth but have delighted in wickedness (2 Thessalonians 2:9-12 NIV).

They perish because they refuse to love the truth. This seems a strange idea at first, but when we think about it, we know it is true. People do believe lies and even seem to prefer them. Why? For one thing, they may *want* the lie to be true. We know from experience that if we tell people what they want to hear, they are more likely to believe us—no matter the truth or error of the statement.

When Dan Rather and crew at CBS ran a story about George Bush that turned out to be based on forged documents, the whole news industry was scandalized. How on earth could the CBS fact checkers not have noticed the problem? The most common explanation at the time was that the news team wanted the story to be true and so they ran it without thoroughly checking it out. Their built-in lie detector had been compromised. But there was probably more to it than that. It fit with an established worldview,[1] a way of looking at people and events. Seeing President Bush as a shirker, a college frat boy, fit with their view of the world, so they went with it. It was a huge mistake and put a distinguished career on the rocks.

There are so many things that conspire to blind us to the truth. Our psalmist suggests that covetousness is a factor: "Incline my heart to thy testimonies, and not to covetousness" (Psalm 119:36). Greed, for money or for power, can blind a man to the truth. That is a sad commentary. But the truth takes the blinders off, and leads to real wealth in the end.

The psalmist went on to plead, "Turn my eyes away from worthless things; preserve my life according to your word" (v. 37 NIV). These two requests tie the Law of God to the ability to know what is valuable and what is not, to know what is truth and what is not. What would it be worth to always know when a man is lying?

---

1. From the German: *weltanschauung*, "a comprehensive conception or apprehension of the world especially from a specific standpoint," *Mirriam-Webster's Collegiate Dictionary*.

You can come pretty close if you just tune up your love of the truth, and the rewards for doing so are enormous.

> Do not snatch the word of truth from my mouth,
> for I have put my hope in your laws.
> I will always obey your law, for ever and ever.
> *I will walk about in freedom,*
> for I have sought out your precepts (vv. 43-45 NIV).

There is a truth of staggering proportions here. It is the connection between the "word of truth" and walking about in freedom. One of the strangest of Christian theologies is the one that considers the Law of God a "yoke of bondage." The idea derives from an idiosyncratic interpretation of an argument advanced by Paul in his letter to the Galatians. He wrote: "Stand fast therefore in the liberty wherewith Christ hath made us free, and be not entangled again with the yoke of bondage" (Galatians 5:1). Ironically, Paul spoke of not becoming entangled with something that takes away liberty and freedom. The psalmist considered the Law of God as the *guarantor* of freedom. So did Paul. Then there was James:

> For if anyone is a hearer of the word and not a doer, he is like a man who looks at his natural face in a mirror; for once he has looked at himself and gone away, he has immediately forgotten what kind of person he was. But one who looks intently at the perfect law, *the law of liberty*, and abides by it, not having become a forgetful hearer but an effectual doer, this man shall be blessed in what he does (James 1:23-25 NASB).

Some interpreters think they find an argument between Paul and James, but they are being careless. The Psalm gives us the key. Understanding of the purpose of the law is what opens the door. The Law of God is the ground and source of all freedom, of liberty. Those people will be in bondage who cannot bring themselves to live by the Law of God. Returning to the psalmist:

I am a friend to all who fear you, to all who follow your precepts. The earth is filled with your love, O LORD; teach me your decrees. Do good to your servant according to your word, O LORD. Teach me knowledge and good judgment, for I believe in your commands (Psalms 119:63-66 NIV).

Many times we have heard, "A man is known by the company he keeps." If you hang out where the truth is valued and lies are condemned, you will be where you belong. It's important to note the last phrase here: "I believe your commandments." The Commandments of God are his *Testimony*.

Before I was afflicted I went astray, but now I obey your word. You are good, and what you do is good; teach me your decrees. Though the arrogant have smeared me with lies, I keep your precepts with all my heart. Their hearts are callous and unfeeling, but I delight in your law. It was good for me to be afflicted so that I might learn your decrees (vv. 67-71).

The worst thing that can happen to us is to have life too easy. It doesn't matter very much what the affliction is. It can be physical pain. It can be failure in business. It is a rare man who engages in self-examination when everything he is doing is working just fine. Someone who had reason to know once said that the best thing that can happen to a man is to get fired somewhere in his 30s or 40s. It forces self-examination and a readjustment of a man's career and life goals. We can just get a little too comfortable, a little too risk-averse, and spend our entire lives like a cog in a machine.

Twice in my long career, I have had occasion to resign from good, well paying positions to start over. I can honestly say that both these moves were good for me, as uncomfortable as they were at the time. In my case, these occasions forced me to look long and hard at my calling, my relationship with God, and my spiritual growth (or lack thereof). It was good for me that I was afflicted. Affliction set my feet on a better path.

Oh, how I love your law! I meditate on it all day long.
Your commands make me wiser than my enemies,
for they are ever with me.
I have more insight than all my teachers,
for I meditate on your statutes.
I have more understanding than the elders,
for I obey your precepts.
I have kept my feet from every evil path
so that I might obey your word.
I have not departed from your laws,
for you yourself have taught me.
How sweet are your words to my taste,
sweeter than honey to my mouth!
I gain understanding from your precepts;
therefore I hate every wrong path (vv. 97-104 NIV).

These verses are the heart and core of this Psalm. The psalmist loves the law because it gives him an edge in life. What is it worth to be wiser than your enemies, to have more understanding than your teachers, to know things even the gray heads don't know? Why would I not love something like this, and why would I not hate anything that threatened to take it away?

Having come this far, we should begin to understand what happens to our lie detector as life proceeds. We are given the core logic at birth, and then the world goes to work eroding it, often with our consent and cooperation. The ability to recognize truth when we hear it, to spot a liar before he finishes his spiel, is worth a lot in life.

What makes the difference? The next verse answers the question: "Your word is a lamp to my feet And a light to my path" (v. 105). This is the chosen analogy. The law is not a burden we have to carry. It is not shackles around our feet and legs. It is a lamp to light our way so we don't fall down and hurt ourselves. When I hear Christians who should know better refer to this law as a "yoke of bondage," I can only shake my head in wonderment.

Your statutes are my heritage forever; they are the joy of my heart. My heart is set on keeping your decrees to the very end.

I hate double-minded men, but I love your law (vv. 111-113 NIV).

It is ironic that the two richest men in the world, Warren Buffet and Bill Gates are giving away most of their wealth. Neither of them wants their heirs to get too much money or too much power. They may not be going far enough, but that is their call. What the psalmist is saying is that he has taken the testimony of God as his heritage. It is worth far more than the billions these two men might leave behind.

The last sentence in this section is interesting: "I hate double-minded men." That doesn't sound right to me. I think what he is saying is that he hates double-mindedness, in himself or in others. Why put up with ambiguity when you can come down on the side of the right?

It is time for you to act, O LORD; your law is being broken. Because I love your commands more than gold, more than pure gold, and because I consider all your precepts right, I hate every wrong path. Your statutes are wonderful; therefore I obey them. The unfolding of your words gives light; it gives understanding to the simple. I open my mouth and pant, longing for your commands (vv. 126-131 NIV).

This is a man who will never be morally confused. He knows right from wrong with clarity. Why? Because he believes God is right. *It really is that simple.* It is striking to read his words and realize that then, as now, there were those with an anti-law philosophy. In the days of the psalmist, they could not argue that the law was nailed to the cross, but they still found a way to regard the law as void. This fellow panted for the laws of God. Some foolish ones are panting to cast them off.

Yet you are near, O LORD, and all your commands are true.
Long ago I learned from your statutes
that you established them *to last forever* (vv. 151-152).

I said earlier that every child born into the world comes with a built in baloney-detector. Baloney is slang for bologna, a large smoked sausage. In slang it means "pretentious nonsense." Why do we get sucked in by baloney? Because it appeals to our vanity, our idea that we are somehow special, that we have knowledge denied to other people. And, of course, we fall for it because we like to be stroked. It is a part of the permanent condition of man, and it led Paul to write this to Timothy:

But mark this: There will be terrible times in the last days. People will be lovers of themselves, lovers of money, boastful, proud, abusive, disobedient to their parents, ungrateful, unholy, without love, unforgiving, slanderous, without self-control, brutal, not lovers of the good, treacherous, rash, conceited, lovers of pleasure rather than lovers of God—having a form of godliness but denying its power. Have nothing to do with them. They are the kind who worm their way into homes and gain control over weak-willed women, who are loaded down with sins and are swayed by all kinds of evil desires, always learning but never able to acknowledge the truth (2 Timothy 3:1-7 NIV).

This is a truly sad commentary. Here are people who are no longer able to discern between truth and a lie. How do people get that way? Paul, on another occasion, answers:

The weapons we fight with are not the weapons of the world. On the contrary, they have divine power to demolish strongholds. We demolish arguments and every pretension that sets itself up against the knowledge of God, and we take captive every thought to make it obedient to Christ (2 Corinthians 10:4-5 NIV).

We are born with a built-in baloney detector. If it is fine tuned, it can demolish arguments and pretentious nonsense. It can save us more heartache than I can enumerate. The Law of God is the highest expression of the logic of God and man. It is the primary source of renewing and repairing the old baloney detector.

We would do well to use the jigsaw principle in studying biblical law. First get all the pieces right side up. Sort them according to the most obvious principles. Locate the boundaries, the corners, the edges, so you can get a proportion of what you are looking for. And then be patient. Don't try to make pieces fit where they don't belong. Don't throw pieces out because they don't look right. The Bible, like the puzzle, will yield to persistence and patience.

Do not be anxious about anything, but in everything, by prayer and petition, with thanksgiving, present your requests to God. And the peace of God, which transcends all understanding, will guard your hearts and your minds in Christ Jesus. Finally, brothers, whatever is true, whatever is noble, whatever is right, whatever is pure, whatever is lovely, whatever is admirable—if anything is excellent or praiseworthy—*think about such things* (Philippians 4:6-8 NIV).

2

The Purpose of Law

The first of all the commandments is, Hear, O Israel;
The LORD our God is one LORD: And thou shalt love the LORD thy
God with all thy heart, and with all thy soul, and with all thy mind,
and with all thy strength: this is the first commandment. And the
second is like, namely this, Thou shalt love thy neighbour as
thyself. There is none other commandment greater than these
(Mark 12:29-31).

You may take for granted the typesetting on the page you are reading, but in days past, it was a very long and tedious labor to set a book to type. Even after the invention of movable type it was still a hard process and prone to error. Each and every letter and space had to be set in place, batted firmly together and then locked to print pages from the set type. All that is gone now, as there is no longer a typesetting process in producing a book. With the onset of computers, the author's own manuscript provides the basis for the final product.

But imagine what a laborious job it would have been to set an entire Bible to type, and how hard it would be to get it right the first time. Naturally, those early typesetters didn't always get it right, and one example turned up in a 1631 edition of the Bible, ordered by King Charles. The Bible was pretty much correct except for the omission of one little three letter word: not. And that might not have been such a big deal if it hadn't been for where that word was supposed to be. It was in Exodus 20, in the seventh of the Ten Commandments which, in this particular edition, read: "Thou shalt commit adultery."

Some wag dubbed it "The Wicked Bible," and King Charles ordered all 1000 of them recalled and destroyed. There are still 11 copies in existence, and the mind boggles to think what they might be worth at auction.

It would be a Bible for our age, though—the age of recreational sex. And since we are talking about God and the law, it might be worth asking: Why did God outlaw recreational sex? Sex surely is fun and exciting, so why not do it? Was it, as teenagers are apt to ask their parents, because God doesn't want us to have any fun? Or are there consequences, for individuals and for society, if sex isn't kept within boundaries?

One of my first clues to this came, of all places, in a Navy VD[1] film. Watching the film, I learned that many babies went blind soon after birth because of the presence of the gonococcus bacteria in the birth canal. The mother may not have shown any symptoms, even though she had been infected. By the time I saw the film, they were putting silver nitrate on babies' eyes at birth to prevent blindness, but the film was warning about other problems.

At the time I saw the film, there were maybe six or seven significant venereal diseases. Now there are more than 50, and they are much more dangerous than what sailors called, "a dose of the clap." How dangerous? Well, you have surely heard of AIDS. Consider Africa. Over 13 million children have been orphaned in Africa from AIDS. Many of those kids now have AIDS themselves and will die of it. In Africa alone, 24.5 million have died of AIDS. Nearly four million of them were children under fifteen.

You can't solve this problem with a little silver nitrate in the eyes or a shot of penicillin in the rump. They say that the spread of AIDS in Africa is primarily from heterosexual, promiscuous sex. The same thing is going on in your country; the only difference is in the numbers. We may begin to see why God would say, "Thou shalt *not* commit adultery."

But this raises a core question. Did God create sexually transmitted disease (STD) as a trap for man, as a punishment for having too much fun? Hardly. It is more likely that STDs are an example of what can happen when viral and bacteriological strains are given indefinite life to mutate and change. Your body is

---

1. VD, Venereal Disease, what is today called STD, Sexually Transmitted Disease.

teeming with bacteria right now. (Try not to panic. Most of them are harmless and some are even good for you.) When a person has sex with another person, he or she inevitably trades some bacteria with the partner. Bacteria and viruses mutate, and in the lifetimes of a man and a woman they may change a bit. However, the strains of germs exchanged between one man and one woman won't survive the lifetime of that couple. But if we add additional people to the mix and give those strains of bacteria indefinite life, all bets are off.

I don't know if that is how STDs originated, but just take it as an analogy to what *might* have happened. What I do know for certain is this: If we could manage complete monogamy for everyone for a generation or two, we could wipe out all STDs including AIDS. So why blame God for it? It is our problem. We created it. God told us how to avoid it.

So, why did God say, "Thou shalt not commit adultery"? Perhaps, at the highest level, it's for the children. Society has a responsibility to protect children from the stupidity of adults. At another level, it's for our personal health. At still another level, it is for the health of society. No one knows yet what the final impact of AIDS will be on society on the African continent—only that it will be devastating.

So, yes, society has an interest in putting a damper on extra-marital, "recreational" sex. But society has completely lost control. We have lost control because we have lost sight of God and the law.

We begin to get the idea right from the start, when God created the basic unit of society: the family.[1] From the beginning, provision was made for the spin-off of a new family from the old. Why a family? Well it's for the children, of course. And why should we care about the children? Because a society that doesn't care for children will not survive. Moslems living in Europe today are producing ten children for every one produced by Europeans. How long do you think European culture can survive that ratio?

A culture that corrupts their children doesn't deserve to survive, and there are too many ways to corrupt children. They can be corrupted sexually. They can also be corrupted by hatred, as Palestinians are teaching their children to hate the Israelis more

---

1. See chapter 16, "The Oldest Covenant."

than they love life. Then there are the effects of divorce.

Divorce is becoming so common in our country that some 50 percent of all kids are being raised in single parent homes. These children have more difficulty in school, more behavioral problems, more negative self-concepts, more problems with peers, and more trouble getting along with their parents.

And there is no reason we should be surprised at this. Children are frightened and confused by the breakup of the family and by the separation and alienation of the two most important people in their world. They tell us that children commonly think they are the cause of the problem when a family breaks up. Sometimes, children even assume the responsibility for reconciling the problem and healing the breach, often sacrificing themselves in the process.

What is it in children that will cause a normally selfish kid to turn around and sacrifice himself to keep his parents together? What does the child know that the parents don't? Divorce can affect the mental, emotional, and physical health of a child. We've come to a terrible pass in our society when those who were to be protected by marriage are the very ones who sacrifice themselves to save it.

The examples I have cited so far speak strongly to the question of biblical law. They speak not only in terms of individual conduct, but to the concerns of society in at least minimal regulation of individual conduct—as in laws to discourage divorce, and promiscuous sex. Many states had laws against adultery that seem antiquated now, but they were rooted in sound morality and a willingness to take strong measures *to protect children.*

What is important about this chapter is that we have shown the justification for society having a concern for private morality. The Supreme Court of the United States jumped the tracks when it found a "right to privacy" in the Constitution—a right not explicitly stated, and not found by any previous court. Some argue that you can't legislate morality. But in society, sometimes you must, or your social order will unravel. There are limits to any perceived right to privacy.

There are two issues here. One has to do solely with personal morals. The other has to do with the preservation of social order for the sake of maintaining the society and for the sake of the children. The state has an interest in protecting the social order. It was this that accounted for two very different aspects of biblical law. One is personal, the other is social. This is parallel to the classic distinction made between moral law and civil law.

Thomas Aquinas distinguished three kinds of law in the Bible: moral, ceremonial, and judicial. Jesus himself confirmed a twofold division:

> The first of all the commandments is, Hear, O Israel; The LORD our God is one LORD: And you shall love the LORD thy God with all thy heart, and with all thy soul, and with all thy mind, and with all thy strength: this is the first commandment. And the second is like, namely this, You shall love thy neighbour as thyself. There is no other commandment greater than these (Mark 12:29-31).

In Jesus' construct, both moral and civil law[1] fall under the heading of the love of neighbor. Ceremonial law would fall under the heading of the love of God. A temptation arises to use these distinctions to explain why some laws are abolished while others are kept, but who can argue for the abolition of the command to love one's neighbor or to love God? Even the distinction between these commandments is blurred. As John put it: "If a man say, I love God, and hates his brother, he is a liar: for he that loves not his brother whom he has seen, how can he love God whom he has not seen?" (1 John 4:20).

And all these laws are gathered together in the broader definition of "the written law," as opposed to "the oral law." It is the written law that Jesus specified when he said:

> Do not think that I have come to abolish the Law or the Prophets; I have not come to abolish them but to fulfill them. I tell you the truth, until heaven and earth disappear, not the smallest letter, not the least stroke of a pen, will by any means disappear from the Law until everything is accomplished (Matthew 5:17-18 NIV).

With this information in hand, we are prepared to address a singular issue in Old Testament legal studies: The civil law. It is

---

1. Or, following Aquinas, the judicial law.

not uncommon to encounter the argument that the civil law is not binding upon Christians, but that is not, strictly speaking, true. All the civil laws of the Old Testament are part and parcel with the written law, and Jesus said plainly he had not come to abolish them.

What, then, are we to make of, say, the laws regulating slavery? Can a Christian own a slave? The very idea is repugnant, but upon closer examination the answer appears to be, that he can. The laws regulating slavery are part of the written law, and therefore would have to be included in Jesus' affirmation of the law. Some light is shed on the subject by a short letter Paul wrote to a Christian who was in fact, a slave owner. His name was Philemon, and he had a runaway slave named Onesimus.

Philemon was a close friend to Paul, having been converted by Paul on his stay in Ephesus. He was also a strong man of faith, and effective in ministering to the church. So imagine Paul's surprise to find that one of the servants who ministered to him, and whom he had converted there in Rome, was a runaway slave belonging to his old friend Philemon.

I would have thought that the Christian faith would have freed all slaves, but apparently not. Paul determined that he had to send Onesimus back to his master. When you think about it, that is a significant statement about the Christian and the law. Paul opened his letter with his usual salutation, and we learn that Philemon is a significant player in the Christian drama. He is leader of the church in his house and beyond. Thus, in his most diplomatic style, Paul writes to him:

> I appeal to you for my child, whom I have begotten in my imprisonment, Onesimus, who formerly was useless to you, but now is useful both to you and to me. And I have sent him back to you in person, that is, sending my very heart, whom I wished to keep with me, that in your behalf he might minister to me in my imprisonment for the gospel; but without your consent I did not want to do anything, that your goodness should not be as it were by compulsion, but of your own free will (Philemon 1:10-14 NASB).

In that brief statement, "I am sending him back," Paul acknowledges the rights of Philemon under the law to own a slave. Not only did Roman law allow it, so did biblical law. But the nature of the common Christianity of both men added a new element:

> For perhaps he was for this reason parted from you for a while, that you should have him back forever, no longer as a slave, but more than a slave, a beloved brother, especially to me, but how much more to you, both in the flesh and in the LORD. If then you regard me a partner, accept him as you would me (vv. 15-17).

Reading between the lines, it is clear that Paul was forestalling any anger or retaliation for wrongs Onesimus might have done. Paul called in a debt:

> But if he has wronged you in any way, or owes you anything, charge that to my account; I, Paul, am writing this with my own hand, I will repay it (lest I should mention to you that you owe to me even your own self as well). Yes, brother, let me benefit from you in the LORD; refresh my heart in Christ. Having confidence in your obedience, I write to you, since I know that you will do even more than what I say (vv. 18-21).

So Christians could own slaves in societies that permitted it. But they were bound by the written Law of God to go beyond anything required by their society. But there is something interesting to consider here. The civic *enforcement* of law was not the function of any individual, nor of the church. That function had transferred to the state under which the Christian lived. We will discuss this again in the chapter on "The Social Contract."

3

Law and Meaning

*But avoid foolish questions, and genealogies,
and contentions, and strivings about the law;
for they are unprofitable and vain (Titus 3:9).*

In religion, the very existence of a law is an invitation to
legalism. When Paul wrote warning Titus to avoid foolish striving
about the law, he was addressing the then common Jewish custom
of endless debate over fine points of law. It was this kind of debate
that later found expression in the Mishnah[1] and finally the Talmud.

I have to believe that there were some contentions about the
law from the earliest days of the Christian faith. That should not be
surprising, because the earliest church was comprised entirely of
Jews, soon joined by "God Fearers"—non-Jews who nevertheless
believed in the God of the Bible, and loosely practiced Judaism.
We know there were Pharisees who became believers,[2] and we are
fully justified in assuming that there were Sadducees as well. In
fact, there is reason to believe that the new Christian faith cut
across every facet of Judaism. That being the case, it is reasonable
to assume that controversies involving the law followed in due
course. It could hardly have been otherwise.

Consider, then, the dilemma of any Christian who takes the
view that the law has not been abolished. He has firm grounds for

---

1. Mishnah (Hebrew for "repetition") is the first written record of the Jewish Oral Law as it was
held by the Pharisees. It is the first work of Rabbinic Judaism It was redacted around 200 A.D.
by Rabbi Judah ha Nasi.

2. Acts 15:5.

that conclusion, since Jesus affirms it in the Sermon on the Mount:

> Do not think that I have come to abolish the Law or the Prophets; I have not come to abolish them but to fulfill them. I tell you the truth, until heaven and earth disappear, not the smallest letter, not the least stroke of a pen, will by any means disappear from the Law until everything is accomplished (Matthew 5:17-18 NIV).

Some awkward problems present themselves when you try to live by this. For example, the law forbids the mingling of fabrics together in the making of a garment.[1] One fellow, sincerely wanting to do the right thing, became concerned about whether the elastic around the band of the top of the socks would constitute the mixing of fabrics together. The story had it that he removed all the elastic from his socks. I don't know what he used to keep them up.

I have long been an advocate for reading the Old Testament, but once people start reading it seriously, all manner of questions start arising about the law. There is a strong temptation to attempt answers to all those questions and thus create a new Talmud. Resisting that temptation, we still need to find a way to heed what Jesus said, to read the law with understanding and learn what it reveals to us about God, his character, and what he expects of us in living a life.

A friend once asked me, "Why it is that we play hopscotch through the Old Testament, picking up this law and dropping the one right next to it?" I thought the question was reasonable. In essence what he was asking was this: "What are the criteria we use to decide which Old Testament laws we will keep and which we will ignore?" It is an important question because, truth to tell, every serious Christian does precisely that.

Ever since the beginning of the Christian faith, theologians and teachers have attempted to address the question. Various and sundry dissections of the law have been suggested in an effort to rationalize what we do. For example, no one is going to argue that the law, "Thou shalt not steal," is of no import to Christians. But when it comes to a law that requires a blue tassel on the fringes of our clothes, we will probably find dissenters.

---

1. Leviticus 19:19.

Some people try to solve the problem by making a distinction between the Ten Commandments and the rest of the Law. In other words, the Ten Commandments are valid, but the rest of the Law is not. Others attempt to distinguish between the Law of God on the one hand and the Law of Moses on the other, feeling that if a statement can be identified as the Law of God, you should keep it; but if it is part of the Law of Moses, then it's abolished. Still others distinguish between what they call "the moral law" and "the ceremonial law." They try to make the distinction based upon whether or not it is a ceremony, a ritual, or a sacrifice. These, they argue, are done away whereas the other aspects of the law are not.

Still another denomination contends that all of the law was nailed to the cross, including the Ten Commandments. They then go on to explain that nine of the commandments were "reinstated" in the New Testament. It is the Sabbath commandment that didn't make the cut.

With typical wrongheadedness, we often make big issues out of things that aren't very important while we give too little attention to more serious matters. It is tempting to ask, "Do I have to do this?" rather than ask, "What does this mean? What lies behind it? What is the underlying principle? How might it apply in real life?"

Too few people ever get around to asking the immortal, "Why?" To me, that is the truly interesting question when it comes to the law. When I read the Old Testament and encounter an obscure law, I stop and ask, "Why did God say that?" I can't see any way to apply the law in the here and now, but the natural question that follows is, "Why was this a law in the first place?" I have come up with some intriguing questions, though not quite so many answers.

I spotted a bumper sticker once that proclaimed proudly, "God said it, I believe it, and that settles it for me." That makes life much simpler, but the fellow driving the car might well be wearing wool and Dacron slacks. He probably has no idea that God handed down a law of mixed fabrics. Yes, God said it. Yes, he believes it. But so far, he hasn't done it. He has likely overlooked the importance of understanding those things that God has said. Solomon wrote: "Wisdom is supreme; therefore get wisdom. Though it cost all you have, get understanding" (Proverbs 4:7 NIV).

Blind obedience may be better than no obedience at all.

Sometimes you don't know the reason behind a law until the consequences come home to roost. But still, obedience with understanding is better. Without it, you may cause actual harm in your attempts at righteousness.

A guiding light for me is that passage in Jeremiah cited on the very first page of this book: ". . . Let not the wise man boast of his wisdom or the strong man boast of his strength or the rich man boast of his riches, but let him who boasts boast about this: that he understands and knows me . . ." (Jeremiah 9:23-24 NIV).

It seems to me that it is in the study of the Law of God that we have a great opportunity for coming to understand the character of God, what he stands for, and why he did some of the things he did.

The Basic Assumption: No Bad Laws

I have approached the study of the law with a basic assumption. One should always be alert to an author's assumptions, so I'm giving you one of mine right up front. I am assuming that God would not and did not ever give man a law that was bad for man.

Readers of the King James Version may object, citing Ezekiel: "Wherefore I gave them also statutes that were not good, and judgments whereby they should not live" (Ezekiel 20:25 KJV). But this flies in the face of the character of God and what we see and know of God. As it happens, the King James guys got it wrong. Read it in context in another version:

> Because they had not obeyed my laws but had rejected my decrees and desecrated my Sabbaths, and their eyes lusted after their fathers' idols. I also gave them *over to* statutes that were not good and laws they could not live by (Ezekiel 20:24-25 NIV). [1]

God did not hand down a set of bad laws when they disobeyed the original. He gave them up to other laws, including the laws they made for themselves. So I can retain my premise. All of God's law, as originally written, was good for man. Then, I can ask an

---

1. "That God would give Israel 'statutes that were not good' means that Israel would choose to live according to the world's ordinances that brought misery and death." *Expositor's Bible Commentary*, on Ezekiel 20:24.

important question about any given law: "Why is this law good?" Proceeding along these lines, I find some interesting questions and some important answers.

Here is another premise I bring to the study of the law: The Law of God is not arbitrary. I get the impression that some people think God sat back one day and said to himself, "Now let's see. These people need some laws. And I must determine what is going to be right and what is going to be wrong."

Some seem to approach the law like teenagers fighting a parent's rules. They think God said, "This act is fun so I will make it wrong." God, they think, doesn't want us to have any fun. If God were arbitrary, he could have taken the things that were fun and made them right and taken the things that were not fun and made them wrong. That would have made life a lot simpler for all of us, not to mention a lot more fun.

I think we can all agree that God, who made man, knows man. And as an old mentor of mine used to put it, "the Bible is God's instruction book to man." He compared the Bible to the instruction book that comes along with a new car. It tells you what kind of oil to put in it, what pressure should be maintained in the tires, what grade of fuel you must use, what periodic maintenance is needed, and how to operate all the features. If you accept the premise that the Bible is God's instruction book, then it follows that God, having created man, then began to communicate to man a way of life, a way of living, and things to do that were good for man, things that would save him from hurt, from trouble, and from the heartache that might come his way. And so, we proceed from this premise to the conclusion that when God speaks to man, he tells him something that is good for man.

But, there is a fly in the ointment. As you begin to read through the law, you're going to occasionally find laws that are a little bit, well, annoying. You will find others that are deeply and profoundly troubling. I don't recall the occasion when I first read the Old Testament laws concerning slavery, but I recall vividly how I felt. I came across this law:

> And if a man strikes his male or female slave with a rod
> and he dies at his hand, he shall be punished. If, however,
> he survives a day or two, no vengeance shall be taken; for

he is his property (Exodus 21:20-21 NASB).

Here was my question: "How could God take such a callous view of human beings and see them treated as chattel, as property? Why would He do that?" I won't answer that question right here, but the laws regarding slavery still fall within the assumption that God never gave to man a law that was bad for him. And, since they are a part of the written law, they haven't gone away.

Our problem is not so much that we are getting the wrong answers as it is that we keep asking the wrong questions. Take this common question, for example: "Is the Law of Moses binding upon Christians?" There are two problems with semantics in the question. What, exactly, does the questioner mean by "the Law of Moses," and how does the word "binding" apply? Here is another misleading question: "Is keeping the Fourth Commandment [the Sabbath] required for salvation?" The question implies that there are some laws that *are* required for salvation, an assumption that is theologically unsound. Just change the commandment by one notch and think about the implications: "Is honoring your father and mother required for salvation?"

The error in this line of questioning is that it does not recognize that the purpose of the law is not, and never has been, the achievement of salvation. It was not a salvation issue for Jews, and it is not for Christians. Proceeding from this basic fact, we can ask what a person means when he asks if a given law is "binding" upon Christians. What does the word "binding" mean? Does it mean God requires it of us? If we don't do it, what happens to us? The question is just another way of asking, "Is this or that law required for salvation?" And that assumes a role for the law that God never intended the law to play.

The best way to get at this question is to illustrate it with one of those Old Testament laws. Try this one: "Do not muzzle an ox while it is treading out the grain."[1] Is a Christian "bound" by this law? It is hard to get at the question by trying to decide what category of law it is. Is it the moral law? Is it ceremonial? There is no ritual involved in the law, and how can it be a question of morality if you feed an ox while he's actually working instead of feeding him before?

1. Deuteronomy 25:4 NIV.

There are more questions. Is this the Law of Moses or is it the Law of God? How would that affect our answer as to whether it is binding? Being where it is in Deuteronomy, it would be part of the Law of Moses. But what if I don't have an ox? Do I need to go out and buy one? The question is absurd, but nevertheless, it's the one that has to follow if we are asking if this law is binding upon us. As it happens, Paul reached back in one of his letters, grabbed this law, and revealed in the process an entirely different way of thinking about the law. He said this:

> For it is written *in the Law of Moses*: "Do not muzzle an ox while it is treading out the grain." Is it about oxen that God is concerned? Surely he says this for us, doesn't he? Yes, this was written for us, because when the plowman plows and the thresher threshes, they ought to do so in the hope of sharing in the harvest. If we have sown spiritual seed among you, is it too much if we reap a material harvest from you? (1 Corinthians 9:9-11 NIV).

One question is answered. This law falls in the category of the Law of Moses. Make a note, though, Paul said it is *written* there, and that turns out to be more important than you might think. Paul did not see it as an animal rights law. It is not, he said, because God is concerned about the animal. It is for our sakes that it is written (he mentions it twice), and it is written so we can understand that it is right and fitting *to compensate our minister*.

You can't argue that this law was nailed to the cross (the common reason for dismissing a law we don't like). Paul wrote this 25 or more years after everything was nailed to the cross that would ever have been nailed there. Nor can we argue that it is solely Jewish. The law was being applied to a *Gentile* church. Plainly, it was not nailed to the cross, and it was not "abolished."

It may be worth looking a little further into Paul's usage. He took this law out of its Old Testament context, and applied it here as an *authority* for what he is telling this church of Gentiles. In the broader context, Paul was talking about his own example of avoiding offenses:

> Am I not free? Am I not an apostle? Have I not seen Jesus
> our LORD? Are you not the result of my work in the LORD?
> Even though I may not be an apostle to others, surely I am
> to you! For you are the seal of my apostleship in the LORD.
> This is my defense to those who sit in judgment on me.
> Don't we have the right to food and drink? (1 Corinthians
> 9:1-4 NIV).

It is an odd statement on its face, but when taken in context, it is clear enough. The word rendered "right" is *exousia*, which means "authority" or "privilege." And as the theme is developed through the chapter, it becomes clear that he meant he had the right to eat and drink at their expense. He appealed to the practice of the other apostles who traveled with a wife and did not work at an ordinary job. "Who ever goes to war at his own expense?" he asked. Then he said something very strange when viewed in the light of modern Christian belief. He appealed to the Law of Moses as an authority. But then the Old Testament was the only Scripture they could appeal to. This is the *meaning* of the law of the Ox:

> Do I say this merely from a human point of view? Doesn't
> the Law say the same thing? For it is written in the Law of
> Moses: "Do not muzzle an ox while it is treading out the
> grain." Is it about oxen that God is concerned? Surely he
> says this for us, doesn't he? Yes, this was written for us,
> because when the plowman plows and the thresher
> threshes, they ought to do so in the hope of sharing in the
> harvest. If we have sown spiritual seed among you, is it too
> much if we reap a material harvest from you? (vv. 8-11
> NIV).

It is worth emphasizing that Paul did not appeal to the teachings of Jesus. He didn't appeal to the Sermon on the Mount. He didn't appeal to Peter, or the Jerusalem elders. He appealed to the law, and specifically to the Law of Moses. Does this make the Law of Moses somehow binding upon Christians? This was said to people just like us. There were people in Corinth who were not even in agriculture. They may have been craftsmen, merchants, or mine workers. They may have owned vineyards, where they didn't use animals for their work. Yet Paul wrote that the law was written for their sakes—and ours.

Mind you, a Gentile church was told that a segment of the Law of Moses was "written for our sakes." It was written, not for oxen, but for the underlying principle:

> If others have this right of support from you, shouldn't we have it all the more? But we did not use this right. On the contrary, we put up with anything rather than hinder the gospel of Christ. Don't you know that those who work in the temple get their food from the temple, and those who serve at the altar share in what is offered on the altar? In the same way, the LORD has commanded that those who preach the gospel should receive their living from the gospel (vv. 12-14 NIV).

I wouldn't have thought that the church or the Gospel was what God had in mind when he handed down that law of the ox. But in a simple, two line statement God laid down a principle that can stand through all the ages, and across all national or cultural boundaries. It is applicable in any circumstance of human endeavor, that a man should be paid fairly and promptly for what he does.

Now a legalist[1] might have been very careful to ensure that his oxen were not muzzled, while at the same time he failed to pay the man who followed the oxen and tended to them.[2] This kind of thinking comes about because men don't understand the underlying principle of the law. It is not enough to obey the letter. One must understand the *meaning* of the law.

This is important because a man might be careful to buy clothes that are 100 percent wool, thereby establishing his righteousness, while he is sleeping with another man's wife. If the law is your salvation, you had better keep it all. You can't just cherry-pick the laws that appeal to you, or that are easier for you. Then there is the fellow who dismisses all Old Testament law and ends up in the same place as the legalist.

---

1. A person who is a strict, literal, or excessive practitioner of conformity to the law or to a religious or moral code

2. James 5:4.

Now listen, you rich people, weep and wail because of the misery that is coming upon you. Your wealth has rotted, and moths have eaten your clothes. Your gold and silver are corroded. Their corrosion will testify against you and eat your flesh like fire. You have hoarded wealth in the last days. Look! The wages you failed to pay the workmen who mowed your fields are crying out against you. The cries of the harvesters have reached the ears of the LORD Almighty (James 5:1-4 NIV).

Try another example of Old Testament law: "When you build a new house, make a parapet around your roof so that you may not bring the guilt of bloodshed on your house if someone falls from the roof" (Deuteronomy 22:8 NIV).

Why on earth, in an age of pitched roofs, would we need to put a parapet around our roof? No one is going up there except repairmen, and they have their own skills and insurance. Maybe this is a law we can safely ignore. Well, not if you have a flat roof and easy access to that roof. If children climb up onto that roof and fall off, you are liable. The principle underlying this law is *personal liability*. You may not have a flat roof, but you might easily have an elevated deck behind your home. My home is built on a slope, and the back edge of the deck is eight feet above the ground. If anyone fell from that deck, they might well be hurt. I have an obligation to protect my family and guests from falling off the edge of that deck, and that obligation is implicit in the law of parapets. Why would it be abolished? It is implicit in the law that it would apply in any comparable situation in any age.

This law would probably be categorized as civil law by those who divide the law into compartments. But there is nothing wrong with civil law. In fact, one should be held accountable for creating a hazard and for negligence.

So here is a biblical law, thousands of years old, that still has application in the 21st century. The reason some might think it doesn't apply is because, in our society, flat roofs are a rarity. But if a person is free to build one, the law requires the parapet. It isn't a matter of legalism, but responsibility for any hazard you create.

It is easy to forget that, in many parts of the world to this day, there are people who not only have flat roofs, they have stairways that go up to them. They go up and sun. The air is fresher up there. They go up and sit in the evening. In fact, I stayed once in a home in Jerusalem that was just so. I think some visitors actually slept on the roof of that house at night because it was so cool once the sun had gone down and the evening breeze began to blow. And it did have a balustrade all around the edges so there was no danger of falling off.

There are, to be sure, parts of the law that would have no application for a man. For example, a single man need not concern himself with the laws that might apply to a married man. And laws that pertained to a particular priesthood would have no application if that priesthood were no longer in existence. In the same way, if there's no Temple, then many of the laws pertaining to the Temple might not have an application. Then, some laws are not applicable because they deal with administrative penalties. Take this one:

> If men who are fighting hit a pregnant woman and she gives birth prematurely but there is no serious injury, the offender must be fined whatever the woman's husband demands and the court allows. But if there is serious injury, you are to take life for life, eye for eye, tooth for tooth, hand for hand, foot for foot, burn for burn, wound for wound, bruise for bruise (Exodus 21:22-25 NIV).

The idea of cutting off a man's hand because he caused the loss of a hand is troubling. So troubling that some interpreters have said that the meaning of the law was that the man had to pay the value of the hand. In any case, it should be clear that only a governmental authority could administer such a penalty, either literal or monetary. A church, existing in a land where there is a civil government, has no right to impose civil or criminal penalties. The law is not abolished. But it cannot, it must not, be privately enforced. That has always been true of laws of enforcement.

Nevertheless, the principle is still there. If you cause bodily harm to another through an act of carelessness, anger or neglect, you are responsible. And in the New Covenant, you are held responsible, not merely to the letter of the law, but to the spirit of the law, whether there are civil penalties or not. We'll talk more later about administrative law and how it affects the relationship between man and God, but for now, I want to look further into the way we *understand* the law.

4

Understanding Law

O how I love I thy law! it is my meditation all the day.
You, through your commandments have made me wiser
than mine enemies (Psalm 119:97-98).

The 119th Psalm is revealing, not only because of the psalmist's love of the law, but because he *thought* about the law. For a legalist, meditation is not required. The law is the law. If you break it, you are punished. If you are not overtly breaking it, you go free. For the Pharisee, it was enough that he count the leaves from his mint plant and tithe one out of ten. Jesus said this about that:

> Woe to you, scribes and Pharisees, hypocrites! For you pay tithe of mint and anise and cummin, and have neglected the weightier matters of the law: justice and mercy and faith. These you ought to have done, without leaving the others undone (Matthew 23:23).

Finding the tithe in the law is a simple matter. So is justice. But where is the law regulating mercy or faith? Far be it from me to suggest that mercy and faith are absent from the law, but a legalist, who only looks at the letter of the law, may never find them. Rather he may cite: "He that despised Moses' law died without mercy under two or three witnesses" (Hebrews 10:28). This man might very well miss the idea of faith that is conveyed through the law, as well as the lessons conveyed in the application of the law. Jesus' rebuke of the Pharisees was sharp.

You blind guides! You strain out a gnat but swallow a camel. Woe to you, teachers of the law and Pharisees, you hypocrites! You clean the outside of the cup and dish, but inside they are full of greed and self-indulgence (Matthew 23:24-25 NIV).

You actually work so hard to get certain technicalities of the law correct, said Jesus, that you never look below the surface of the law, at the deeper undercurrent, at the underlying meaning. There is a law of love, a law of faith, and a law of mercy contained in the law, but you have to think about it to see them.

It may be surprising to realize that neither Jesus nor the apostles made a distinction between the Law of Moses and the Law of God, nor did they distinguish the sacrificial law or the ceremonial law. Generally speaking, they just used the word "law" as though everyone knew what they were talking about. And for the most part, their readers did. They spoke of "the law" and in that law is the love of God, the mercy of God, the compassion, and the faith of God. All these things the Pharisees seemed unable to grasp.

"Woe unto you, scribes and Pharisees, hypocrites! for ye make clean the outside of the cup and of the platter, but within they are full of extortion and excess" (v. 25 KJV). I don't know why the NIV changed "extortion" to "greed" for the Greek word *harpage* denotes pillage, extortion, ravening, spoiling. Jesus decried the custom of those Pharisees, who would tithe meticulously, while threatening some poor soul with exposure if he didn't pay up. The practice was detestable, and yet these men, who appeared to be righteous, who were the pillars of the community, who flaunted symbols of righteousness, and with great sweeping gestures of generosity toward their fellow man, would turn and steal, lie, and cheat. They kept the letter of the law, while they shattered the underlying intent and the spirit of the Law of God.

He went on to say, "Woe to you, teachers of the law and Pharisees, you hypocrites! You are like whitewashed tombs, which look beautiful on the outside but on the inside are full of dead men's bones and everything unclean" (v. 27 NIV).

Everyone knows that biblical prophecy is highly symbolic. What does not seem so widely understood is that the law is also symbolic. It has meaning that reaches beyond mere words. And this is what I have been driving at all along. When I ask, which laws are applicable to Christians today, my answer is (brace yourself), *all of them are*. But the key lies in understanding that the law is often symbolic. Sometimes, the law cannot be applied for one reason or another, but that does not imply abolition or repeal. Paul's example of not muzzling the ox is an apt illustration. It is written for our sakes, and it is written so we can apply the principle in our dealings with one another. Many aspects of the law are proverbial. That is, they are used like axioms or aphorisms. If I say, "Don't kill the goose that lays the golden egg," nearly everyone will know what I mean. It is a figure of speech, a metaphor, and it is applicable whether you have a goose or not.

For some reason, when faced with a law, people are prone to ask, "Do I have to do this in order to be a Christian?" Or, "Do I have to do this to make it into the kingdom of heaven?" I feel a far better question is, "What does this law mean? What is the intent, the spirit of the law? How might it instruct me in living my life?" When we start reading the law that way, we will be much further along than we were when we thought legalistically—which both law keepers and law rejecters are apt to do. Returning to the Sermon on the Mount, we need to look at what Jesus said one more time:

> Do not think that I have come to abolish the Law or the Prophets; I have not come to abolish them but to fulfill them. I tell you the truth, until heaven and earth disappear, not the smallest letter, not the least stroke of a pen, will by any means disappear from the Law until everything is accomplished (Matthew 5:17-18 NIV).

Heaven and earth still being there, does that mean I can't wear wool and Dacron slacks? No it doesn't and we will explain why presently. Unfortunately when people think of any part of the law being abrogated, they seriously miss the point. But if we acknowledge that not one word of the law has passed away, we come smack up against another question, "What does it mean?" That is where the truth is to be found. Jesus continued:

> Whosoever therefore shall break one of these least commandments, and shall teach men so, he shall be called the least in the kingdom of heaven: but whosoever shall do and teach them, the same shall be called great in the kingdom of heaven. For I say unto you, That except your righteousness shall exceed the righteousness of the scribes and Pharisees, ye shall in no case enter into the kingdom of heaven (vv. 19-20 KJV).

It is not enough to follow the letter of the law, to go through the motions and then say, "I have fulfilled the Law of God, I'm worthy of salvation." Jesus said that unless your righteousness goes beyond that, you're not going to see the kingdom of heaven at all.

What is expected of us is that we look beyond the statement, "you shall not muzzle the ox that treads out the corn," and realize that we have an obligation, not merely to animals, but to men. We are required to be honest with workers, to pay them what they are due, to give them what is theirs. It's an eternal principle, not something that can be abolished simply because times have changed, or even because the relationship between God and man has changed. This has to do with the relationship between man and man. As long as there are two men, there will be a necessity for one man who has another working for him to be honest with his employee.

Jesus continued: "You have heard that it was said to the people long ago, 'Do not murder, and anyone who murders will be subject to judgment'" (v. 21 NIV). Here is something fundamental. A man might say, "I have never killed a man. I couldn't do that." Does that mean that the commandment "thou shalt not kill" poses no issue for him? Hardly, because Jesus said that if you hate a man, you are guilty of a violation of the underlying spirit and intent of that commandment. He went on to say, "But I tell you that anyone who is angry with his brother will be subject to judgment. Again, anyone who says to his brother, 'Raca,' is answerable to the Sanhedrin. But anyone who says, 'You fool!' will be in danger of the fire of hell" (v. 22 NIV). Both of these exclamations were violent epithets.

This simple teaching of Jesus was given as a subheading under the commandment, "You shall not murder." It is an elaboration of

41

the principle, of the spirit of that law. It is a part of what the Sixth Commandment is saying to mankind. It won't work in the judgment to say that we haven't broken the commandment, when in truth, we all have.

When we get down to what the Ten Commandments are all about, when we get below the superficial, the mere letter of the law, we see something more. When we grasp what is really involved in not bearing false witness, in honoring our father and mother, in being honest and generous, all of us will have to confess that we are guilty. We will come to realize that we have indeed broken the law and become sinners, dependent upon the grace of Christ.

The Sermon on the Mount is rich with illustrations of this principle, so much so that it is hard to understand how anyone could miss it. Because of the temptations of the flesh, we tend to remember longer a statement like Jesus' teaching on adultery:

> You have heard that it was said, "Do not commit adultery."
> But I tell you that anyone who looks at a woman lustfully
> has already committed adultery with her in his heart (vv.
> 27-28 NIV).

It makes it much harder to stand in judgment and say you haven't broken the Seventh Commandment. Christ came, in the words of Isaiah, to "magnify the law and make it honorable" (Isaiah 42:21 KJV). The statement is better rendered, to "exalt the law and make it glorious." It is a far cry from dismissing it entirely.

When we really get down to brass tacks, which of us will be able to say to God, "I am clean"? Which of us can say, "I have not sinned"? The truth of the matter is that the commandments of God reach so much deeper into us than we imagine. Jesus made that clear as he continued the Sermon on the Mount. Most Christians are very familiar with what Jesus taught in that sermon. But now we need to take a look at the underlying laws which are not so familiar. Take the law of lost animals:

> If you see your brother's ox or sheep straying, do not ignore
> it but be sure to take it back to him. If the brother does not
> live near you or if you do not know who he is, take it home

with you and keep it until he comes looking for it. Then give it back to him. Do the same if you find your brother's donkey or his cloak or anything he loses. Do not ignore it (Deuteronomy 22:1-3 NIV).

Could anything be more Christian? But there is no statement of that law in the New Testament. Is it therefore no longer applicable to a Christian? Imagine yourself walking along a road in the country when a strange dog joins you on your walk. He is wearing a collar, so he is somebody's pal; but today, he has decided to join your walk. This actually happened to my wife and me one day. The dog followed us all the way home and started acting as if he were our dog. So we gave the big fellow some water, put him in the back yard, and began calling neighbors. Finally, we located the dog sitter who was supposed to have been caring for the dog while the owners were on a cruise. The dog had gotten out due to the sitter's carelessness and might well have been lost to the owner.

Now, if we had just ignored the dog, if I had said, "Oh, I'm in a hurry. I haven't got time. The owner will find him sooner or later. I'm not going to let on that I even saw it," would I have obeyed the law? After all, the law didn't say anything about a dog.

We thought about this after the fact and pondered what it was that motivated us to take care of this fellow and restore him to his owner. We didn't even think about it at the time. Part of the motivation was empathy. How would we feel if our dog was lost? (We knew well how that felt.) But part of it was the law applied in a Christian sense. It had become internalized. We felt responsible for our neighbor's animal.

This law in principle has an application to every man. I am responsible for trying to help protect my neighbor's property and to keep it secure for him. I should do this even if I don't know who the owner is. I should bring the animal home, water him and feed him, and when the owner is located, I should give it back to him. The dog we found, by the way, turned out to be a valuable bird dog, and was barely a year old.

The law goes further than that. "You shall not see thy brother's ass or his ox fall down by the way, and hide thyself from them: thou shalt surely help him to lift them up again" (Deuteronomy 22:4). Here is a fellow in trouble, with a hurt animal, trying to get the critter up again. You can't pretend you didn't see. You can't dodge behind the hedge and avoid the issue. No, you are supposed to walk right up to him and then stop and help.

"Well," I can hear someone say, "no one around here has farm animals, so the law has no application for me." Really? Suppose your neighbor is trying to put a tarp on a wind-damaged roof all by himself. Should you help?

Now of course, all this is covered by the golden rule. We should do to others what we would want them to do for us. But the law explains and illustrates the golden rule for us. It does not *limit* the law to these literal examples.

When I thought about this, it occurred to me that this law is never reiterated in the New Testament. Instead, it is illustrated in a way that underlines what Paul said about not muzzling the ox. The illustration is the familiar parable of the good Samaritan.[1]

It seems a man was on his way to Jericho when he was set on by a gang of thieves. They stole his clothes and everything he had, wounded him, and left him half dead. While he lay there, two religious men came along, saw him, and avoided him. In the words of Jesus, they "passed by him on the other side." So, what did they do that was so wrong? It wasn't any of their business.

Then along came another man. A Samaritan. He felt sorry for the man, tended to his wounds, helped him up on his own animal, and took him to an inn to recover. Not only that, the Samaritan paid his expenses and left money to see to it that the man was cared for until he was well. Why would the Samaritan do that? What is not often noticed is that the Samaritans also had the law—the Samaritan Pentateuch.[2] The Samaritan's conscience was informed by the law in Deuteronomy. The Priest and the Levite who left the man there may have been within the letter of the law, but the Samaritan understood the meaning of the law—our obligation to help our fellow man. Odd, isn't it, that the despised Samaritan understood the law better than the legalistic Pharisee?

There is another issue that arises from this same chapter in Deuteronomy. "The woman shall not wear that which pertains to a

1. See Luke 10:30 ff.

2. The Samaritan Pentateuch is a version of the first five books of the Old Testament which the Samaritans preserved from ancient times. It is the only part of the Hebrew Bible the Samaritans have ever accepted as authoritative.

man, neither shall a man put on a woman's garment: for all that do so are abomination unto the LORD thy God" (Deuteronomy 22:5). Years ago, I answered a letter from a lady who was worried about whether she could wear her husband's parka while milking her cows. This kind of question arises because we tend to think too literally when it comes to law. If she had thought about the underlying principle, she would never have needed to ask. And yet, there are still some absurd situations which arise in churches about this issue. I heard of one church that was planning a skating party and some ladies wondered if it would be okay for them to wear slacks or jeans. The deacons got together to talk this over. There was the obvious problem with skirts if a woman should fall. And yet, in their view, women should not wear pants. So they had a conflict between rules about modesty and rules about women wearing pants.

So what is the law trying to tell us? It seems simple enough. The law suggests we be attentive to gender identity. And it is not a matter of skirts or slacks. Women's slacks and men's trousers are easily distinguished. And there are parts of the world where a man might wear a kilt. Social custom determines what clothing men and women wear, and their clothing should be different. When you encounter a law like this, it is perfectly okay to stop and think it through before you try to apply it. And it is okay to use common sense. Unfortunately, common sense is an early casualty when it comes to making rules in church.

Does God really care if the parka a woman puts on to go out and milk the cows is her's or her husband's? Or does God mind, if her feet get cold, if she pulls out her husband's socks and puts them on because he's got some wooly ones and hers aren't so warm? Is God really going to say, "Aha, now I have her. She has put on the wrong socks"?

I start this process with the assumption that God is not arbitrary, that God is not unkind, that God is love, that he is not trivial or petty, that he never gave man a law that was bad for him. If you can disprove that premise, you've got me. But I'm going to proceed on that and live by it. I believe it as an article of faith. I think that the law is simple enough to understand as to God's intent. Take the next verse as an example:

If you come across a bird's nest beside the road, either in a tree or on the ground, and the mother is sitting on the young or on the eggs, do not take the mother with the young. You may take the young, but be sure to let the mother go, so that it may go well with you and you may have a long life (Deuteronomy 22:6-7 NIV).

I suppose that there are some people who feel that God in heaven is counting these little birds (which, according to Jesus, he really is) and that if you don't handle this right, he will deliberately shorten your days. Hardly. If you think about it, God is saying that the days of man upon the land are dependent upon his attention to ecology. It is important to conserve wildlife, to not destroy species. Is this law still binding? Of course it is, but it is binding because it arises from the nature of things, not because it is enforced by some entity. Is the law meaningful in the 21st century? Ask any environmentalist. And it is the meaning that is important. We are supposed to think about the environment, to take reasonable steps to preserve species.

It isn't that easy to show the meaning of all the laws in the Old Testament, but that doesn't mean the meaning isn't there. It may mean nothing more than that we have not been paying attention.

Consider this one, for example: "Thou shalt not plow with an ox and an ass together" (Deuteronomy 22:10). Now I am no authority on agriculture, and I didn't immediately see the problem. I did hear one fellow opine that the fertilizer which fell from the two animals differed in some important way, and it would be bad for the ground to mix them. I fear I was rather rude in my response to that theory. Another gentleman pointed out the obvious, the animals were of such disparate sizes that it simply wouldn't work. *No one would ever think of doing that.* I could see that, but all that did was raise another question. Couldn't man have figured that out for himself? If you simply can't make that combination work, why would it be necessary to hand down a law? The answer to that came out of the blue.

Years ago, when I was Dean of Students at a college in England, a fellow member of the faculty and I were discussing a young man who was, as young men are wont to do, pursuing one of the female students. I told my friend, "I know that relationship doesn't look right, I have a feeling it's not going to work. Why do I feel that way?" My friend replied: "It's simple—'you shall not plow with an ox and an ass together.'" Since the young man's behavior somewhat resembled one of the named animals, we were both vastly amused.

As it happened, my friend had put his finger on what this law was really about. There can be such differences between two elements, be it the size or pulling power of two animals, the personalities of two individuals, the abilities of two business partners, or even the religions of two persons, that the relationship is *unworkable*. It is obvious that Paul draws on this law when he uses the word "yoke" as he did: "Be ye not unequally yoked together with unbelievers: for what fellowship hath righteousness with unrighteousness? and what communion hath light with darkness?" (2 Corinthians 6:14).

This raises an interesting distinction. I have heard people ask of this or that passage: "Is it a law, or is it a principle?" I decided to look it up. Here's what I found:

Principle: A comprehensive and fundamental law, doctrine, or assumption, the laws or facts of nature underlying the working of an artificial device, a primary source, an underlying faculty or endowment.

There's more, but this will serve our needs. As the question was asked, a law was inflexible, while a principle was optional. But as we become more familiar with biblical law, the roles are reversed. It is the underlying principle that is inflexible. It is the principle that is the fundamental thing. The enforceable stuff is built on the principle. But these are just words. What can we take away from this that means anything in life?

Laws like those I have cited create axioms, aphorisms that imply a universal, underlying truth. In this case, it is a law that there can be such great differences between two people that they should not attempt to be tied together in any way that does not give them the freedom to walk. That law makes as much sense today as it did when Moses wrote it down.

So, what happens if you break it? A loss of salvation? A denial of your eternal reward? No, what breaking this law gives you is heartache, financial loss, and if you are plowing, some busted up harness. As it happens, that is what most of the law is about. It is about life, not salvation. It is optional only in the sense that you can decide to break it and bear the consequences. There will be consequences, and they may not go away just because you are sorry.

As it happens, the verse about plowing immediately precedes the law I cited earlier about wearing a garment of mixed fabric. It suggests that both laws are saying the same thing in different words. What the law is about is recognizing diversity (a good, modern term), and realizing that there are some diversities that just cannot be bridged.

We know that Christ spoke in parables. We know that the parables were not to be taken literally, but were intended to convey a deeper meaning. It was a meaning that was conveyed to some and hidden to others. It seems that God did much the same thing with the law.

Years ago, I heard a Christian teacher suggest the law of mixed fabrics might have been intended to demonstrate that the practice of interracial marriage was wrong. At the time, I thought he was stretching things a bit. But if you take the premise and think it through, you may notice that there is no law in the Bible prohibiting marriage between races, per se. There is a prohibition of marrying into other cultures for religious reasons. I think there is very good reason for that.

But I traveled to South Africa many times in the days of apartheid and had ample opportunity to observe the absurdity of attempts to define and enforce racial separation. So many humiliating and debasing decisions were made in that era. They drew a difference between black and colored, for example. They even had to have court decisions on how black is black. Then there were the people from India who lived in South Africa (Ghandi lived there for a while). So they had to have a separate racial category for Asians. Chinese people were allowed to marry Indians, but not blacks. People were found to be colored, black, or white, based on a court decision. That is what happens when you try to enforce racial divisions.

Nevertheless, cross-*cultural* marriages are headed for rough sailing. Perhaps God, in his love, knowing what man was like, knowing that all men had a common ancestry and therefore could mate, yet knowing how many heartaches were in store for cross-cultural marriages, had to find a way of expressing the principle in a way that did not *require or admit* to enforcement. Making a prohibition against interracial marriage in the law would have created an untenable position. So what he did was to convey to those who were willing to hear it, that there are some mixtures that just aren't going to work. Not merely in marriage, but in business, in agriculture, even in fabrics. It left the final decision in the hands of those who would have to suffer the consequences, and thereby denied enforcement rights to the government (or to the church).

On the other hand, interreligious marriage was a different matter altogether. Defining religious differences was a simple matter, and it was not merely the individual who would suffer from bringing another religion into Israel, but the entire social structure.

Now I don't believe that any of these laws were "abolished," not even the ceremonial laws. After all, they are a part of the written law which Jesus said could not pass away as long as the creation endures. In ceremony, perhaps more than anywhere, symbolism becomes extremely important. And while it is possible to change the ceremony, the underlying meaning remains intact. Consider the Passover lamb as a case in point. The original Passover lamb was symbolic of the Messiah who would suffer and die. What Jesus did at the Last Supper (which was a Passover supper) was to change the symbols. He did not change the law. He still had to die, to be sacrificed. He still had to pay the penalty for our sins and, at that supper, he instituted new symbols. Instead of a lamb, it would henceforth be unleavened bread and wine.

I think every Christian church, even those who believe the ceremonial law was abolished, maintains one central rite. Call it communion, the LORD's Supper, the Eucharist, it is still a rite, and it still has its roots in the Passover. We can believe that Jesus changed the symbols of the Passover, but we aren't allowed to think that he abolished the law of the Passover. After all, it is written down with jots and tittles intact.

It is hard to argue that the ceremonial law was abolished while retaining the spiritual concept of washing in the waters of baptism. Whether your church sprinkles, pours, or immerses, it has a rite of baptism. The underlying meaning of washing and baptism is the same—the purification from sin. Only the symbols have been changed.

In the information age, we have all become familiar with computers, and the word "icon" has returned to our language. It is a Greek word, *eikon*, which means "a usually pictorial image." In computer usage, it has come to refer to a graphic symbol on a computer screen that suggests the availability of a given function— even a set of instructions which can be carried out with one click of a button. It is not hard to imagine that the icon can be altered without changing the function it implies.

One of the most striking illustrations of this principle is found in the laws of the Sabbath day, and the holydays. Once a person commits to the Fourth Commandment, and the admonition to not do any work, it is only natural to start asking questions about what constitutes work. It is too easy to focus on the letter of the law and never come to understand the underlying meaning of the law. The Pharisees who challenged Jesus and his disciples on an issue of Sabbath observance didn't understand this. They saw the disciples, walking through a field of grain, plucking grain and eating it. "Behold, thy disciples do that which is not lawful to do upon the sabbath day" (Matthew 12:2). They were, by the legal definition of the Pharisees, harvesting grain. Jesus replied:

> Have ye not read what David did, when he was hungry, and they that were with him; How he entered into the house of God, and did eat the showbread, which was not lawful for him to eat, neither for them which were with him, but only for the priests? Or have ye not read in the law, how that on the sabbath days the priests in the temple profane the sabbath, and are blameless? (vv. 3-5).

This is an important issue. Jesus did not argue that the law was no longer in effect, nor did he argue that David did not break it. He implied that human need, in this case hunger, could override the written law. Yet what David did was unlawful. Two things happen when you break a law. One is consequences, the other is punishment. Jesus implied that there would be no punishment for David's decision. But there were serious consequences arising from that decision. Several good men lost their lives.[1]

Then Jesus added the statement about the priests. No one could argue with the fact that their duties on the Sabbath involved work and were therefore, technically, unlawful. Yet they were blameless, having been commanded to do these services every day. It is possible for two laws to come into conflict and leave you with a decision. The letter of the law won't help you very much. The meaning of the law will serve you better.

Concerning the holydays, there are those who will say, "Well, I think the holydays are nice and all that, but I don't necessarily think they have to be kept." Yet I ponder how much of the truth about God's plan I would understand today had I not kept them. The holydays provide a framework of sorts, like a line of seven pegs along a wall, upon which you can hang the things you learn. They create a relationship between the things that God is doing and give meaning to the events of history.[2]

And so I have to understand that the Law of God is profoundly symbolic and pregnant with meaning. So much of the time we are asking the wrong questions about the law. Rather than asking, "Is it binding upon me today?" we should ask, "What does it mean for me today?" Much of the time, you will not know the answer. It is tempting to call someone and ask for a ruling. If you called me, I would likely reply, "I really don't know. Your explanation sounds as good as any." But the study of the law can provide a fascinating topic for conversation with others who are doing the same. If we are looking for the meaning rather than a ruling, we will be a long way down the road.

When you grasp these things, you will find yourself understanding the psalmist when he cries, "O how love I thy law! it is my meditation all the day. Thou through thy commandments hast made me wiser than mine enemies: for they are ever with me (Psalms 119:97-98 KJV). There would never be a time when the psalmist would not have enemies. But he grasps the truth that the law made him smarter than his enemies. He thought about it all the time. Every time he came up against a problem, he started thinking about how the law might clarify the issues. The result was: "I have more understanding than all my teachers: for thy testimonies are

---

1. You can read the story in 1 Samuel 21.

2. See *The Thread, God's Appointments with History*, Ronald L. Dart, Wasteland Press, 2006.

my meditation. I understand more than the ancients, because I keep thy precepts" (vv. 99-100).

Jesus said that many prophets and righteous men had, in the past, wanted to know the things that the disciples were only then learning. Some things take more time than others. Sometimes we have to grow to the place where we can understand. Other times, we have to gain enough experience for things to make total sense to us. We learn through facing situations, making decisions, and observing the results. Later, we may have the chance to share that experience with others who will combine our experience with theirs. Sometimes it can take a generation before issues become entirely clear.

I think I understand far more of God and his plan than I did 40 years ago, and much of the increase in understanding came from giving attention to the Law of God. It did not come from slavish obedience to the letter of the law, though I traveled for a while down that road. It came rather from an understanding of the law, how it applied, and what it meant. So much came from simply learning to ask the right questions.

There is a logic in asking seriously, "What did God mean by that law? I can't believe he cares whether my new suit is Dacron and wool. So why did he say that?" We are servants of God and more. We are his friends, and he is not interested in causing us hurt. When we learn that, and learn to respect his judgments, we will gain an enormous edge in life.

> I have kept my feet from every evil path so that I might obey your word. I have not departed from your laws, for you yourself have taught me. How sweet are your words to my taste, sweeter than honey to my mouth! I gain understanding from your precepts; therefore I hate every wrong path. Your word is a lamp to my feet and a light for my path (Psalm 119:101-105 NIV).

Looking back over my life, I feel I was making my way down the road in the dark, like a man on his hands and knees feeling his way. Now that I am asking better questions about the law and looking for God's intent, it is like someone turned on a light and dispelled the darkness. Now I can see where I am going. I can stand up and walk.

One of the most important ideas to emerge from this study is what the New Testament writers really meant when they spoke of the Law of God, the Law of Moses, and the traditions of the Jews. Here we find the primary reason why Paul is so commonly misunderstood.

5

Jewish Law

*Stand fast therefore in the liberty wherewith Christ
hath made us free, and be not entangled again
with the yoke of bondage (Galatians 5:1).*

Some readers of the English Bible have a curious habit. They
like to find the meaning of the words and then insist that they
always carry exactly the same meaning, and no other, everywhere
they are found. Why we do that isn't clear. After all, English
doesn't work that way. Why should Greek and Hebrew? We
understand that words have denotations and connotations, and the
meaning of a word can vary with context. It can also vary
depending on who is using the word. Some theological discussions
can sound like Alice and Humpty Dumpty:

> "When I use a word," Humpty Dumpty said, in rather a
> scornful tone, "it means just what I choose it to mean—
> neither more nor less."
> "The question is," said Alice, "whether you can make
> words mean so many different things."
> "The question is," said Humpty Dumpty, "which is to be
> master—that's all. . .They've a temper, some of them—par-
> ticularly verbs: they're the proudest—adjectives you can do
> anything with, but not verbs—however, I can manage the
> whole lot of them! Impenetrability! That's what I say!"[1]

---

1. *Through the Looking Glass*, Lewis Carroll.

Sometimes I think impenetrability is the object of some religious discussion. Semantics raises its head again and again, making it possible to carry on an argument indefinitely. For all I know, that may be the objective: endless argument.

But I digress. There are two terms used in discussions of biblical law that leave non-Jewish readers at sea. They are "The *Torah*," and "The Law of Moses." The New Testament gives us reason to believe that the meaning of these terms depends entirely on who is using them, as well as the context. "*Torah*" is a singularly confusing word. If you look it up in an English dictionary, the first definition is, "the five books of Moses constituting the Pentateuch." That, naturally, is the written law. The second definition is, "the body of wisdom and law contained in Jewish Scripture *and other sacred literature and oral tradition*" [emphasis mine]. The expression, "The Law of Moses," carries the same ambivalence.

There is a story behind this, but in order to tell the story, I have to call your attention to something Paul wrote to the Galatians. He began his letter with a striking statement.

> I want you to know, brothers, that the gospel I preached is not something that man made up. I did not receive it from any man, *nor was I taught it*; rather, I received it by revelation from Jesus Christ. For you have heard of my previous way of life in Judaism, how intensely I persecuted the church of God and tried to destroy it. I was advancing in Judaism beyond many Jews of my own age and was extremely zealous for the traditions of my fathers (Galatians 1:11-14 NIV).

This is where Paul placed "Judaism" firmly in his past. All this seems to be very important to Paul, because he will end this section with an unusual affirmation: "I assure you before God that what I am writing you is no lie" (v. 20 NIV).

It was that excessive zeal that led him to persecute the first Christians. Nothing Paul said here is particularly difficult, but there is a common misconception lurking in the background. Not everyone agrees on what the word "Judaism" means. In modern usage, Judaism is the religion of the Old Testament. Abraham is called a practitioner of Judaism, never mind that Judah, after whom Judaism was named, would not be born for two more generations.

As it happens, that is not how Paul used the term. And in fact, Judaism, per se, was a relatively late form of the worship of God, one that grew up after the exile of the Jewish people in Babylon. Prior to that captivity, there was no "Judaism." The religion of Abraham, and indeed the religion of Israel all the way through the monarchy was never identified by name. It was not an "ism." It was not merely a religion. It was the faith and practice of those who worshiped the one and only God. It was simply the worship of Jehovah, or Yahweh, if you prefer, by name.

The consequence of this is that the modern reader is apt to miss what Paul is driving at when he speaks of his "previous way of life in Judaism," and also likely to miss the point of what was happening in Galatia.

It was Jacob Neusner who began to get this in focus for me. "Judaism is a religion," said Neusner, "and every religion is a story." It is a story that a group tells to explain where it came from, where it is going, what it is, in accord with God's plan.[1] He describes what he calls "the Generative Myth," the story that Judaism tells about itself, and addresses the origins of what is today called "Rabbinic Judaism."

> Christianity began in the first five centuries C.E. (the Common Era = A.D.). With roots deep in the pre-Christian centuries, Rabbinic Judaism, the particular Judaism that would flourish from the first century to our own times, made its classical statement in that same period of about five to six hundred years.[2]

Neusner recognizes that many identify Rabbinic Judaism with the normative Judaism of the first century. He also points out that the record does not support that claim. There were many "Judaisms" extant in the first century.[3] But in the process of explaining all this, he develops a theme that may shed some light

---

1.   Jacob Neusner, *Judaism When Christianity Began, a Survey of Belief and Practice,* (Westminster John Knox press, 2002), 1.

2. Ibid., 6.

3. Most notably, the Judaisms of the Pharisees, Sadducees and Essenes.

on the issues before us. The "Generative Myth" of Judaism is expressed in the collection of wise sayings of the great Rabbinic sages called "Sayings of the Fathers." According to Neusner:

> The opening allegation is that Moses received Torah—Instruction—at Sinai. But it is not then claimed that Moses wrote the entire Torah in those very words we now possess in Scripture. Rather, Moses received Torah and handed it on to Joshua, and so on in a chain of tradition. That the chain of tradition transcends Scripture's record is clear when we reach "the men of the great assembly," who surely are not part of the biblical record.[1]

The Jewish story is that Moses received both written and oral instruction. The Oral Law, they say, has been passed down from generation to generation, and forms an important part of the *Torah*, the Law of Moses. This presents an important distinction for Christians, because Scripture says that Moses wrote down *everything* God told him:

> And Moses came and told the people all the words of the LORD, and all the judgments: and all the people answered with one voice, and said, All the words which the LORD hath said will we do. *And Moses wrote all the words of the LORD* . . . (Exodus 24:3-4).

What is important is this: *In Rabbinic Judaism, tradition transcends Scripture.* This fact underlies the ongoing conflict between Jesus and the Rabbis. Judaism sees a line of tradition from Moses through the sages to later generations. Jesus challenged that tradition head on. The conflict is best illustrated by one particular encounter. Some of the scribes and Pharisees came to Jesus asking why his disciples transgressed "the tradition of the elders" by eating without properly washing their hands (Matthew 15:2). There are two terms here that we need to understand before moving on. The terms are: "scribes," and "the tradition of the elders." The scribes are what Jewish scholars call "the sages," while "the

---

1. Ibid., 7.

traditions of the elders" are what Jews call "the Oral Law." [1] To the Pharisees, the disciples of Jesus were offending against the Oral Law as defined by the sages. Jesus' reply cuts sharply across this idea.

> Jesus replied, "And why do you break the command of God for the sake of your tradition? For God said, 'Honor your father and mother' and 'Anyone who curses his father or mother must be put to death.' But you say that if a man says to his father or mother, 'Whatever help you might otherwise have received from me is a gift devoted to God,' he is not to 'honor his father' with it. *Thus you nullify the word of God for the sake of your tradition*" (Matthew 15:3-6 NIV).

The Pharisees, who seem to be the progenitors of Rabbinic Judaism, would have admitted frankly that the traditions of the elders did indeed transcend the Scriptures. Jesus flatly rejected that idea.

> You hypocrites! Isaiah was right when he prophesied about you: "These people honor me with their lips, but their hearts are far from me. They worship me in vain; their teachings are but *rules taught by men*" (vv. 7-9 NIV).

Thus Jesus characterizes the Oral Law: "Rules taught by men."[2] The Jews could not miss the stark contrast between their approach and that of Jesus. When they interpreted the law, they cited other sages, other rabbis. Here's an example of Talmudic reasoning:

> Talmud of Babylonia tractate Baba Mesia to Mishnah tractate Baba Mesia 4:10.I.15:/59a-b.
> A. There we have learned: If one cut [a clay oven] into parts and put sand between the parts,
> B. Rabbi Eliezer declares the oven broken-down and

---

1. It is by no means certain that the term "Oral Law" was even in use at this point. If it was, then the absence of the term in the New Testament text is significant. The writers deliberately refused the expression, calling it what it was: tradition.

2. Compare with Paul, Colossians 2:20-22.

therefore insusceptible to uncleanness.

C. And sages declare it susceptible. . .

F. Said Rabbi Judah said Samuel, "It is because they surrounded it with argument as with a snake and proved it was insusceptible to uncleanness."[1]

This is a long discussion of an issue among the sages, and the points are lettered A through X. No less than five different Rabbis are cited by name with their arguments for or against the proposition, some citing still other rabbinic sources. Now contrast this with the teaching of Jesus:

Ye have heard that it was said by them of old time, Thou shalt not kill; and whosoever shall kill shall be in danger of the judgment: *But I say unto you . . .*" (Matthew 5:21, 22a).

Jesus does this over and over again in the Sermon on the Mount. Note well, he does not say "you have read," nor "it was written." It was almost an article of faith that the Oral Law should not be written, and it was a momentous decision when it finally was. Jesus' approach would have jarred many of his listeners, and Matthew takes note of it:

And it came to pass, when Jesus had ended these sayings, the people were astonished at his doctrine: For he taught them as one having authority, *and not as the scribes* (Matthew 7:28-29 KJV).

Lest we misunderstand the import of what Neusner is saying, and how this affects our understanding of the distinction, here is what he goes on to say:

Putting this together, we may say that the generative myth of Rabbinic Judaism, tells the story of how Moses received Torah in two media, in writing and in memory, the memorized part of the Torah being received and handed on a process of oral formulation and oral transmission.[2]

---

1. Cited, Neusner, 21.

2. Neusner, 7.

The "memorized portion of Torah" came to be called the Oral Law. In the New Testament, it is, "the traditions of the elders." But there is more. According to Neusner, "What emerges is now clear, the masters of Rabbinic Judaism stand in a chain of tradition from Sinai. Their teachings *form part of the Torah God gave to Moses at Sinai*" [emphasis mine].

You may want to read that again, because it really does say what it seems to say. The teachings of the sages of first century Judaism are said to be part and parcel of what God handed down to Moses himself. The generative myth of Rabbinic Judaism holds that Scripture, the written law, is only *part* of Torah, only *part* of the Law of Moses. The conflict generated by this myth underlies the entire argument that arises from the New Testament relative to the law. It is what prompted Jesus' statement in the Sermon on the Mount—the one I will cite so often:

> Do not think that I have come to abolish the Law or the Prophets; I have not come to abolish them but to fulfill them. I tell you the truth, until heaven and earth disappear, *not the smallest letter, not the least stroke of a pen,* will by any means disappear from the Law until everything is accomplished (Matthew 5:17-18 NIV).

In referring to letters and strokes of the pen, Jesus made a sharp distinction. He was talking about the written law. He offered no such permanence to the Oral Law or Jewish tradition, and his audience would have quickly picked up on that. I realize what enormous problems I raise here, for there is much in the written law that is simply untenable in the modern world, but we discussed that in preceding chapters.

Judaism, as such, grew out of the period when Persia was the dominant force in the Middle East. It was the Babylonians who carried the House of Judah captive. Babylon was later conquered by the Persians, and it was the Persian kings who allowed the Jews to return home and establish themselves once again in Jerusalem. Not very much is known about Jewish life in this period, but there was a body of men called, "The Great Assembly." Adin Steinsaltz writes of this group:

The exact nature of the great assembly is unclear; it may have been a permanent institution with legislative and executive powers, or merely a generic name for all the scholars of a given period. In fact, with few exceptions, the names of the sages and outstanding personalities of this age are unknown. The same cloud of obscurity envelops the activities of the members of the great assembly, and nothing is known of their conduct or methods. But, culturally and spiritually speaking, this period was a decisive one in the annals of the Jewish people. It gave Judaism its unique and well-defined spiritual framework, which has survived, despite changes and modifications, throughout the centuries in the Holy Land and the Diaspora.[1]

The Great Assembly probably traced its function to the original 70 elders appointed by Moses to render judgments about the law, and it would likely have been the precursor of the Sanhedrin of the first century. Nicodemus, who came surreptitiously to see Jesus is called an *archon*, a ruler of the Jews. I presume he was a member of that important assembly. Steinsaltz elaborates:

The members of the Great Assembly actually collected holy writings, decided which books would be canonized in the Bible, which chapters of each book should be selected, and gave the Bible its definitive form and style. The completion of the Bible, one of the greatest projects of the Great Assembly, also marked the beginning of the reign of the Oral Law.[2]

By the time Jesus came on the scene, there were two political parties who divided along this fault line, and who struggled for influence among the people. On the one hand were the Pharisees who believed that the Oral Law was of divine origin and carried authority equal to that of the written law.[3] On the other hand were the Sadducees who rejected the authority of the Oral Law. It isn't

---

1. Adin Steinsaltz, *The Essential Talmud*, (Basic Books, 1976), 14-15.

2. Ibid.

3. When one speaks of "Jewish Law," one is generally speaking of the Oral Law, which has long since been committed to writing and is not strictly oral any longer.

clear whether the Sadducees rejected it out of hand, or merely refused to use it for making rulings.

With this background, we can return to the Sermon on the Mount and see what we make of what Jesus had to say. In affirming the permanent nature of the written law, he is establishing common ground and heading off an accusation that might come his way. He affirms the written law, but he makes no such affirmation of the Oral Law, embarking immediately on a challenge of the "traditions of the elders."

> I tell you the truth, until heaven and earth disappear, not the smallest letter, not the least stroke of a pen, will by any means disappear from the Law until everything is accomplished. Anyone who breaks one of the least of these commandments and teaches others to do the same will be called least in the kingdom of heaven, but whoever practices and teaches these commands will be called great in the kingdom of heaven (Matthew 5:18-19 NIV).

Jesus had to establish this distinction, because he was about to part company with the sages of an earlier generation. He was going to say, not only that they were wrong, but that they transgressed the written law by their interpretations. The practice of the Pharisees was not merely a matter of opinion or interpretation, but an active setting aside of the written law, of Scripture. It may be hard to get your mind around it, but realize that, for the Jew of that time, tradition was deemed part of the Law of Moses. It was the prevailing belief of the Pharisaic establishment that everything the sages said was part of that law, even the conflicts of interpretation, in some curious way. Having established that he had no quarrel with the *written* law, Jesus began to challenge the Oral Law, as we have just seen.

Now we are equipped to consider a particular conflict in the early church, one that has generated much confusion. The first mission of Paul and Barnabas represents a major turning point in the history of the faith. Up to this point, very few Gentiles had been converted, and these all were people who believed in the God of the Bible before they ever heard of Jesus. They were Gentile practitioners of Judaism, commonly called "God Fearers." The pattern, then, that Paul and Barnabas followed on this journey was to go first to the synagogue in every city and announce the good news that the Messiah had come in the person of Jesus. To their surprise, everywhere they went the Jews rejected the Gospel wholesale. Only a handful believed.

But when they left the synagogue in defeat, they were thronged by the God fearing Gentiles who did believe. Paul and Barnabas taught them, baptized them, and went on their way. When they returned to Antioch, the church received, with great joy, the news that God "had opened the door of faith to the Gentiles." But then a fly showed up in the ointment.

> Some men came down from Judea to Antioch and were teaching the brothers: "Unless you are circumcised, according to the custom taught by Moses, you cannot be saved." This brought Paul and Barnabas into sharp dispute and debate with them. So Paul and Barnabas were appointed, along with some other believers, to go up to Jerusalem to see the apostles and elders about this question. . . . When they came to Jerusalem, they were welcomed by the church and the apostles and elders, to whom they reported everything God had done through them. Then some of the believers *who belonged to the party of the Pharisees* stood up and said, "The Gentiles must be circumcised and required to obey the law of Moses" (Acts 15:1-5 NIV).

Here I come back to the theme I opened with at the beginning of this chapter. When most Christian readers come to this passage, they think the expression "the Law of Moses" was referring to the first five books of the Old Testament. But now, thanks to Jacob Neusner, we can see this from another angle. What these believing Pharisees were talking about was broader than that. They were talking about the whole of what they called *Torah*, oral and written. For them, the worship of God was part of a system that included *all* the traditions of the elders, some of which were explicitly rejected by Jesus. Neusner again:

What we see at the end is what we saw at the outset: Judaic religious systems rest squarely on the Hebrew Scriptures of ancient Israel. The Rabbinic sages read from the Written Torah forward to the Oral Torah.[1]

This is what I had long assumed to be the case. That the traditions of the Jews that formed what they call the Oral Law, were the accumulated *judgments* of the sages. I had never imagined that they considered them on a par with, or even above, the written law. I assumed that the traditions grew out of generations of precedents established by the interpretation of the written law. Neusner:

> Then are the rabbis of the Oral Torah right in maintaining that they have provided the originally oral part of the one whole Torah of Moses our Rabbi? To answer that question in the affirmative, sages would have only to point to their theology in the setting of Scripture as they grasped it.[2]

What you see reflected in Paul's writings is a conflict, not with the Law of God, but with the rabbis of the Oral Torah. Now with all this in mind, I can return to Paul's statement I cited before and parse it: "But I certify you, brethren, that the gospel which was preached of me is *not after man*" (Galatians 1:11).

If we accept that the problem in Galatia was that sect of believers who followed Judaism, then this statement fits perfectly. My Gospel, said Paul, does not arise from human tradition: "For I neither received it of man, neither was I taught it, but by the revelation of Jesus Christ." (v. 12). This is in contrast with what Neusner said about the Rabbis:

> Rabbinic Judaism is thus the Judaism that sets forth the whole teaching of Sinai, written and oral, and that points to its sages, called rabbis. . . who in a process of discipleship acquired ("received") and transmitted ("handed on") that complete Torah, oral and written, that originates with God's

---

1. Neusner, 185.

2. Neusner, 188.

instruction to Moses.[1]

Paul, then, used the language of Judaism to emphasize that what the sages did was emphatically not what happened to him: "I neither received it from man, nor was I taught it." Paul admits that he had been a serious practitioner of the Oral Law.

> But when God, who set me apart from birth and called me by his grace, was pleased to reveal his Son in me so that I might preach him among the Gentiles, I did not consult any man, nor did I go up to Jerusalem to see those who were apostles before I was, but I went immediately into Arabia and later returned to Damascus. Then after three years, I went up to Jerusalem to get acquainted with Peter and stayed with him fifteen days. I saw none of the other apostles—only James, the LORD's brother. I assure you before God that what I am writing you is no lie (vv. 15-20).

This last is striking. It is very strong and apparently it had to be. The statement represents a major break from the Jewish tradition of *receiving* from one sage and *passing on* to another. What Paul is establishing is that *the Gospel was a matter of revelation, not tradition.* This was in sharp contrast to the troublemakers in Galatia, who were apparently of the same stripe as those at the Jerusalem conference of Acts 15. Developing the theme a little further, Paul cites an instance of Peter's behavior in Antioch.

> When Peter came to Antioch, I opposed him to his face, because he was clearly in the wrong. Before certain men came from James, he used to eat with the Gentiles. But when they arrived, he began to draw back and separate himself from the Gentiles because he was afraid of those who belonged to the circumcision group. The other Jews joined him in his hypocrisy, so that by their hypocrisy even Barnabas was led astray. When I saw that they were not acting in line with the truth of the gospel, I said to Peter in front of them all, "You are a Jew, yet you live like a Gentile and not like a Jew. How is it, then, that you force Gentiles

---

1. Ibid, 8.

to follow Jewish customs?" (Galatians 2:11-14 NIV).

This is heart and core of what the Jerusalem conference was all about and it also serves as a good illustration of the struggle for the heart and soul of the early church. By this time in the first century, the Jews had created a whole new set of rules for their relationships with Gentiles. These rules, in many cases, ran directly contrary to the written law. The law was explicit. Strangers were to be fully assimilated into Israelite society, as we will see in chapter ten. There was to be one law for the stranger and the home born. Strangers were even allowed to offer sacrifices and to share fully in the worship of God. But by the time of the second Temple, all that had changed.

What Peter was shown—in no uncertain terms—was that the Gospel was to go to Gentiles. He was forced to acknowledge that Jewish law was wrong on this issue. He told Cornelius:

> You are well aware that it is against our law for a Jew to associate with a Gentile or visit him. But God has shown me that I should not call any man impure or unclean (Acts 10:28 NIV).

Against whose law? Peter called it "our law." We will walk through this in a later chapter. Gentiles were to be fully assimilated into the Israelite community. But by this time in history, Jewish tradition had led the Jews to separate themselves from Gentiles. As Paul continued his rebuke of Peter, the theme of justification emerges.

> We who are Jews by nature, and not sinners of the Gentiles, Knowing that a man is not justified by the works of the law, but by the faith of Jesus Christ, even we have believed in Jesus Christ, that we might be justified by the faith of Christ, and not by the works of the law: for by the works of the law shall no flesh be justified (Galatians 2:15-16).

Implicit here is the belief of the Pharisees that doing the works of Judaism made a man just before God. Paul denied that explicitly and repeatedly. The only thing the law has to do with justification is that it creates an awareness of a need for justification. But for some versions of Judaism, one only comes to God through the law. Neusner:

> But it is only through scripture that Judaism takes the measure of events and occasions in God's self revelation. Scripture, the written part of the *Torah* or teaching of Sinai, preserves whatever can be known about how God has revealed himself. It is the writing down of the encounter— and the contents of encounter. If, therefore, people wish to know God, they meet God in the *Torah*. That guides them, to be sure, to know and evaluate and understand God's ongoing revelation of the *Torah*. Study of the *Torah* in the chain of tradition, formed by the relationship of disciple to master, from the present moment upward to Moses and God at Sinai, then affords that direct encounter with God through his revealed words that Judaism knows as revelation.[1]

Take a moment to consider the implications of that statement. It is not only Scripture, but the entire chain of tradition, that Judaism knows as revelation. If you are wondering how it is possible for sages of the first century to become a part of *Torah* that was given to Moses at Sinai, so am I. For better or for worse, here is what Neusner tells us about how that works.

> Both Judaism and Christianity for most of their histories have read the Hebrew Scriptures in an other-than-historical framework. They found in Scriptures words, paradigms— patterns, models—of an enduring present, by which all things must take their measure; they possessed no conception whatsoever of the pastness of the past. In departing from Scriptures' use of history to make a theological point—as the progression from Genesis through Kings means to do—Rabbinic Judaism invented an entirely new way to think about times past and to keep all time, past, present, and future, within a single framework.[2]

---

1. Neusner, 16.

2. Ibid.

One begins to understand what Jesus was driving at when he told the Jews they were making the commandments of God of no effect, by their tradition. This *suspension of time* is, quite frankly and unashamedly, an invention of Rabbinic Judaism. Paul spoke of this sort of error in his letter to Titus: "Not giving heed to Jewish fables, and *commandments of men*, that turn from the truth" (Titus 1:14). The comparison between Paul's battles and what we now know of Judaism is instructive. Neusner went on:

> For that purpose, a model was constructed, consisting of selected events held to form a pattern that imposes order and meaning on the chaos of what happens, whether past or present or future. Time measured in the paradigmatic manner is time formulated by a freestanding, (incidentally) atemporal model, not appealing to the course of the sun and moon, not concerned with the metaphor of human life and its cyclicity either.[1]

Jewish sages, if I understand what he is saying, step outside of time and become participants in the creation of the Torah God gave to Moses. If you found that hard to follow, you are not alone. Neusner has lapsed into philosophical jargon. It is what happens when men try to explain something that the facts won't support. We get a lot of that in politics—and religion.

If there is one thing that emerges from a careful reading of both the law and the New Testament, it is that during the entire period when the New Testament was being written, throughout all the existing churches, the Sabbath, the holydays, and indeed the written law, were honored. The Oral Law was dismissed as mostly irrelevant and utterly without authority.

As is often the case with unsupportable law, the Rabbis resorted to sanctions to enforce it. It is the freedom from Jewish sanctions that Paul is so exercised about in his letters. "Stand fast therefore," urged Paul, "in the liberty by which Christ has made us free, and do not be entangled again with a yoke of bondage" (Galatians 5:1).

Galatians is a little more complicated than that, but this is a start. "Thou shalt not steal" is not a yoke of bondage (unless you

---

1. Ibid.

are a congressman, perhaps).

> For if anyone is a hearer of the word and not a doer, he is like a man who looks at his natural face in a mirror; for once he has looked at himself and gone away, he has immediately forgotten what kind of person he was. But one who looks intently at the perfect law, *the law of liberty*, and abides by it, not having become a forgetful hearer but an effectual doer, this man shall be blessed in what he does (James 1:23-25 NASB).

I think the reason for James' choice of words is the underlying conflict between the controls of Judaism and the liberty of the Christian.

6

Moses and the Constitution

Let me not be understood as saying that there are no bad laws, nor that grievances may not arise for the redress of which no legal provisions have been made. I mean to say no such thing. But I do mean to say that although bad laws, if they exist, should be repealed as soon as possible, still, while they continue in force, for the sake of example they should be religiously observed. —Abraham Lincoln

It is surprising at times where insights will come to you. I was browsing the Internet and came upon a speech by a Supreme Court Justice of these United States, and it helped me understand some things about biblical law that I had not gotten quite straight.[1] Christian people have a lot of difficulty with the law and sometimes take shortcuts in trying to understand it. One of the most common approaches is to divide the law into types. Thomas Aquinas divided the law into three types: moral, ceremonial, and judicial. Something like this is widely accepted by Christian people, allowing that the moral law continues, while the ceremonial and judicial have passed away.

So, how did Justice Scalia help me with this? The title of his speech was, "A Theory of Constitution Interpretation." It seems to me that the big problem Christians have with biblical law is not so much the application of law, but the *interpretation* of law. You cannot justly apply it if you don't understand what it means. Scalia

---

1. The speaker was Antonin Scalia, at The Catholic University of America, Washington, D.C., Oct. 18, 1996.

began his speech by asking, "What is the object of the court?"

> This is a matter of interest to not only judges and lawyers, but any intelligent American citizen, philosopher or not. What do you think your judges are doing when they interpret the Constitution? It's sad to tell you after 200 years, there is not agreement on this rather fundamental question: What is the object of the enterprise?

Well, I can't say I am surprised, but what is not obvious is that this is not merely disagreement about the interpretation of a given law. Decisions have always been handed down in terms of, say, a five to four vote by the justices. But I think what Justice Scalia was saying is that there is no agreement on the object of the court— what are they there for?

In his speech, I learned something about constitutional law that I didn't have straight. I thought that the Constitution should be interpreted on the basis of "original intent" and I assumed that Justice Scalia thought the same way. Not so. I learned that there is a marked difference between "original intent" and "originalism," and the difference is more important than I had realized. Here is how Scalia explained it:

> The theory of originalism treats a constitution like a statute, and gives it the meaning that its words were understood to bear at the time they were promulgated. You will sometimes hear it described as the theory of original intent. You will never hear me refer to original intent, because as I say I am first of all a textualist . . . If you are a textualist, you don't care about the intent, and I don't care if the framers of the Constitution had some secret meaning in mind when they adopted its words. I take the words as they were promulgated to the people of the United States, and what is the fairly understood meaning of those words.

It is interesting to consider how that principle might apply when studying biblical law. What did the words mean to the people who first heard them? This is a tough challenge, because we are dealing with both linguistic and cultural issues in trying to get at the meaning of a given law. Still, in most cases, if we ask what these words meant when they were spoken by the LORD to Moses and when Moses wrote them down, we have at the least found a legitimate starting point.

It is striking to me that when you start examining law in any historical context, you keep coming upon the same principles. And so, following the judge's example, we take the words of the text as they were originally handed down from Sinai and we consider how they might have been understood by the people who heard them. We can look for what Scalia calls, "the fairly understood meaning of those words."

With the Bible, this is crucial, because we are looking at many laws that had a meaning in that culture that does not naturally carry over into our own. Let me give you an example:

> Speak to the Israelites and say to them: "Throughout the generations to come you are to make tassels on the corners of your garments, with a blue cord on each tassel. You will have these tassels to look at and so you will remember all the commands of the LORD, that you may obey them and not prostitute yourselves by going after the lusts of your own hearts and eyes" (Numbers 15:38-39 NIV).

It is evident that the custom in ancient times of wearing that fringe or tassel had meaning. Studies indicate that this custom was as well understood in that culture as the yellow ribbon is in ours, and it tended to serve a similar purpose—to make a public statement about who you are and what you stand for. [1] The yellow ribbon has come to mean you have a loved one in the military serving far away. I think it may have originated with the yellow stripe down the leg of a cavalryman's uniform, and his lover wearing a yellow ribbon in support of him. The custom has morphed into various other applications, such as the pink ribbon for breast cancer awareness. The blue tassel for Israel seems to fall in a similar category. It made a public statement that "I am a commandment keeper and a servant of Jehovah."

---

1. See Milgrom, Jacob, "Of hems and tassels: Rank, authority and holiness were expressed in antiquity by fringes on garments," *Biblical Archaeology Review*, v. IX, # 3, May/June 1983, pp. 61-65.

I met a gentleman not long ago who was wearing a pair of tassels woven of white and blue. But I suspect he was wearing them, not so much as a sign to others, but merely because God said do it. I doubt seriously that one person in 10 whom he met would know what that tassel was supposed to mean, and thus it becomes meaningless. I have heard that some wear that blue ribbon on their underwear which makes it all the more irrelevant. The fellow I met had his tied to his belt under his jacket, and you could easily miss it. The Israelites were supposed to wear them in plain view. In some ancient societies, the tassel, not necessarily blue, was a sign of rank or status and they wanted it to be seen.

So here is what we have, in the meaning of the words *to the people who first heard them*: "In the tassels you ordinarily wear on your garments, you will always include a thread of blue." Thus you remind one another of your God, his commandments, and his ways. It is worth noting that blue was one of the dominant colors in the decor of the Tabernacle. Thus it was a double tie to the worship of Jehovah. In a strange way, it is not unlike school colors.

For a society that does not wear tassels at all, the meaning of the law is lost. Even if you decide to wear a loop of blue ribbon on your lapel, people may realize that it means something, but will not know what. In the society of the time, it identified commandment keepers and worshipers of Jehovah to one another and it connected them to the Tabernacle.

In a way, it was part of the social contract of Israel. Two Israelites in a market in Damascus could spot one another by the ribbon of blue in the tassels on their robes. Circumcision, also a part of the social contract, couldn't quite serve the same purpose.

It is tempting to dismiss the law of tassels as an Old Covenant practice that has passed away. The problem is that what we call the Old Covenant may still have application to an Israelite.[1] Thus, we can understand what Jesus meant when he said the law was not going away.

Simply think of this as a custom of the time that no longer carries the meaning it once did. If you customarily wear tassels, then put a ribbon of blue in them. But if the custom doesn't exist, there is no requirement to create it. It is also worth noting that this was a voluntary provision. I have not seen in the Bible anything

---

1. We'll discuss that later in chapter 19, "Israel and the Covenant."

resembling "tassel police."[1] Even if breaking the law was sin, compliance was still up to the individual.

Let me return to Scalia's view of the Constitution. He noted that he does not use legislative history in interpreting the law:

> The words are the law. I think that's what is meant by a government of laws, not of men. We are bound, not by the intent of our legislators, but by the laws which they enacted, which are set forth in words, of course. As I say, until recently this was constitutional orthodoxy. Everyone at least said that: That the Constitution was that anchor, that rock, that unchanging institution that forms the American polity. Immutability was regarded as its characteristic. What it meant when it was adopted it means today, and its meaning doesn't change just because we think that meaning is no longer adequate to our times. If it's inadequate, we can amend it. That's why there's an amendment provision. That was constitutional orthodoxy. When I say constitutional orthodoxy, I don't mean its just judges and lawyers. Judges and lawyers are not very important. It's ultimately the American people. What do they think this document is?

Now here we come across something rather different. God's law is immutable, and there is no amendment process. But there is latitude for judgments to be made as to the implementation of the law. In some cases, there were courts where one could take difficult cases. In most cases, the elders of a given city sat in the gate (the equivalent of your county court house), and judged. But it was inevitable that hard cases would arise. What do you do when the matter is too hard for you?

> Then shalt thou arise, and get thee up into the place which the LORD thy God shall choose; And thou shalt come unto the priests the Levites, and unto the judge that shall be in those days, and inquire; and they shall show thee the sentence of judgment (Deuteronomy 17:8-9).

---

1. The idea that compliance with any part of the law was voluntary, though, gives some people the willies. "How can it be a law, if it is voluntary?" But compliance is always voluntary if you have any choice in what you do.

This passage, all by itself, should tell us that the letter of the law was not the answer to every issue. Otherwise, there was no need for a judiciary. The law made provision for judges, due process, cities of refuge, and other issues important in governing a people. Moreover the decision of the Supreme Court was final:

> And thou shalt do according to the sentence, which they of that place which the LORD shall choose shall show thee; and thou shalt observe to do according to all that they inform thee: According to the sentence of the law which they shall teach thee, and according to the judgment which they shall tell thee, thou shalt do: thou shalt not decline from the sentence which they shall show thee, to the right hand, nor to the left (vv. 10-11).

What is interesting about this system was that the choice of going to court was up to the individuals who were in dispute. If they could settle it themselves, they were free to do so. But once they brought it to the court, they were bound on penalty of death to accept the court's decision. To do otherwise was considered a defiant sin. I suspect this had a positive effect on compliance with the court's decisions.

So the meaning of the Law of God is immutable, but the judgments made under that law are not. Times and circumstances can change, and while the judgment still serves as a precedent, it can be changed. This is what Jesus was doing through much of the Sermon on the Mount. He made it plain that he was not abolishing the written law. But he certainly was correcting a lot of bad judgments that had been made by Jewish courts.

Then there is the interesting case of a woman who had been caught in the act of adultery.[1] The Pharisees brought her to Jesus, not following due process (after all, it was none of his business; he was not a judge), but trying to cast Jesus in conflict with Moses.

Jesus declined to judge the woman, and in the process, illustrated a basic misunderstanding about biblical law. The Law of Moses required due process, just as our own Constitution does. If a man caught his wife in adultery, he couldn't just take her out and kill her himself. There was a judiciary, and the woman had rights.

---

1. John 8:1 ff.

She could not be deprived of life without a hearing. Furthermore, some assume that under the Law of Moses, an adulterer had to be stoned. Not necessarily. Joseph did not think to have Mary, the mother of Jesus, stoned when he found her with child, and the Law of Moses allowed for divorce instead of death.[1]

In any case, someone had to want to carry out the penalty. The witnesses were to be the ones who cast the first stones. If they wouldn't do it, no one else could. Jesus added one more criterion. If you were going to stone this woman, you had to be innocent yourself. Now that is not in the law. That is a judgment. And since it comes from Jesus himself, it carries a lot of weight.

Scalia presented an interesting illustration of the principles involved in originalism, citing the Nineteenth Amendment adopted in 1920 which gave women the right to vote. Scalia noted that, as an abstract matter, there was no need for an amendment to the Constitution. There was, after all, an equal protection clause right there on the page. So why the national campaign of the suffragettes to get a new constitutional amendment? Why didn't they just go to court on the basis of the equal protection clause? According to Justice Scalia, "Because they didn't think that way."

"Equal protection," he suggested, "could mean that everybody has to have the vote. It could mean a lot of things in the abstract." He went on to explain:

> It could have meant that women must be sent into combat, for example. It could have meant that we have to have unisex toilets in public buildings. But does it mean those things? Of course it doesn't mean those things. It could have meant all those things. But it just never did. That was not its understood meaning. And since that was not its meaning in 1871, it's not its meaning today. The meaning doesn't change.

Scalia made another interesting point about the original intent of the framers of the Constitution. Their intent mattered not in the least. What was important was what the people who ratified the words thought they meant, because it was only in the ratification that the Constitution became the law. This may also be important in

---

1. See Deuteronomy 24:1ff.

thinking about the Ten Commandments. The people were, in a sense, ratifying the commandments when they agreed to a covenant in which the commandments played a part. What did *they* think the words meant?

One area which I have intuitively not trusted is the argument that the opinions of the Supreme Court should "reflect the evolving standards of decency of a maturing society." It took Scalia to explain why this is a bad idea:

> Now you know that Pollyanaish attitude is not the attitude that is possessed by people who adopt a bill of rights. People who adopt a bill of rights know that societies not only evolve, they also rot. And they are worried that future generations may not have the integrity and the wisdom that they do, so they say, "Some things we are going to freeze in, and they will not change."

Common sense should tell us that is true, but common sense does not often prevail in political wars. The battles in the political arena are not about truth and justice, but about acquiring and retaining power. Scalia goes on:

> We believe, the court believes, and worst of all the American people believe that not only the 8th amendment but the whole Bill of Rights, the whole Constitution, "reflects the evolving standards of decency of a maturing society." Or, to put it more simply, the Constitution means what it ought to mean.

He said another thing that rather surprised me: "This is not, I caution you, a liberal versus conservative issue." In truth, new rights are being created all the time on both sides. "So it's not liberal/conservative. It's modernist versus the traditional view of the Constitution."

And this is a mistake I think we make all the time in talking about our political situation. There is a presumption in our society that modern equals good. We forget that societies do not always evolve upward. They also rot. Thus the need for stability, somewhere. It comes most naturally in the words of the written law. And this may be the reason why Jesus said what he said about it. Here it is yet again:

> Do not think that I have come to abolish the Law or the Prophets; I have not come to abolish them but to fulfill them. I tell you the truth, until heaven and earth disappear, not the smallest letter, not the least stroke of a pen, will by any means disappear from the Law until everything is accomplished (Matthew 5:17-18 NIV).

The written law, to Jesus, including the law about hems and tassels, was not going away. But then, he proceeded in that same message to interpret the various laws in terms of their original *meaning*. The application of the law, the judgments made on the law can change. Scalia again:

> And finally I will mention the last deficiency of non-originalism. And that is, in the long run, it is the death knell of the constitution. As I suggested earlier, the whole purpose of the constitution[sic] is to prevent a future society from doing what it wants to do.

And in an important way, that is precisely why Old Testament law cannot be cast aside. It is there to prevent a future *church* from doing what it wants to do. And we could provide a whole list of churches that are doing what they want to do without regard to what the Law of God says they should do. Scalia:

> That's the whole purpose. To change, to evolve, you don't need a constitution, all you need is a legislature and a ballot box. Things will change as fast as you want. You want to create new rights, destroy old ones? That's all you need. The only reason you need a constitution is because some things you don't want the majority to be able to change. That's my most important function as a judge in this system. I have to tell the majority to take a hike. I tell them, "I don't care what you want, but the bill of rights [sic] says you cannot do it."

And the reason Jesus did not lay aside the written law is because there were some things he didn't want the church to go changing. Scalia went on:

> Now if there is no fixed absolute, if the Constitution evolves to mean what it ought to mean today. What makes you think the majority is going to leave it to me or to my colleagues to decide what it ought to mean? . . . So at the end of this long process, this great evolution from stuffy old originalism to an evolutionary constitution we arrive at the point where the meaning of the constitution [sic], the most important part of the constitution [sic], the bill of rights [sic], is decided upon by the very body that the bill of rights is supposed to protect you as an individual against. Namely, the majority.

There is, I think, a lesson in all this for the church. We have been tempted to interpret Scripture, not in terms of what the words mean, but in terms of what we think they *ought* to mean. And thus, we have made ourselves the arbiters of right and wrong. That has happened to the nation. And it seems to be happening to the churches. And we steer our ship, not by the stars, but wherever the winds and currents take us.

7

Freedom and the Law

You cannot use law to hold back a moral landslide.
It simply won't do it. You'll just add to the laws. – Os Guiness

When the framers of the American Constitution first gathered, they faced a fundamental question. The question was not merely, can we create a free republic? The question was, can we create a free republic that will *remain* free? Those men knew their history, and they knew that history was against them. On the day the Constitution was to be signed, Benjamin Franklin wanted to address the assembly but, old man that he was, he was too weak to stand. So his speech was read by James Wilson of Pennsylvania. It is a speech of profound wisdom, but there was one statement that echoes down through time and is entirely relevant to the topic at hand. It is a long sentence, and deserves careful thought:

> In these sentiments, Sir, I agree to this Constitution with all its faults, if they are such; because I think a general Government necessary for us, and there is no form of Government but what may be a blessing to the people if well administered, and believe farther that this is likely to be well administered for a course of years, and can only end in Despotism, as other forms have done before it, when the people shall become so corrupted as to need despotic Government, being incapable of any other.

Ben Franklin did not rule out the possibility of the American experiment ending in despotism. But he felt it would only go that way when the people were no longer capable of any other form of government. It had happened through history over and over again, and he felt it might well happen again. The odd thing about the statement to me was the idea that a people might *need* a despotic government, that there might be people incapable of living free.

For Ben Franklin and the Founders, the first step in gaining freedom—the American Revolution—was past. They had now taken the next step and drafted a constitution. But the biggest challenge lay beyond their horizon: sustaining freedom—a challenge Ben Franklin knew well enough. Why? Because he was a student of history.

According to Os Guinness, "The Framers knew their history in a way many modern political leaders to their shame don't." What they understood was this: "If you have a corruption of customs, the Constitution itself will be subverted. People will follow the same laws, but with a different rationale, and you'll see a steady decline."[1]

If he was right, law is not enough to sustain freedom. We believe in the rule of law in this country, and the idea was carefully drawn as a distinction from the rule of a king. What we may not have realized is that the law can become just as tyrannical as any king.

How would that happen? Well, just look at how the courts are interpreting the law. We are no longer being governed by all the people, but by the law as interpreted by a few judges. And what is guiding the judges, the Constitution or the customs of the time? In recent years the courts have been increasingly influenced in their decisions, not by the words of the Constitution, but by the evolving morality of the times.

Dr. Guiness went on to ask: "What was the Framers' solution to this? Many people think it's the Constitution and law. It isn't. That's only half the answer. The other half is quite clear, and incredibly overlooked today, even among scholars. It's what I call the Little Triangle of Assumptions."

His triangle of assumptions is simple enough, and it is entirely

---

1. Os Guinness, "Contours of a Christian Worldview," Speech given February 12, 2004, in the Longworth House Office Building, Washington. Cited in *The Washington Times*, March 16, 2004. Guinness is the author of 11 books, and is a keen Christian apologist and cultural critic.

compatible with Ben Franklin's statement. The three sides to his triangle are:

1. Freedom requires virtue.
2. Virtue requires faith of some sort.
3. Faith requires freedom.

In Navy firefighting school, I learned about the triangle of fire. For a fire to burn, three things are required: temperature, fuel and oxygen. The concept of firefighting in any circumstance, from the flight deck to a steel compartment below decks, was this: Remove any side of the triangle, and the fire goes out.

So it is with Os Guinness' little triangle of assumptions. Remove one side from the triangle, and all is lost. He argued that if freedom has to be guarded by laws, it will eventually be lost, because every new law takes away some freedom.

There was also a sound logic behind the Framers' insistence on religious liberty. Virtue cannot be maintained in the absence of some kind of faith. The argument is not that law is unnecessary, but that the rationale behind the laws is crucial. And that without *virtue*, the whole structure of society may come unraveled.

Continuing to think in threes, Guinness went on to say that we have three massive contemporary menaces to faith and freedom. Three menaces that will, if the Framers were correct, eventually affect the system and freedom will not survive. The menaces are:

1. The idea that faith, character, and virtue are fine if you want them, but they have no place in the public square.
2. A breakdown in the transmission of values.
3. A corruption of customs.

Nancy Pearsey addressed the first of these by warning that Christians are cooperating in their own marginalization.[1] Faith, they think, need have nothing to do with their education, their jobs, their careers. They find a way to compartmentalize their lives and restrict faith to the private sphere.

The second menace, the breakdown in the transmission of values, began with the banning of prayer and Bible reading from

---

1. Nancy Pearsey, *Total Truth, Liberating Christianity from Its Cultural Captivity,* 2004.

the public schools. How can you teach right from wrong without some standard of right and wrong?

The third, a corruption of customs, has moved on apace for a long time now. Guinness dates the beginning to the 1960s, when many foundational assumptions were being "profoundly eroded or under assault. What is life? Is there such a thing as truth? What's a family? What's a marriage? What's justice more than power?"

He sees freedom in America "tilting towards evil," and warns: "If not reversed, your children and grandchildren will experience the consequences. No great civilization survives if it cuts its relations to its roots. We are on the edge of doing that. As faith goes, so goes freedom. As freedom goes, so goes the United States." He went on to ask: "Are we beyond the point of hope? I'm personally an optimist. Things are not nearly as bad here as they have been in times past, and they have been turned around."

> When faith went in [Germany], it produced the most horrendous evil the world's ever seen. I wouldn't bet that we are yet to see an American evil of monumental proportions unless there's a turning back. You cannot use law to hold back a moral landslide. It simply won't do it. You'll just add to the laws. You've got to rejuvenate the culture.[1]

"A moral landslide" is a pretty good description of what we have seen in recent years, and the decline seems to be accelerating. Obscenity and nudity on the public airways finally stung Congress to action to start fining broadcasters who insult the public. But the problem with Congress is that they only have one tool to work with: the law. And every law passed by Congress is, in some small way, an infringement on freedom. You can hear the howls coming from those whose ox is being gored this time, but I can't help wondering when someone will decide that we can't teach the Bible over the public airways. And don't think that's not possible. The government owns the airways just like it owns the courthouse. And it is not such a great step from banning the Ten Commandments in the courthouse to banning the Gospel from radio.

Let me return to Os Guinness' idea that freedom requires virtue

---

1. Os Guinness, op. cit.

and that if freedom has to be guarded by laws, it will eventually be lost. The Apostle Paul said something like this in his second letter to the Corinthians. He was addressing a local problem and then, in what seems like an aside, he tossed in one of his more profound theological statements.

> . . . Or do we need, like some people, letters of recommendation to you or from you? You yourselves are our letter, written on our hearts, known and read by everybody. You show that you are a letter from Christ, the result of our ministry, written not with ink but with the Spirit of the living God, *not on tablets of stone but on tablets of human hearts* (2 Corinthians 3:1-3 NIV).

He shifted his point of reference from letters of commendation to the letter of the law. He was himself a minister of the New Covenant, not the old. He spoke of the differences between his ministry and that of Moses. Tablets of stone, to nearly any reader, suggests the Ten Commandments, and Paul spoke of *those commandments* as written, not on stone tablets, but on the heart. It was here that Paul began the theme that Os Guinness will echo centuries later. External laws cannot hold back a moral landslide. They can only erode our freedoms. In my opinion, this was the fundamental error of first century Judaism. With the Oral Law, the Mishnah and the Talmud, they built a fence around the law. In the process, they took away freedom after freedom, and that was precisely what Paul was driving at in his epistles when he talked about liberty and freedom. He was not urging freedom from the law, but from the laws written by men to enforce the law that was written in stone.

"Laws written in the heart" is a pretty good definition of virtue. You can't make the letter of the law work without the Spirit. This was Paul's fundamental premise:

> Not that we are competent in ourselves to claim anything for ourselves, but our competence comes from God. He has made us competent as ministers of a new covenant—not of the letter but of the Spirit; for the letter kills, but the Spirit gives life (vv. 5, 6).

Laws are necessary, but when virtue has fled, they can't hold. In the absence of virtue, the letter of the law can only take away freedom. It will require more laws to enforce it and in the end, they will kill freedom. The law, as we may be seeing now, can be as much a tyrant as any dictator. There is nothing wrong with the law, as such. Paul acknowledged that it was glorious. But he also said that the ministration of the spirit is even more so. In fact, without virtue and without the Spirit, all the law can do in the end is condemn us—for we will break it. Continuing:

> Now if the ministry that brought death, which was engraved in letters on stone, came with glory, so that the Israelites could not look steadily at the face of Moses because of its glory, fading though it was . . . (v. 7).

As Paul was not himself the New Covenant, but a minister of it, so Moses was not himself the Old Covenant. Paul chose an odd construct in calling the Old Covenant a "ministry that brought death," but of course it did bring death. The law was never an instrument of salvation. It is the definer of right and wrong and, in the Old Covenant, it was combined with a ministry of *enforcement*. It was not living *within* the law that brought death. Honoring one's father and mother could hardly bring death. Dishonoring them could, in certain circumstances. It is only in the breach that either law or covenant becomes a "ministry of condemnation."

> Therefore, since we have such a hope, we are very bold. We are not like Moses, who would put a veil over his face to keep the Israelites from gazing at it while the radiance was fading away. But their minds were made dull, for to this day the same veil remains when the old covenant is read. It has not been removed, because only in Christ is it [the veil] taken away. (vv. 12-14 NIV).

Paul has a way of mixing his metaphors, so it is sometimes necessary to explain what he is saying. The Old Covenant was a good thing. It made it possible for Israel to continue as a civil society. But the law alone was not enough, not if it remained external to the people. *There is no set of laws that can be written to govern a people who do not wish to be governed by those laws.* We learned that in the years of Prohibition, but seem to have forgotten it in the modern world.

For Israel, the law was everything. But they could not see beyond the law. They had a veil over their eyes which blinded them to the spirit of the law. What this means to me is that the Christian can read the Old Testament law *without* the veil. He can see clearly what God is saying to us and can *internalize* the law: "Even to this day when Moses is read, a veil covers their hearts. But whenever anyone turns to the LORD, the veil is taken away" (vv. 15-16).

This chapter of the letter to Corinthians is commonly misunderstood. When Moses was read (which happened Sabbath by Sabbath in synagogues everywhere), the Jews did not see what lies within, behind, and underneath the law. Their eyes were veiled. But, said Paul, when one turns his heart to the LORD, the veil—not the law—is taken away. Thus one can see the real spirit of the law behind the letter. The veil is a strange metaphor, but it seems to say that Judaism never truly understood the law. And far from saying that the law is taken away, when anyone turns to the LORD, their understanding of the law becomes clearer—the veil is lifted.

Now the LORD is the Spirit, and where the Spirit of the LORD is, there is freedom. And we, who with unveiled faces all reflect the LORD's glory, are being transformed into his likeness with ever-increasing glory, which comes from the LORD, who is the Spirit (vv. 17, 18).

The key to understanding the matter is this. The letter of the law does not convey liberty. The Spirit of the LORD conveys liberty. Not a few religious movements in the past have tried to manage their flocks according to the letter of the law. As a result, they have stifled the work of the Spirit among God's people, and destroyed their liberty in Christ.

So Paul and Os Guiness were saying the same thing. Freedom requires virtue, an internalizing of the law; and if freedom can only be guarded by external laws, it will eventually be lost.

Guiness' other point was this: "Virtue requires faith of some sort. This is is the simple reason that the Framers argued there should be religious liberty."

This is inescapable. Without faith, without God, we become our own arbiters of what is right and what is wrong. So, first Congress, and then the courts start deciding right from wrong for us and, in the process, squeeze our liberties into oblivion. We will follow the "evolving standards of morality" around in an ever tightening circle until all our liberty is gone.

We have long since tossed God out of the schools and our kids are taught that we have no designer, no guarantor of our freedoms, no final arbiter of right and wrong. We have to look to ourselves; there is no God to save us.

Finally, Guinness' third assumption in his little triangle is that faith requires freedom. "If that triangle is perpetual, then freedom has a chance of defying the odds and keeping alive." Without freedom, faith will be squeezed to nothing.

So the question is still before us: Will we survive as a civilization, or will we, like all the great ones before us, go into decline? Everyone knows about Rome. And while we don't think about it very often, the great Islamic Empire of a thousand years ago is now reduced to the cowardly killing of women and children in a vain attempt to achieve their objectives. There was a time when the Islamic Empire was even greater than Rome's or Alexander's. But it is gone.

In our own time, we have seen the disappearance of the British Empire. So, why should we assume that we are any better? That which might have made us better—faith—has been tossed aside. As we have already heard from Os Guinness:

Law alone won't do it without faith. Because without faith, you have no basis for the law. Benjamin Franklin said one more thing that echoes in our own generation:

Much of the strength and efficiency of any Government in procuring and securing happiness to the people, depends, on opinion, on the general opinion of the goodness of the Government, as well as of the wisdom and integrity of its Governors.

No one has contributed more to the diminishing of respect for the wisdom and integrity of our governors than the governors themselves. Day by day the political machines, created and controlled by those who govern, continue to trash the reputations of those who oppose them.

You would think Peter was speaking of our generation when he spoke of "them that walk after the flesh in the lust of uncleanness, and *despise* government. Presumptuous are they, selfwilled, they are not afraid to speak evil of dignities" (2 Peter 2:10).

In our day, the "general opinion of the goodness of the Government" is in tatters. Government is the joke of the late night comedians. How can a generation of lawmakers, so despised by so many, reverse a moral landslide? Have we, in Ben Franklin's words, "become so corrupted as to need despotic Government, being incapable of any other"?

8

Divorce Law

Moses because of the hardness of your hearts
suffered you to put away your wives:
but from the beginning it was not so (Matthew 19:8).

Divorce is painful. If you have been through a divorce, you need no one to tell you that. Not only do the children get hurt, there are the grandparents, the family, the friends. And no one can tell of the pain, of the anger that comes in the middle of the night to the two people who once loved each other above all others. Once this wreckage is strewn across the lives of a family, it can never all be cleaned up. The pain and the hurt may be healed, the guilt may go away, but life will never be quite the same again.

The heart and core of Christianity is forgiveness and healing, and yet the effects of divorce seem terribly hard to shake. Jesus could heal a withered arm. He could give sight to the blind. He could make the crippled walk. He could make the deaf hear. What we now have to consider is whether he can, or will, heal the broken lives of the victims of divorce.

Human beings are not machines. When they are cut they bleed. When they are divorced they hurt. So the hurting ones turn to Jesus, not only for forgiveness, but for understanding and for guidance. The Pharisees came to Jesus to hear his interpretation of the law: "Is it lawful for a man to divorce his wife for any and every reason?" (Matthew 19:3 NIV). There were two major schools of thought at that time. One believed that a man could divorce his wife for almost any reason; the other held that some form of unchastity was the only ground. The Pharisees wanted to know where Jesus stood on the question.

He gave them an answer, though it was not what they expected or wanted. He allowed that men should not divorce their wives at all: "Have you not read," he replied, "that he which made them at the beginning made them male and female, and said, For this cause shall a man leave father and mother, and shall cleave to his wife: and they two shall be one flesh? Wherefore they are no more two, but one flesh. What therefore God has joined together, let not man put asunder" (Matthew 19:5-6).

Jesus' answer was unequivocal and clear, and the Pharisees understood it well enough. Marriage was in the design of God from the beginning and it was permanent. Man was commanded not to "put asunder" what God had joined together. Not only was Jesus opposed to divorce for every cause, he was opposed to divorce for *any* cause.

The Pharisees were taken aback by his reply, and they challenged it immediately: "Why did Moses then command to give a writing of divorcement, and to put her away?" (v. 7). They felt they were on firm ground, because the Law of Moses plainly permitted divorce, and Jesus knew it. He could only acknowledge the truth of what they said: "Moses because of the hardness of your hearts suffered you to put away your wives: *but from the beginning it was not so*" (v. 8).

This statement of Jesus is crucial. With it he establishes what may be the single most important fact in the entire discussion: There was a law "from the beginning," an original law, if you will, and it differed in significant ways from the Law of Moses. Here is the Law of Moses on the issue:

> When a man hath taken a wife, and married her, and it come to pass that she find no favour in his eyes, because he hath found some uncleanness in her: then let him write her a bill of divorcement, and give it in her hand, and send her out of his house (Deuteronomy 24:1).

Jesus said this law was given because of the hardness of men's hearts. In other words, the law was given in response to a set of conditions existing at the time. Jesus established beyond question that the law stated in Deuteronomy 24 was a judgment—that is to say, an application of the law to a set of circumstances.

Moses specified a case where a man had found some "uncleanness" in his wife. The Hebrew expression here rendered "uncleanness" means "matter of nakedness." The same expression is used extensively in Leviticus 18 and 20 and there it refers to illicit sexual relationships. In other words, if a man's wife has an affair, he can put her away.

It is sometimes objected that "uncleanness" in this passage cannot mean adultery, because the law required the death penalty for adultery.[1] The fact is that, although the death penalty was authorized, it was not always required. When Joseph found Mary with child, he assumed it was the result of an illicit affair. Since he was a "just man," i.e., one not afflicted with hardness of heart, he was minded to "put her away," to divorce her, privately (Matthew 1:18-19). On another occasion, Jesus declined to authorize the stoning of a woman taken in the very act of adultery (John 8:3).

The question Moses faced was simple. When sin had entered the picture and destroyed the very foundation of marriage, when a man's wife has slept with another man and he can no longer trust her or live with her, yet he does not want to stone her, what should he do? The answer, given with all the authority of God's law, is found in Deuteronomy 24. The man was to make a written document of divorce, give it to the woman, and send her away. She was then free to marry another man.

One primary purpose of this judgment was to protect the rights of the divorced woman. This was not an age when women could readily enter a work force, and there was no welfare as we know it. When her husband put her away, her right to remarry was a right to food, shelter, and clothing. It is not often realized that in the ancient world, women were often treated as chattel. This law not only gave the woman the right to remarry if she were divorced, it prevented the first husband from taking her back against her will. The second marriage terminated the first husband's property rights (verse 4).

This underlines one other effect of this judgment. There is no case for breaking up a second marriage on the pretext that a woman is somehow bound to the first husband. The second marriage, whether it was right or wrong, ended the first husband's rights. She

---

1. Leviticus 20:10

91

was not deemed to still be married to the first husband.

Divorce was not a part of the original intent of God's constitution for man. Even under Moses, it was a "necessary evil," a step taken to alleviate the damage of failed marriages, and keep some semblance of order in the home for the sake of the children and for society at large.

When Jesus restated the original intent of marriage, did he reject the Law of Moses on this subject? Not at all. When his statement was challenged by the Pharisees, and when he had acknowledged that Moses had indeed given them a law regulating divorce, he went on, "And I say to you, Whosoever shall put away his wife, except it be for fornication, and shall marry another, commits adultery: and whoso marries her which is put away commits adultery" (Matthew 19:9).

The original word for "fornication" is *porneia*, and it denotes illicit sexual relations. The King James Version renders the word, "fornication," which is generally thought of as premarital sexual intercourse. But that is not all it means. *Porneia* includes premarital sex, and adultery.[1] In other words, *porneia* in Jesus' statement corresponds to "some uncleanness" in Deuteronomy 24. This means that Jesus accepted the judgment of the Law of Moses on divorce and rejected the rabbinical idea of "divorce for every cause."

But why make an exception at all? After all, the law is the law. Why compromise it with judgments and exceptions? The disciples still did not understand. Their conclusion was, "If that is the case of the man with his wife, it is good not to marry" (v. 10). That doesn't seem to follow, but at least it prompted Jesus to explain further. In the process, he gave us the reason for the exception clause.

> But He said to them, "Not all men can accept this statement, but only those to whom it has been given. For there are eunuchs who were born that way from their mother's womb; and there are eunuchs who were made eunuchs by men; and there are also eunuchs who made themselves eunuchs for the sake of the kingdom of heaven. He who is able to accept this, let him accept it" (Matthew 19:11-12 NASB).

1. Presumably, it would also include homosexual acts.

The idea Jesus advanced here is a little obscure at first, but it is firmly based in God's original intent: "And the LORD God said, it is not good that the man should be alone" (Genesis 2:18). Man was a good piece of work, but what was included in the design of man was what Freud called the libido (the sexual urge, to you and me). Actually it is not just sex drive, but the drive to love, to be close, to touch, to be intimate with another human being. Most human beings cannot flourish without it.

If Jesus' disciples were talking about permanent celibacy when they said it was good for a man not to marry, they seem to have missed the point entirely. But if they were talking about the man who is *divorced*, that it is good for *him* not to marry, then the discussion becomes rational.

What Jesus was saying in his curious discussion about "eunuchs" is that some men and women cannot remain celibate. Thus, Jesus and Moses both conclude that when a marriage is broken by sexual sin by one of the partners, it is not necessary for the offended party to live alone for the rest of his or her life. But, at least as far as this judgment goes, if a man and a woman divorce for any other reason, they must not marry another. If they do, it is adultery. As Paul put it, "And unto the married I command, yet not I, but the LORD, Let not the wife depart from her husband: But and if she depart, let her remain unmarried, or be reconciled to her husband: and let not the husband put away his wife" (1 Corinthians 7:10-11).

A couple who are divorced do not have to live celibate lives. They have an option—*they can be reconciled.* In this case, the sexual urge can serve to bring two people back together. But it does not require a lot of imagination to realize that there are problems with this. In fact, Paul had to deal with a problem that Jesus did not address—the problem of marriages divided, not by infidelity, but by religion. The Corinthians had written Paul about several questions, and he was systematically addressing them. Unfortunately, we do not have the letter from the Corinthians to Paul. It would be of enormous value in understanding the Corinthian letters, but we can still draw some inferences from what we read.

The subject of divorce and remarriage is addressed in the

seventh chapter and is introduced by the curious statement, "Now concerning the things of which you wrote to me: It is good for a man not to touch a woman." Since we know that it is not wrong for a man to touch a woman,[1] we must assume he was referring to a question arising from their letters. Indeed, later in this chapter, he acknowledged that much of what he was saying was said only because of the "present distress" (verse 26).

Having made this statement, he went on to acknowledge the physical needs of men and women. He knew that any attempt to impose celibacy would lead to fornication. In verses three through six, he outlined the intimate responsibilities of husbands and wives to one another.

Like Jesus, Paul knew that the ability to remain celibate was a gift that some had and some did not: "For I would that all men were even as myself," he wrote, "but every man hath his proper gift of God, one after this manner, and another after that. I say therefore to the unmarried and widows, It is good for them if they abide even as I. But if they cannot contain, let them marry; for it is better to marry than to burn" (vv. 7-9). Note that the word "unmarried" is the same word used in verse 11 for divorced women. The "unmarried and widows" in this passage are two categories of formerly married women. Paul says, if they cannot control themselves, "let them marry."

But Paul stood opposed to divorce: "And unto the married I command: yet not I, but the LORD, Let the wife not depart from her husband: But and if she departs, let her remain unmarried, or be reconciled to her husband; and let not the husband put away his wife" (vv.10-11).

Having said all this, he was still left with a problem—not a few of the Greek converts were married to unbelieving mates. These were not Christian husbands with different doctrinal beliefs, but pagans who did not believe in Jesus Christ at all. What was a woman to do if she was abandoned by such a man?

Paul began by saying, "But to the rest speak I, not the LORD," (v. 12). He was rendering a *judgment*. His judgment in this matter follows: "If any brother hath a wife that believes not, and she be pleased to dwell with him, let him not put her away. And a woman

---

1. "Marriage is honourable in all, and the bed undefiled: but fornicators and adulterers God will judge (Hebrews 13:4).

who has a husband that believes not, and if he be pleased to dwell with her, let her not leave him. . . But if the unbelieving depart, let him depart. A brother or a sister is not under bondage in such cases; but God hath called us to peace" (verses 12-15).

Was Paul adding another "exception clause" for divorce? In the first place, he declared that religious differences are no excuse for breaking up a marriage. Marriage is just as binding for Christian/pagan marriages as it is for marriages between converted mates.

However, this was not the case if the unbelieving mate abandoned the marriage. When that happened, a brother or sister was not "under bondage." In other words, they were free—loosed from the marriage bond. Paul spoke of marriage in terms of "binding and loosing" twice more in the chapter. Once in verse 27, "Art thou bound unto a wife? Seek not to be loosed. Art thou loosed from a wife? Seek not a wife," and again in verse 39, "The wife is bound by the law as long as her husband lives." Paul plainly said that a woman deserted by an unbelieving mate was not bound to her husband—she was free to remarry.

Then it would seem that Paul was indeed adding another exception to the one given by Moses and Jesus. Did he have the right to do that? There are some things to consider. First is Jesus' statement to all the Apostles that they had the power to make "binding and loosing" decisions (Matthew 16:19 and 18:18). Nowhere is this wording more appropriate than in matters of marriage and divorce. Second, there is a strong presumption that a pagan mate who abandons his Christian wife will not remain celibate—that he will commit sexual sins and thus invalidate marriage. Just because the wife cannot prove it should not condemn her to a life of celibacy, or worse, to a life of sin because she cannot remain celibate.

Perhaps the most important thing to understand is that Moses, Jesus, and Paul were not creating "exception clauses." They were rendering judgments. Jesus was addressing essentially the same people Moses addressed. Paul was not. Had Jesus addressed the Corinthian church directly there is no reason to think He would have said anything differently from Paul.

But Paul had one more difficulty to address; that of the divorce and remarriage that is already an established fact. One or both of a married couple had divorced a previous mate without legitimate grounds. Paul addressed the problem this way:

> Brethren, let every man, wherein he is called, therein abide with God. Now concerning virgins I have no commandment of the LORD; yet I give my judgment, as one that hath obtained mercy of the LORD to be faithful. I suppose therefore that this is good for the present distress, I say that it is good for a man so to be. Art thou bound unto a wife? Seek not to be loosened. Art thou loosed from a wife [divorced]? Seek not a wife. But and if thou marry, thou hast not sinned (verses 24-28).

This passage speaks to the newly converted at the time of his calling. It assumes that reconciliation with the former mate is out of the question.

The time of a person's calling is pivotal. One's whole life turns on the point of baptism, because at baptism we die to the past. This is just as true of divorce as it is of any other sin. In another letter, Paul says: "Know ye not, brethren, (for I speak to them that know the law), how that the law hath dominion over a man as long as he lives? . . . But if the husband be dead, she is loosed from the law of her husband" (Romans 7:1-2).

Compare this with what he said in an earlier chapter: "Know ye not, that so many of us as were baptized into Jesus Christ were baptized into His death? Therefore we are buried with Him by baptism into death; that like as Christ was raised up from the dead by the glory of the Father, even so we should also walk in newness of life. Knowing this, that our old man is crucified with Him, that the body of sin might be destroyed, that henceforth we should not serve sin. For He that is dead is free from sin" (Romans 6:3-7).

There is no requirement for the man or woman who is baptized to go back and try to make up for all the sins of the past. As far as the law is concerned, they are dead. The penalty has been exacted. No former obligations, including the penalty for divorce, can be enforced. They are free to walk in a new life. There is never a case for splitting up an existing marriage and home to try to right some past wrong. God hates divorce, and He hates second and third ones as he does the first.

There will always be questions about divorce and remarriage that will require judgment. What about a woman who learns she has married an alcoholic, or a child abuser? What if she fears for her life? Naturally she can flee to a crisis center, but can she divorce such a man? Almost certainly. This is the reason God established a set of judges under Moses (Deuteronomy 17:8-13), and under Christ (Matthew 16:19 and 18:18).

Those who judge righteous judgment will always take the high ground of Jesus' statement first: "Have ye not read, that He which made them at the beginning made them male and female, and said, For this cause shall a man leave father and mother, and shall cleave to his wife; and they twain shall be one flesh? Wherefore they are no more twain, but one flesh. What therefore God hath joined together, let no man put asunder."

But if they remember Jesus' caution, "I will have mercy and not sacrifice," they will also work to bind up the brokenhearted and to heal the spirit wounded by divorce. Divorce is not the unpardonable sin. The ravages of divorce can be forgiven and healed like any other wound.

It is not my intent to make the judgment for people considering divorce or remarriage, but to give them the knowledge to make that judgment for themselves. In the end, those who have to live with the decision should be the ones to make it.

For the rest of us, it is not our decision to make, and we should not attempt to influence the outcome. Those who make the decision will answer to God and God alone. And they have enough pain without the rest of us adding to it.

9

The Avenger

Let every soul be subject unto the higher powers. For there is no power but of God: the powers that be are ordained of God (Romans 13:1).

As we saw in the last chapter, divorce has long been a perplexing subject. This chapter is not about divorce, but the discussion about divorce opens a door to understanding another, very different, issue:

> When a man hath taken a wife, and married her, and it come to pass that she find no favour in his eyes, because he hath found some uncleanness in her: then let him write her a bill of divorcement, and give it in her hand, and send her out of his house (Deuteronomy 24:1).

The meaning of this seems obvious to me, but there has been an incredible range of interpretation ranging from the severe to the absurd. I have read some tortuous explanations of this verse, but there really is no question what Moses meant by this. It does not mean that if the man finds his wife doesn't wash often enough or keeps a dirty house, he can divorce her. What it does mean is that, if a man finds his wife has been adulterous, he can legally put her away. Furthermore, once she has been another man's wife, he can never take her back.

Of special interest is the expression, "you shall not cause the land to sin" (v. 4). This means that there is a *societal* interest in keeping marriage sacred.[1] The law is first and foremost for the sake of the children. Society has a vested interest in protecting children, because they are the future of the society. Sexual relationships were regulated because unbridled sex can bring an entire country to the brink of ruin. There is, however, one major objection to the interpretation I have offered here. It arises from another law on adultery:

> If a man be found lying with a woman married to an husband, then they shall both of them die, both the man that lay with the woman, and the woman: so shalt thou put away evil from Israel (Deuteronomy 22:22).

So, what is this thing about divorce for sexual uncleanness? If the woman was guilty of adultery, why was she not stoned? A common assumption is that the law was inexorably and always applied in the letter. That does not appear to be the case for two reasons. One is that there may not be the two witnesses that are required. The other is that there may be no one who wants the death penalty carried out. Consider these two related passages. One we have discussed, the other we have not.

> If a damsel that is a virgin be *betrothed unto an husband,* and a man find her in the city, and lie with her; Then ye shall bring them both out unto the gate of that city, and ye shall stone them with stones that they die; the damsel, because she cried not, being in the city; and the man, because he hath humbled his neighbour's wife: so thou shalt put away evil from among you (vv. 23-24).

Couple that with this:

> Now the birth of Jesus Christ was on this wise: When as his mother Mary was espoused to Joseph, before they came together, she was found with child of the Holy Ghost. Then Joseph her husband, *being a just man,* and not willing to make her a public example, was minded *to put her away*

---

1. The expression, "the land," is used in a variety of applications in Hebrew texts. In some contexts, as in this one, it refers to the nation, the society, the social contract.

privily (Matthew 1:18-19).

There are some important things here to think about. Joseph was not a scofflaw. He was a just man. He could have made her an example but decided not to, and thus arises an insight into the law: Mercy was allowed. Joseph would have been deemed the offended party. It was his call, and no one else's. Now let's add one more insight.

Jesus came to the Temple early one morning and immediately drew a crowd. He sat down and began to teach. While he was talking, there was a disturbance and the scribes and Pharisees entered, dragging a woman with them. They stood her in the middle of the crowd and said to Jesus: "Master, this woman was taken in adultery, in the very act" (John 8:4).

That the woman was caught in the act was important. Witnesses were required in all capital cases.[1] Guesswork was not permitted and they knew it. Her accusers went on:

> Now Moses in the law commanded us, that such should be stoned: but what sayest thou? This they said, tempting him, that they might have to accuse him. But Jesus stooped down, and with his finger wrote on the ground, as though he heard them not. So when they continued asking him, he lifted up himself, and said unto them, He that is without sin among you, let him first cast a stone at her (vv. 8:5-7).

The motive of the Pharisees in bringing this case had nothing to do with justice or the law. They were looking for a cause to accuse Jesus, but he wasn't biting. Now they had to deal, not with Jesus, but with the law. While the whole crowd could participate in stoning, under the law the witnesses had to go first. What came at issue here was *mercy*. Sinners, if they are not in denial about their own sins, can be the most merciful of people. Jesus stripped away all denial. All that was left was mercy.

> And they which heard it, being convicted by their own con-science, went out one by one, beginning at the eldest, even unto the last: and Jesus was left alone, and the woman

---

1. Deuteronomy 17:6

standing in the midst. When Jesus had lifted up himself, and saw none but the woman, he said unto her, Woman, where are those thine accusers? hath no man condemned thee? She said, No man, LORD. And Jesus said unto her, Neither do I condemn thee: go, and sin no more (vv. 9-11).

This is crucial in understanding issues of the law. The condemnation of the poor sinner was *a matter of choice*. God himself does not routinely kill adulterers, or we would have suffered massive depopulation by now. One of the most evil approaches to the Law of God is to remove the mercy option. To be sure, there are some crimes where mercy is simply not possible.[1] But to make the law automatic and inexorable is to make God into someone entirely different from who he is.

Not a few struggle with this issue. One approach is to divide the law into various compartments—this law is in effect and that one is not—playing hopscotch through the law. There are, though, two significant divisions in what is called, "The Law of Moses." The divisions are commonly called *moral* and *civil*. The division is problematic because some conclude that the civil law is abolished while the moral law remains. The problem is that the civil law is written, and Jesus said the written law would continue as long as heaven and earth remained. What people are describing by the term "civil law" is administrative law—the laws describing who is to administer and enforce the law, and how they are to go about it.

There is in the Bible a basic law that differentiates between right and wrong, and applies to man, whenever and wherever he finds himself. The obedience to this law is personal and between a man and his God. For example, consider this promise made to Isaac.

And I will make thy seed to multiply as the stars of heaven, and will give unto thy seed all these countries; and in thy seed shall all the nations of the earth be blessed; Because that Abraham obeyed my voice, and kept my charge, my commandments, my statutes, and my laws (Genesis 26:4-5).

---

1. Hebrews 10:28.

101

Long before Moses, there was a complete system of law, but there appears to have been no civil administration of that law. There is another set of laws that became necessary for men to live together in a community. These laws were administrative.

For example, we have in this country a basic law that condemns murder. Then there is another set of laws controlling how we deal with the murderer. In our society, these are familiar: Trial by jury, due process, laws of discovery, chain of evidence, etc. These laws can actually vary from state to state. If you have ever sat on a jury, you have seen these laws applied by the court.

Now take this back in time to Israel in the days of the judges. Living in the land of Israel, an adulterous relationship occurs. Say, Baroc ben Ephraim learns that his wife has been sleeping with Juda ben Mannaseh down the road. By law, Baroc could gather the elders, establish the case, cast the first stone and have them both executed.

Now let's move the case to Alexandria and Egyptian law. The underlying moral law is still very much in effect. Adultery is wrong. Baroc can divorce his wife. But Egyptian administrative law may have had no provision for capital punishment for this offense. This underlines a major source of misunderstanding. An assumption is made that the administrative law, sometimes called the civil law, was abolished in Christ. Problem is, the administrative law was part and parcel of the written law—that part of the law that Jesus said would last as long as heaven and earth remain.

But the administrative law may not be enforceable if there is no administration. The law remains, but it can only serve as a *precedent* for the will of God in a given time and place. A man or a woman may commit adultery and escape the death penalty, but the law remains to teach us how truly damaging the act is to human relationships. And in that way, it suggests a call for forgiveness and mercy, and it reveals why the call for mercy is needed.

Of what I have said so far, this is the sum: Old Testament law is not nearly as inflexible as many seem to think. There were judges, priests, elders, and an entire administration. Some penalties were at the discretion of these people and there could be extenuating circumstances.

I was discussing this with a group and someone pointed to the example of David and Bathsheba. Should they not have been executed for their crime? One obvious reason why they were not is that David was the head of state. There was no one above the king who could sit in judgment of him and call for his execution. God could have killed him, of course, but God had delegated judgment to a civil administration and was not willing to take it back. I think there is something very important in that simple fact. *Even when civil government is corrupt, it is still the authority which has been authorized to judge.* Paul faced this issue in an altogether different time and place:

> Everyone must submit himself to the governing authorities, for there is no authority except that which God has established. The authorities that exist have been established by God. Consequently, he who rebels against the authority is rebelling against what God has instituted, and those who do so will bring judgment on themselves (Romans 13:1-2).

And what was the governing authority when Paul wrote these words? Since he was writing the churches in Rome, it would seem that it was Roman authority he was describing as God's servant, the bearer of the sword, and an "agent of wrath to bring punishment on the wrongdoer" (v. 4). The agent is, in the Greek, the *ekdikos*, literally, the executor of justice. In Old Testament terms, he was "the avenger."

This raises an interesting distinction, not unlike our two Israelites living in Alexandria. Adultery was still a sin against God and neighbor, but Egyptian law controlled in matters of execution. So, living in the Roman Empire, the state became the avenger.

Who, in Mosaic Law, was the avenger? By the time of the monarchy, the state was the avenger, but in the period between Joshua and Samuel, it was different. Here is what the law required in these, the freest of times:

> Speak unto the children of Israel, and say unto them, When ye be come over Jordan into the land of Canaan; Then ye shall appoint you cities to be cities of refuge for you; that the slayer may flee thither, which killeth any person at unawares. And they shall be unto you cities for refuge from the avenger; that the manslayer die not, until he stand

before the congregation in judgment. And of these cities which ye shall give six cities shall ye have for refuge (Numbers 35:10-13).

This is an early example of due process. Intentional murder was one thing. Manslaughter something else. But of special interest in this passage is the word "avenger." In Hebrew, the word means "redeemer." It is the same word in the familiar, "For I know that my *redeemer* liveth, and that he shall stand at the latter day upon the earth."[1]

The "redeemer" is a synonym for the next of kin who has the right to redeem his brother from slavery, or in this case to redeem his blood from the man who took it. It is revealing of what lies behind the death penalty under Moses' law—a sharp distinction between vengeance and retribution.

When Paul uses the term "avenger," good Hebrew that he was, it was used in the sense of the redeemer, of the balancer of the books. In Rome, the state was the avenger of blood, and there were no cities of refuge. In the time of the judges, it was different. Under that administration, there were cities designated as cities of refuge. If you accidently killed a man, you were guilty of manslaughter. If you went to one of the cities of refuge without delay, the avenger could not take your life. The cities were to be conveniently placed:

Lest the avenger of the blood pursue the slayer, while his heart is hot, and overtake him, because the way is long, and slay him; whereas he was not worthy of death, inasmuch as he hated him not in time past (Deuteronomy 19:6).

In other words, the killing was accidental, not premeditated. What is interesting here is that person with the legal right to redeem could legally take the life of a killer. It is not mere vengeance. It is retribution. A balancing of the books. Furthermore, you had to have the legal right of next of kin to do the deed. This is the Israelite law of manslaughter. It had a penalty short of death. He had to stay in that city of refuge until the death of the High Priest. Only then could he leave. But what if it was not manslaughter? What if it was premeditated murder? It was dealt with according to due process.

---

1. Job 19:25

> But if any man hate his neighbour, and lie in wait for him, and rise up against him, and smite him mortally that he die, and fleeth into one of these cities: Then the elders of his city shall send and fetch him thence, and deliver him into the hand of the avenger of blood, that he may die (vv. 11-12).

Mercy was not an option for the elders of the city. The *avenger* might extend that mercy, but not the civil administration. There is one more thing about this. As in our Constitution, no man could be deprived of life or liberty without due process. And at least two witnesses were required.

> Whoso killeth any person, the murderer shall be put to death by the mouth of witnesses: but one witness shall not testify against any person to cause him to die. Moreover ye shall take no satisfaction for the life of a murderer, which is guilty of death: but he shall be surely put to death. And ye shall take no satisfaction for him that is fled to the city of his refuge, that he should come again to dwell in the land, until the death of the priest. So ye shall not pollute the land[1] wherein ye are: for blood it defileth the land: and the land cannot be cleansed of the blood that is shed therein, but by the blood of him that shed it (Numbers 35:30-33).

There are some interesting things about this law. One is that you couldn't pay off the elders to get them to let you go. Another very important issue is that a minimum of two witnesses was mandatory. One was not enough. Therefore, judicial execution was probably infrequent in those days. Did they allow circumstantial evidence into court? Probably not to the extent that courts do today. It is doubtful if O.J. Simpson would have been convicted under the law of Moses, just as he wasn't under United States law. It may be that Scott Peterson, convicted of the murder of his wife and unborn son, would not have been found guilty under Israelite law.

Our Constitution requires that no man should be deprived of life or liberty without due process of law. The same was true in

1. This is another instance where the word, "land," refers to the social structure of a land, a nation. It isn't the acreage that is corrupted, it is the social contract.

Israelite law. I worry a bit about our system these days. I think the office of the prosecutor is the weak link. In the time of the Judges of Israel, there was one very important difference. When a crime came to trial, the judges were to make diligent enquiry. If witnesses or accusers had testified falsely, the penalty they had sought to impose would be carried out on the accuser.[1] This should have a chilling effect on authorities who are tempted to plant false evidence to get a conviction. It is an unfortunate truth that the authorities have, on occasion, cooked the evidence to get a man they were sure was guilty. In such a case, then the District Attorney or the officers guilty of that should go to jail for the same term they were trying to pull off for the accused. If you are ever called to serve on a Grand Jury or a Petit Jury, hold the prosecutor's feet to the fire and be sure he proves his case. Scott Peterson may well have killed his wife and unborn child. But he should not be convicted of murder merely because he is a proven louse, or because the jury has been led to hate him as a result of prosecutorial manipulation.

So, let me take my summary a bit further. There is much about Old Testament law that we do not understand. We know that not one word of it has been abolished. We also know that we have to draw a line at the point of administration, and thus the *enforcement*, of the law. The enforcement of the law has not been abolished, but the authority to enforce has been given to the state.

Now I want to get a little closer to the original language of something Paul wrote. Peter observed that Paul was hard enough to understand, even by those who read Greek. That difficulty is magnified for us, and nowhere more so, than in his letters to Corinth. But the struggle is essential in dealing with the topic at hand. Consider this, for example:

> And such trust have we through Christ to God-ward: Not that we are sufficient of ourselves to think any thing as of ourselves; but our sufficiency is of God; Who also hath made us able ministers of the new testament; not of the letter, but of the spirit: for the letter kills, but the spirit giveth life (2 Corinthians 3:4-6).

---

1. See Deuteronomy 19:16-19.

The word for "ministers" in this passage is the Greek, *diakonos*. It is closely related to *diakonia*, which is usually rendered "ministry." The root of both words is *diokos*, "to pursue." A deacon is a servant, but not necessarily a menial servant. He may have the duty of pursuing justice, for example, as a "civil servant." He may be an administrator, one who executes public affairs, as distinguished from a policy maker or legislator.

In this context, I think Paul's use of diakonia would be better rendered, "administration." Look at it this way:

But if the *administration* of death, written and engraven in stones, was glorious, so that the children of Israel could not stedfastly behold the face of Moses for the glory of his countenance; which glory was to be done away: How shall not the *administration* of the spirit be rather glorious? For if the *administration* of condemnation be glory, much more doth the *administration* of righteousness exceed in glory (vv. 7-9).

The glory in Moses' face would fade over time. And the administration of death would also be replaced by the administration of the Spirit. Paul and the other apostles were able administrators of the new covenant.

What I think is too often overlooked in Paul's writing is his rejection of the *diakonia,* the administration, of the Jewish establishment. Their administration was corrupt. Moses' administration was glorious, and adequate for the governance of a nation, but was not intended to govern the heart of man.

All this comes together to shed light on a widely misunderstood teaching of Jesus. On two separate occasions, he told his disciples, "I tell you the truth, whatever you bind on earth will be bound in heaven, and whatever you loose on earth will be loosed in heaven" (Matthew 18:18). This is the moment when Jesus replaces the Jewish administration of the assembly of God's people. In its place, for the church, he creates a new administration based on the apostles: "Again, I tell you that if two of you on earth agree about anything you ask for, it will be done for you by my Father in heaven. For where two or three come together in my name, there am I with them" (vv. 19-20).

Thus, unilateral administration of the church is set aside. It takes two or three leaders to judge a matter. What we are seeing is a change of administration.

10

Immigration Law

The stranger that is within thee shall get up above thee very high; and thou shalt come down very low. He shall lend to thee, and thou shalt not lend to him: he shall be the head, and thou shalt be the tail (Deuteronomy 28:43-44).

I would not presume to advise the French on what to do about their Muslim populations. After the riots of not-so-distant memory, after the French cleared their streets of burnt-out cars, after they had finished rebuilding the burned schools, there was no shortage of talking heads on television handing out free advice with all the confidence of hindsight. Frankly, I get a little tired of all the worn out generals and colonels and ex-CIA operatives treating us to their expertise, and advising a government that no longer needs or wants their advice. If they're so smart, why aren't they running the country? Now, there's one very useful book on the market. I think it may be the most important book written so far about terrorism, about Islam and about what we're facing in the world. It's Tony Blankley's, *The West's Last Chance: Will We Win the Clash of Civilizations?* Blankley can't resist offering advice any more than any other pundit, but before he does, he offers facts and analysis that I hadn't seen anywhere else. I came away from his book far less confused about what is going on than I was before I read it.

Most Americans pay little attention to what goes on in Europe and our media does very little to help. When Muslim hoodlums were burning thousands of cars across French cities, including

109

Paris, we got a lot of pictures of burning cars, of young thugs throwing Molotov cocktails at the police, but we got very little understanding about what was going on or why. And when they did try to tell us why it was happening, for the most part, they got it wrong.

In fairness to the media, they're in the business of making money. It is all too easy to forget that, when you're watching news programs. If we get bored with the program and switch off, they can't sell their commercials so they keep the news buzzing with action. And their analysis is more combative than it is enlightening. That's what made Tony Blankley's book such an eye opener. Some time ago he wrote in *The Washington Times*:

> When, seven months ago, I finished writing my Book, *The West's Last Chance: Will We Win the Clash of Civilizations?*, London had not been attacked by Islamic terrorists, the Tate Museum in London had not removed an art exhibit because it offended radical Muslim sensibilities, and France had not yet experienced the explosion of violence from elements of its Muslim populations in its no-go zone communities. The fact that I predicted all these events in my book was not the result of clairvoyance. It was merely the result of a normally intelligent person looking at the facts and their rather obvious implications without the blinding effect of a politically correct mentality.[1]

And for me, it was the *facts* that were riveting. Part of the shock was realizing how much we in this country simply do not know about what has been happening in Europe. We don't read the European press and it seems the news hounds in this country don't read it either. They had to take notice, finally, when Paris was burning, but even then they left us in the dark, probably because that's where they were. Political reporters in this country pay attention to what heads of government do overseas—chancellors, presidents, prime ministers. They follow all these people around and report to the world on what these leaders are doing and saying. But if the press has a clue as to what the man in the street is thinking, they don't bother telling the rest of us.

1. Tony Blankley, "Islamist Threat in France," *The Washington Times*, November 9, 2005.

According to Tony Blankley, events in Europe, going on right now in the streets and coffee houses, are telling a different story. They're telling careful observers that the people our newsmen are covering now in Paris and Bonn, heads of governments, are going to be turned out of office in the not-too-distant future. The man in the street is fed up and governments are already leaning to the right across Europe. They have to pay attention to where the man in the street is going because these are the people who vote.

Blankley went on to say that the Muslim parts of Paris, Rotterdam and other European cities are already labeled no-go zones for ethnic Europeans, including armed policemen. As the Muslim populations and their level of cultural and religious assertiveness expand, European geography will be claimed for Islam. Continuing to quote:

> Europe will become pockmarked with increasing numbers of little Falujahs that will be effectively impenetrable by anything much short of a United States Marine Division. Thus as the fundamentalism expands into Europe and, perhaps to a lesser extent, American Muslim communities, not only will Islamic cultural aggression against a seemingly passive and apologetic indigenous population increase, the zone of safety and support for actual terrorists will expand as well.[1]

There are parts of Europe where this is already the case. According to a German news magazine, "The veil of multiculturalism has been lifted, revealing parallel societies where the law of the state does not apply." Now think about that. It is true in Europe, but not so true here—yet. In Europe there are zones where the laws of the German state for example, or the laws of the French state simply do not apply. They can't be enforced and the people who live there enforce their own cultural laws. This is not merely the future; in Europe, it is now. And as Tony Blankley observed, all this stuff is third or fourth page news to American news sources. Nobody is paying any attention. In the waning days of the new French insurrection, Blankley wrote this:

---

1. Ibid.

Soon the violence of the last two weeks will be seen as the opening of an event of world historic significance. Even when the current violence subsides, even when the French government attempts to placate its radical Muslim population by offering more welfare benefits and programs, it will not be the end of the story. A new benchmark of the possible will have been established. The flaccid and timorous response of the French government will only increase the radicalizing Muslim's contempt for western cultural weakness.[1]

Tony Blankley went on to cite Paul Belien writing from Brussels about the same time, who observed: "It is not anger that is driving the insurgents to take it out on the secularized welfare states of old Europe, it is hatred. Hatred caused not by injustice suffered, but stemming from a sense of superiority. The youths do not blame the French; they despise them."

This is something no one in this country seems to grasp. Whenever you pick up the news magazines or you hear the comments by the talking heads, people are trying to explain why it is that the Arabs are so angry at the injustice they have suffered; about the way that they have been treated by the host country. And that's all people in this country seem to understand. Most of the media have missed the story completely. Talking heads criticize the French for isolating the Muslims in their country in ghettos, but that is not the picture seen from Europe.

Paul Belien goes on to report: "Look what a typical radical Muslim leader, the leader of the Brussel's based Arab-European League has to say: 'We reject integration when it leads to assimilation. I don't believe in a host country. We are at home here and whatever we consider our culture to be also belongs to our chosen country. I'm in my country; not the country of westerners.'"[2] Where was he? He was in Belgium. Or, consider the statement of a radical German-Islamist that Tony Blankley recounted in his book. This from a German Muslim:

---

1. Ibid.

2. Paul Belien, cited by Tony Blankley, op. cit.

Germany is an Islamic country. Islam is in the home, in schools. Germans will be outnumbered. We Muslims will say what we want; we'll live how we want. It's outrageous that the Germans demand that we speak their language. Our children will have our language, our laws, our culture.[1]

I said I would not presume to advise the French. I don't know enough. But the difficulties Europe is having with immigrant populations serve to throw *biblical* immigration law into sharp relief. The Bible offers solutions that can be summarized by two simple, easy-to-understand, principles: (1) drive out or destroy the incorrigible elements who will not be assimilated; (2) welcome and *assimilate* the rest.

The Palestinians are exhibit number one of a people who could not/would not assimilate with Israel. And the problem in ancient times is the problem today. It was a competing religion. Then it was Baal. Now it is Allah.

Shortly after handing down the Ten Commandments and an assortment of judgments apropos of the circumstances they faced in the wilderness, God added this:

Behold, I send an Angel before thee, to keep thee in the way, and to bring thee into the place which I have prepared. Beware of him, and obey his voice, provoke him not; for he will not pardon your transgressions: for my name is in him. But if thou shalt indeed obey his voice, and do all that I speak; then I will be an enemy unto thine enemies, and an adversary unto thine adversaries (Exodus 23:20-22).

This is a good start. God would be an enemy of their enemies. Israel was headed toward the promised land. They would have to fight for it, but God would fight on their side: "For mine Angel shall go before you, and bring you in unto the Amorites, and the Hittites, and the Perizzites, and the Canaanites, the Hivites, and the Jebusites: and I will cut them off" (v.23).

What Israel would face was a particular set of people with whom they were to attempt no accommodation, no assimilation. Their cultures, particularly their religions, were simply

---

1. Tony Blankley, *The West's Last Chance, Will We Win the Clash of Civilizations?* 75.

incompatible. The people were also corrupt beyond imagination. Just how corrupt they were will be discussed in the next chapter. The six listed tribes were people who would never assimilate with Israel but would, in the end, corrupt them if they stayed. God goes on to develop the theme:

> You shall not worship their gods, nor serve them, nor do according to their deeds; but you shall utterly overthrow them, and break their sacred pillars in pieces. But you shall serve the LORD your God, and He will bless your bread and your water; and I will remove sickness from your midst. There shall be no one miscarrying or barren in your land; I will fulfill the number of your days (Exodus 23:24-26 NASB).

Every vestige of their *religion* was to be eradicated from the land, for it would undermine the laws God gave them—laws that had a lot to do with health as it turned out. Implicit in this statement is that there would be health issues in assimilating with a pagan population.

> I will send My terror ahead of you, and throw into confusion all the people among whom you come, and I will make all your enemies turn their backs to you. And I will send hornets ahead of you, that they may drive out the Hivites, the Canaanites, and the Hittites before you. I will not drive them out before you in a single year, that the land may not become desolate, and the beasts of the field become too numerous for you. I will drive them out before you little by little, until you become fruitful and take possession of the land (vv. 27-30 NASB).

We will learn later that this transition plan also required Israel to fight. It wasn't going to be easy, but God would fight on their side. Just how big was this land to be? "And I will fix your boundary from the Red Sea to the sea of the Philistines, and from the wilderness to the River Euphrates; for I will deliver the inhabitants of the land into your hand, and you will drive them out before you" (v. 31).

But for this to work, no deals could be made with these people, no treaties, no covenants, *and zero tolerance for their religion.* They were not even allowed to take residence in Israel (vv. 32-33).

Now as brutal as this is, the alternative was to become corrupted and eventually destroyed from within by the people they didn't drive out. This is the picture Tony Blankley is drawing for us in Europe right now. The Europeans have invited these people in to provide a work force. But many are people who refuse to assimilate. They won't learn the French language, nor will they learn German. They want to have their own government, their own schools, their own religion. It is their stated goal to eventually make Europe their own country. But consider what God said to Israel: "You had better get rid of these people." There are some religions and some cultures that are completely incompatible, incorrigible, and corrupt.

Now in the modern politically correct way of thinking about this, it sounds like Israel was to be a racist, exclusive, xenophobic society, but that's not the whole story. In Israelite law, aliens were not only welcome in Israel, they were to be treated with respect and consideration. They were to have all the rights, privileges and responsibilities of one who was Israelite born. That said, *Israel was not to become a multicultural society.*

The word "multicultural" is going to be very much in the news, and we need to think long and hard about the issues it raises. "Multicultural" is not synonymous with multi-racial. You can have all kinds of people of different nationalities, races and ethnic groups living together in one culture. But once you allow the cultures to separate in an attempt to create a multicultural society, as Europe has done (and as some in this country believe we should do), you are headed for trouble. What the Law of God said to the aliens who lived among them was, "If you are going to live here, you will have to become part of the culture."

Israel was given explicit instructions regarding strangers, aliens who had come to sojourn among them: "Thou shalt neither vex a stranger, nor oppress him: for ye were strangers in the land of Egypt" (Exodus 22:21). But wait. What about those people they were to drive out? These instructions seem contradictory.

We need to pause here to get some terms straight. The word, "Gentile," is commonly used to describe any person who is not a

Jew, but that is not the correct usage in the Old Testament. In fact, the singular "Gentile" isn't found there. It is always "Gentiles." The Hebrew word is *goy*, in the sense of a massing of people, and it means "nation." Usually, it is a foreign nation, but Israel is also spoken of as a *goy*, a nation.[1]

Goy is not the word for "stranger." The word for stranger is *ger*, derived from the verb *guwr*, which means "to sojourn." The people who lived in Canaan before the conquest were tribes of people who were often at war with one another. It was a way of life. There was no way these people could have been assimilated into Israel en masse. On the other hand, the stranger is an *individual* who can easily be assimilated. Attempting to take in an ethnic group that worshiped another God would be a disaster.

But the stranger, the sojourner, who arrives in Israel for trade or for work was to be treated as a guest. That said, the stranger was bound by the laws of the land: "Ye shall have one manner of law, as well for the stranger, as for one of your own country: for I am the LORD your God" (Leviticus 24:22). If that law were applied today, we would say to people who come to live among us, "You are welcome here, but you must live under our laws, learn our language, go to our schools, and accept our culture. All this is required, but then we will treat you like one of us." There is more:

> For the LORD your God is God of gods, and LORD of lords, a great God, a mighty, and a terrible, which regards not persons, nor takes reward: He executes the judgment of the fatherless and widow, and *loves the stranger*, in giving him food and raiment. Love ye therefore the stranger: for ye were strangers in the land of Egypt (Deuteronomy 10:17-19).

When we have immigrants who come to our country, God says we should love them, because he loves them. We are not to reject them or persecute them, but to treat them well. That said, there is no call to leave them as a completely isolated, separate culture in our midst. They must, in return for our hospitality, accept our culture and our laws. There is more:

---

1. See Exodus 33:13.

Also thou shalt not oppress a stranger: for ye know the heart of a stranger, seeing ye were strangers in the land of Egypt (Exodus 23:9).

And thou shalt not glean thy vineyard, neither shalt thou gather every grape of thy vineyard; thou shalt leave them for the poor and stranger: I am the LORD your God (Leviticus 19:10).

The stranger is entitled to your welfare program on the same basis as those born in the land. But in Israel, welfare was not brought to you. You had to work to get it. Israel was to love the stranger, to accept him as one born in the land. That said, the stranger was expected to respect the religion of the host country. When it came to the Sabbath, they were told to shut down their work:

But the seventh day is the Sabbath of the LORD thy God: in it thou shalt not do any work, thou, nor thy son, nor thy daughter, thy manservant, nor thy maidservant, nor thy cattle, *nor thy stranger* that is within thy gates (Exodus 20:10).

There was, in Israel, both cultural and religious assimilation. You were welcome to come and set up shop, but not to keep it open on the Sabbath. This is not the religious assimilation that says you have to believe what we believe. You just have to practice what we do. Israel was not to be a multicultural society. To strangers they said, "You're welcome here, but you must assimilate, you learn the language, you learn the culture, you live by our laws, or you get out."

The reason was the protection of their religion. It was possible for a stranger to participate fully in the religion of Israel if he chose to do so. And this is something that it seems hardly anybody understands.

And thou shalt say unto them, Whatsoever man there be of the house of Israel, or of the strangers which sojourn among you, that offereth a burnt offering or sacrifice, And bringeth it not unto the door of the tabernacle of the congregation, to offer it unto the LORD; even that man shall be cut off from among his people" (Leviticus 17:8-9).

What a surprise. Far from being banned from the temple, as they were by the first century, strangers were actually permitted to offer a sacrifice. But, if he does it and does not bring it to the door of the Tabernacle, to offer it to Jehovah, that man shall be deported—i.e., cut off from the social contract. In other words, if you're going to worship our God, you must worship our God the same way the rest of us do. Our civil laws and our religious laws apply to you just like it would if you were home-born.

> And this shall be a statute for ever unto you: that in the seventh month, on the tenth day of the month, ye shall afflict your souls, and do no work at all, whether it be one of your own country, or *a stranger that sojourns* among you (Leviticus 16:29).

The cultural and religious assimilation of strangers included the most common aspects of daily living—even to the point of fasting on the Day of Atonement.

If I could summarize God's Law for the modern nation, it is to avoid multiculturalism like the plague. Require the people who immigrate to France to become French, speak the language, learn the culture. The same thing is true here. If a person wants to immigrate to this country, he should learn English and respect our culture, our history, and our religion.

And it's that last that's part of the problem. France, the government more than the people, has walked away from their religious faith. Here in America, there are those trying to take us down the same path. *And if you expect the strangers to assimilate with your culture, you have to have a culture.* That is a warning that God gave to Israel that should be taken very seriously. In a long discourse, he said to them:

> And it shall come to pass, if thou shalt hearken diligently unto the voice of the LORD thy God, to observe and to do all his commandments which I command thee this day, that

the LORD thy God will set thee on high above all nations of the earth (Deuteronomy 28:1).

The LORD shall cause your enemies that rise up against thee to be smitten before your face: they shall come out against you one way, and flee seven ways (v. 7).

But it shall come to pass, if thou wilt not hearken unto the voice of the LORD thy God, to observe to do all his commandments and his statutes which I command thee this day; that all these curses shall come upon thee, and overtake thee (v. 15).

The stranger that is within thee shall get up above thee very high; and thou shalt come down very low. He shall lend to thee, and thou shalt not lend to him: he shall be the head, and thou shalt be the tail (vv. 43-44).

A multicultural society is an unstable society and it will fall to those who know who they are and who know where they're going. That is the danger France is facing today and the United States will be facing tomorrow.

Tony Blankley believes that Europe has three choices: One, the government gets on top of this, restricts civil liberties for Muslims, takes all necessary action from imprisonment to deportation, and puts an end to the problem.

Two, rising vigilantism by the man in the street will lead to much bloodshed but will solve the problem that way. Vigilantism is on the rise in Europe and we don't hear very much about this in this country. It's much bigger in Europe than most Americans realize. Tony Blankley's hope is that it will begin to put the pressure on the governments in Europe who will turn and do the right thing.

Three, Europe will roll over and accept the eventual domination by Islam, which, at last, will leave the United States completely isolated.

I suppose I could say that Tony Blankley is optimistic long term, but he seems to expect a lot of bloodshed and some radical changes in western society. According to him, mainstream opinion in Europe has recently abandoned political correctness and wants to halt the inroads of Islam from Norway to Sicily. Governments, politicians, and media are laying aside doctrines of diversity, insisting that Islamism (as the French call the fundamentalist form that pervades the housing estates) is incompatible with Europe's liberal values.

Even a left-wing French intellectual, such as commentator Jacques Juilliard, said that the left's long-standing tolerance has been used as an agent for the penetration of Islamic intolerance. That is a stunning admission and a warning for everyone. In this country, I don't look for a change in national direction from mere persuasion. We can argue about this till hell freezes over and nothing will change. But let one dirty bomb make lower Manhattan uninhabitable for a thousand years, and hell will freeze over.

11

The Pagan Feminine

*Do you not see what they are doing in the towns of Judah
and in the streets of Jerusalem? The children gather wood,
the fathers light the fire, and the women knead the dough
and make cakes of bread for the Queen of Heaven. They
pour out drink offerings to other gods to provoke me to
anger (Jeremiah 7:17-18 NIV).*

I don't know if you have read the novel, *The Da Vinci Code*,
but I am reasonably sure you have heard of it. The book created its
own cult following, but it wasn't really new at all. It is truly
fascinating to watch an ancient pagan cult attempt to rise again in
the modern world.

Another fascinating element is how a work of fiction can be
taken as fact in some quarters. The first and most important thing to
know about *The Da Vinci Code*, is that it is fiction. It is not
historical fiction, it is fiction-fiction; it does not have a veneer of
fiction, it is fiction all the way through, and it combines another
form of fiction, conspiracy theory, to spice things up.

One reader said that she found herself constantly doing Internet
searches to find out if the things being described in the novel are
real or not. I laughed, because I initially found myself doing the
same thing. But even when you find something that is really there,
on examination, you find that it is once again a veneer.

One of the ideas developed in the book is the assumed
suppression of the sacred feminine. It is an old idea, and has found
a lot of repetition in literature, especially in the occult. But the

suppression of the pagan feminine really happened. It is discussed quite frankly in the Bible. What had to be squelched in all its many forms was Asherah worship. Something like it still persists in the modern world. Here is how the idea is characterized by one website, called Teen Witch:

> Asherah—The original bread of life. Hebrew and Canaanite women molded loaves of this figure which were blessed and ritually eaten, the precursor of the communion wafer. Her idols were found under every green tree, were carved from living trees, or erected as poles or pillars beside roadside altars. Crude clay images of her as tree of life later evolved into the more refined Syrian Artemis. Ancient sexual rites (dismissed to this day by male scholars as cult prostitution) associated with worship of Asherah insured that matrilineal descent patterns, with their partnership rather than dominator values, would continue. Hebrew priestly iconoclasts finally uprooted Asherah, supplanting matrifocal culture with patriarchy. Our Judeo-Christian inheritance of this law of the Levites, passed on by the Roman Empire, is one source of present-day sex inequality.[1]

I don't know how old this posting is, but it sounds like the idea was borrowed whole from *The Da Vinci Code*—or vice versa. Whatever the case, it is true indeed that Hebrew and Canaanite women did what is said here, and Jeremiah was dead serious about it. Here is what God told him:

> So do not pray for this people nor offer any plea or petition for them; do not plead with me, for I will not listen to you. Do you not see what they are doing in the towns of Judah and in the streets of Jerusalem? The children gather wood, the fathers light the fire, and the women knead the dough and make cakes of bread for the Queen of Heaven. They pour out drink offerings to other gods to provoke me to anger. But am I the one they are provoking? declares the LORD. Are they not rather harming themselves, to their own

---

1. http://www.teenwitch.com/deity/canaan/asherah.htm.

shame? (Jeremiah 7:16-19 NIV).

Of course, we know all too well that the Israelites were to drive out the Canaanites and *not* to adopt any of their religious customs. What we read in the Teenwitch summary is the whining one would expect from a people whose gods have been defeated. The irony is that Asherah worship was *not* uprooted. It persisted all the way to the fall of Jerusalem. Asherah worship even turned up among the refugees who fled to Egypt after that. Jeremiah was among those people, and it became necessary for God to speak to them about this persistent error.

> Thus saith the LORD of hosts, the God of Israel; "Ye have seen all the evil that I have brought upon Jerusalem, and upon all the cities of Judah; and, behold, this day they are a desolation, and no man dwelleth therein, Because of their wickedness which they have committed to provoke me to anger, in that they went to burn incense, and to serve other gods, whom they knew not, neither they, ye, nor your fathers. Howbeit I sent unto you all my servants the prophets, rising early and sending them, saying, Oh, do not this abominable thing that I hate" (Jeremiah 44:2-4).

What was so terrible about what Israel was doing? They had burned incense to other gods, but that hardly seems to call for such dire punishment upon a nation. "Why," God asks, "commit ye this great evil against your souls, to cut off from you man and woman, child and suckling, out of Judah, to leave you none to remain" (v. 7).

Here is a good place to stop and try to understand what was really going on. This had to be more serious than a little incense burning and baking bread. It was, after all, bad enough that God turned them over to the worst of the heathen and cut them all off from the land. What had they done, really?

Whatever it was, they would not listen to Jeremiah. They said in reply:

> We will certainly do everything we said we would: We will burn incense to the Queen of Heaven and will pour out

drink offerings to her just as we and our fathers, our kings and our officials did in the towns of Judah and in the streets of Jerusalem. At that time we had plenty of food and were well off and suffered no harm. But ever since we stopped burning incense to the Queen of Heaven and pouring out drink offerings to her, we have had nothing and have been perishing by sword and famine (Jeremiah 44:17-18 NIV).

The insolence is breathtaking, but so is the denial of what happened to them. It is true that they were engaged in Asherah worship at the absolute peak of prosperity. Because they were prosperous at the same time they were worshiping the Queen of Heaven, they confused coincidence with cause. The truth is that they were blessed by God in the land because he had promised to do so. They completely ignored the fact that they were warned, right at the peak of prosperity, that they were sinning. And they ignored the fact that they never repented of the sin right through the fall of Jerusalem.

But what is this all about, and why is Asherah worship such a very big deal? And why haven't we heard elsewhere about this Queen of Heaven, seeing she is so important in Jeremiah? Well, we have, but for some reason the old Bibles paper over it. Take, for example, the King James Version:

Take heed to thyself, lest thou make a covenant with the inhabitants of the land whither thou goest, lest it be for a snare in the midst of thee: But ye shall destroy their altars, break their images, and cut down their groves (Exodus 34:12-13 KJV).

The word here rendered, "groves," is the Hebrew, *Asherah*. The NIV calls these Asherah poles. But what does that mean?

Asherah worship involved what is probably the oldest and surely the most persistent of all the ancient pagan customs—cult prostitution. It is a mixture of two of the most powerful influences on the human psyche—sex and religion. Cult prostitution differs from street prostitution only in its ostensible religious purpose. Truth to tell, it is doubtful how much religion really had to do with it.

Historically, religious prostitution involved a lot of the same dreadful practices that are still in play today. Women do not generally decide to be sex workers as an occupational choice when an alternative is open to them. Often as not, they were sold into it as children and they are sex slaves. The Greeks, who saw more than a thousand cult prostitutes in the temple at Corinth, called them *hierodules*—from the word *hieron*, temple, and *doule*, female slave. (Some say there were about the same number of male and female sex slaves in Greek worship.)

The practice is much older than Greece, though, being traced back to the earliest civilizations. One of the surprising aspects of Asherah worship is its persistence. Every tribe of ancient cultures had a different male deity. Baal, Molech, Dagon, etc. What is surprising is that the one constant in all those cultures was the goddess. She was always and everywhere the same. She was the sacred feminine, consort of the gods, and presumably she slept with all of them.

So this is rather more than incense and hot cross buns. It turns out that it is also more than a little temple sex with a consenting adult. Historically, not many women voluntarily took on the role of a cult prostitute. They were sold into it as children and had never known any other life.

Among the laws concerning relations with alien nations, there is this:

> Be careful not to make a treaty with those who live in the land where you are going, or they will be a snare among you. Break down their altars, smash their sacred stones and cut down their Asherah poles. Do not worship any other god, for the LORD, whose name is Jealous, is a jealous God. Be careful not to make a treaty with those who live in the land; for when they prostitute themselves to their gods and sacrifice to them, they will invite you and you will eat their sacrifices. And when you choose some of their daughters as wives for your sons and those daughters prostitute themselves to their gods, they will lead your sons to do the same (Exodus 34:12-16 NIV).

I think many take this reference to prostitution in a figurative sense. But apparently, it was quite literal. Cult prostitution was indeed the world's oldest profession:

> It was revered highly among Sumerians and Babylonians. In ancient sources (Herodotus, Thucydides) there are many traces of hieros gamos (holy wedding), starting perhaps with Babylon, where each woman had to reach, once a year, the sanctuary of Militta (Aphrodite or Nana/Anahita), and there have sex with a foreigner, as a sign of hospitality, for a symbolic price.[1]

Every woman in that culture had to commit an act of prostitution. So if your sons took a wife from among the heathen, their wives would prostitute themselves to their gods. Literally.

Why would God hate this so much? Well, consider how persistent and destructive it is. It is hard to grasp that even now, in the "modern" world, child sex slaves are quite common. The Anti-Slavery Society works to put an end to the practice, and you can read what is happening on their web site. Sex slavery is all too common, still, in India and Nepal. In years gone by it usually involved parents dedicating their little girls to a Hindu god. Sometimes the parents offered the girls as a sacrifice to appease the gods, or the girls were purchased and offered to the gods. The girls served as slaves or dancers employed by the priests to provide sexual services to men who came to worship. According to the Anti-Slavery Society, times and methods have changed:

> However, nowadays, this original purpose has gone and, after dedication—usually at the age of 5 to 7 years of age—the child is often deflowered by the priest and then sold to the highest bidder, who keeps her as his child concubine. When she grows older and loses the bloom of youth, her buyer usually gets rid of her. The girl then has to work in a brothel which often has a shrine at the door to symbolize her original dedication to Hindu cult prostitution.

---

1. *Wikipedia*, article, "Religious Prostitution."

The British made efforts to suppress hierodulic child prostitution in India—the Indian Penal Code 1860 made it a criminal offence to procure women or girls for that purpose—and it was on the decline throughout the earlier part of the last century. However, there has been a recent revival of these institutions in Karnataka and Andhra Pradesh.[1]

I think, when people imagine temple prostitutes, they think of the kind of woman you might see on a street corner in the red light district. But I get the impression that in all ages, it has been a kind of slavery involving little girls and little boys. It hasn't been only the religion of the Hindus, but everywhere that Asherah has been worshiped. So maybe when God says he hates, loathes, and despises this, and calls it "going a whoring after other gods," we can take his point?

I gather that "eating the sacrifice" says rather more than having a steak, and some aspects of these customs are too vile to discuss here. I will simply tell you that *The Da Vinci Code* alleges that the holy grail is actually Mary Magdalene, and I suspect this is of a piece with some ancient custom.

It seems Israel had not been long in the land until they began to absorb the culture and religion of the people they were supposed to drive out:

And the children of Israel dwelt among the Canaanites, Hittites, and Amorites, and Perizzites, and Hivites, and Jebusites: And they took their daughters to be their wives, and gave their daughters to their sons, and served their gods. And the children of Israel did evil in the sight of the LORD, and forgat the LORD their God, and served Baalim and the Asherah[2] (Judges 3:5-7).

Judah did evil in the eyes of the LORD. By the sins they committed they stirred up his jealous anger more than their fathers had done. They also set up for themselves high places, sacred stones and Asherah poles on every high hill

---

1. http://www.anti-slaverysociety.addr.com/hieroras.htm

2. Substituting for the KJV, "groves."

and under every spreading tree. There were even male shrine prostitutes in the land; the people engaged in all the detestable practices of the nations the LORD had driven out before the Israelites (1 Kings 14:22-24 NIV).

Ahab son of Omri did more evil in the eyes of the LORD than any of those before him. He not only considered it trivial to commit the sins of Jeroboam son of Nebat, but he also married Jezebel daughter of Ethbaal king of the Sidonians, and began to serve Baal and worship him. He set up an altar for Baal in the temple of Baal that he built in Samaria. Ahab also made an Asherah pole and did more to provoke the LORD, the God of Israel, to anger than did all the kings of Israel before him (1 Kings 16:30-33 NIV).

Asherah, or Ashtoreth, was the female consort of every male deity in the world, and a temple to Baal would have included the sacred feminine, i.e., the temple prostitute. King Josiah put a stop to these practices, which also included child sacrifice. In their orgies in Carthage, children were sometimes burned alive to Baal:

[Josiah] did away with the pagan priests appointed by the kings of Judah to burn incense on the high places of the towns of Judah and on those around Jerusalem—those who burned incense to Baal, to the sun and moon, to the constellations and to all the starry hosts. He took the Asherah pole from the temple of the LORD to the Kidron Valley outside Jerusalem and burned it there. He ground it to powder and scattered the dust over the graves of the common people. He also tore down the quarters of the male shrine prostitutes, which were in the temple of the LORD and where women did weaving for Asherah (2 Kings 23:5-7 NIV).

Asherah crops up again and again in the Bible, and she is the "Sacred Feminine" in its original form. It amounts to nothing more than an ancient sex goddess who arranged the selling of little boys and girls as sex slaves. It preys on the weakest and most helpless among us. It is a powerful force for the destruction of marriage and family, and eventually of society. The novel, *The Da Vinci Code* resurrected the old goddess worship, and the movie bid fair to push it even further. But it really boils down to an excuse to justify satisfying one of the oldest cravings of man. Sex without responsibility.

As a footnote to all this, it was not the priests who put an end to Asherah worship among the Hebrews. It was the Babylonian captivity. When the Persians finally allowed the Israelites to return, Asherah worship ceased. Archaeological digs all over Palestine find, in the pre-exile sites, numerous little figurines of the fertility goddess. In the post-exile layers of a dig, they find none. It is one lonely example of a people learning a lesson from history.

12

The Problem with Sin

What then shall we say that Abraham, our forefather, discovered in this matter? If, in fact, Abraham was justified by works, he had something to boast about—but not before God. What does the Scripture say? "Abraham believed God, and it was credited to him as righteousness" (Romans 4:1-3 NIV).

I used to be a teenager. True, it was a long time ago, but I still remember vividly some of the questions about the Bible that troubled me back then. This may come as a surprise, but teenagers have a spiritual life and they really do think about God. Moreover, their questions are important to them. Sad to say, they are too often left unanswered. Faith may survive, but it often gets badly bruised.

I remember as a teenager wondering about some of the stuff I heard from the pulpit and in Sunday School. For example, I heard that it was impossible for man to keep the Law of God perfectly. Then I wondered (but I never asked anyone), why would God give man a set of laws he cannot possibly observe, and then punish him for not observing them? Don't think that is a straw man. That assertion is still rattling around in the minds of many.

I understand grace. I understand what Paul meant when he said, "by grace are you saved." But if you think about it long enough you will realize that doesn't answer the question. Why do you even need to be saved? Why doesn't God just write your sins off the books with the observation, "Oh well, they couldn't have kept the law anyhow"?

My parents didn't punish me for not doing something I couldn't do. If they gave me a rule and I broke it, at least it was a rule I could have kept if I tried. And the punishment fit the crime. They weren't cruel to me. The worst I ever got was a few swats on the behind. I survived.

But my question about God remained over the years: "Why would God give man a set of laws he could not possibly observe, and then punish him for not observing them?"

I don't remember when the answer occurred to me, but in time I came to realize that my question made the assumption that the Law of God was arbitrary. That is to say, the law depended on the individual discretion of God for enforcement and for punishment. But then I realized there were, in fact, two assumptions. One, the law was arbitrary and could just as easily have never been imposed. (It follows naturally from the assumption that the law could be set aside.) Two, the enforcement of the law depends on a sovereign act of God. In other words, God can let me off or punish me at his sole, subjective discretion.

But what if my assumptions were wrong? If they were, then there were two conclusions that might follow. One, the law is not arbitrary after all but arises from the nature of things, the nature of man in particular. Two, the violation of the law has inexorable *consequences*, great and small, that do not depend on the action of any enforcing authority. One of the consequences can be death, but even that doesn't require an act of God. It can come about as a result of alienation from the source of life.

There is a biblical word for this. The word is "sin." John defined it in simple terms: "Whoever commits sin transgresses also the law: for sin is the transgression of the law" (1 John 3:4).

Paul, I think, clarified the issue somewhat: "Now we know that what things soever the law says, it says to them who are under the law: that every mouth may be stopped, and all the world may become guilty before God" (Romans 3:19). Now at first blush, this sounds a little like my first assumption: i.e., God placed everyone under a system of law designed to ensure that everyone becomes guilty. But that doesn't make sense, and I don't see that Paul means that. He went on. "Therefore by the deeds of the law there shall no flesh be justified in his sight: for by the law is the *knowledge* of sin."

Now it begins to come clear. The point of the law is not to *create* sin, but to make us *aware* of sin. There are a lot of issues in life that have negative consequences that we might not know about, so God tells us what they are. Paul continued: "But now a righteousness from God, apart from law, has been made known, *to which the Law and the Prophets testify*" (Romans 3:21 NIV).

That is a surprising statement, when you think about it. Not a few Christians assume that righteousness "apart from the law," is a New Testament thing—that righteousness prior to the New Testament came by the law. But Paul said that righteousness "apart from the law" is witnessed by the law itself (and, incidentally by the prophets). How does the law do that? It presents us with two steps.

Step number one: Faith. You have to believe God. How hard is that? Here is an Old Testament witness from the Book of the Law:

> And God brought Abraham outside, and said, "Look now toward heaven, and tell the stars, if thou be able to number them: and he said unto him, So shall thy seed be." *And he believed the LORD; and he counted it to him for righteousness* (Genesis 15:5-6).

You can't get any more Old Testament than this, and it is stunning in its simplicity. God makes Abraham a promise of incredible scope, and Abraham does something almost as incredible. He *believed* the promise. The implications of this are that Abraham, believing that what God said was true, would order his life to align with that belief. This is what led Paul to write what he did:

> But now the righteousness of God apart from the law[1] is manifested, being witnessed by the law and the prophets; Even the righteousness of God which is by faith of Jesus Christ unto all and upon all them that *believe*: for there is no difference: For all have sinned, and come short of the glory of God (Romans 3:21-23).

---

1. As the NIV.

So, step one is to believe God, in particular the Son of God, Jesus Christ. Step two is to restore the relationship with God that was damaged by sin. Somehow, in the process of thinking this through, it became obvious to me that the law is about life. Thus, the law is complicated and difficult because life is complicated and difficult. The law was given, not arbitrarily, but as a description of the things that hurt people and destroy relationships.

Is the Law of God beyond our reach? No, not in any of its parts. We don't have to steal, but we do. We don't have to lie, but we do. So what is it about sin that is so bad? The problem with sin is that it is a relationship killer. It alienates. Take adultery as a classic example. An indiscretion like adultery is like taking an axe to a tree and cutting great chunks out of it. Even if the adultery is undiscovered, the relationship is damaged, sometimes beyond repair. And it isn't only the relationship with the mate that is damaged. The relationship with God is damaged as well.

Sin involves alienation from God. There is no better illustration of this than the story of Adam and Eve. The happy pair were placed in Paradise, and given very simple instructions: You can eat of all the trees in this garden except one. Leave it strictly alone. How hard could this have been? All they had to do was *believe* God. Think about it. God said that if you eat of this tree, you will die. If they had really believed that, would they have eaten of it? Would you? What they did was a breach of trust. What is your reaction when someone won't believe you, won't trust you? Doesn't it damage the relationship? Or at least reveal that the relationship is already in trouble?

I went on for years accepting a simple equation from the Garden of Eden. God gave Adam one commandment. Don't eat of that tree. Adam broke the commandment and God expelled the first couple from the garden. Then one day, I was studying the Book of Hosea and found that God, through the prophet, condemned the men of that generation and saying this of them: "Like Adam, they have broken the covenant—they were unfaithful to me there" (Hosea 6:7 NIV).

A covenant is not mentioned in the creation story, but it is implied. God gave Adam a commandment and presumably Adam agreed. Then, he broke covenant with God. This seems to be a much more serious matter than for a person to sin when not in covenant with God.

So Adam and Eve ate of the Tree of the Knowledge of Good and Evil. And they died. But here is what is interesting about this story. *God did not kill them.* He simply separated himself from them—and incidentally, cut them off from the Tree of Life. What this says to me is that the result of this sin was not *punishment* from God, but the *consequence* of being alienated from God.

This is underlined by what happened when Cain killed his brother Abel. God did not kill him either. He exiled him. And Cain, and all the rest of the children of Adam and Eve, died. They died because they were away from God—the source of all life. This is what the "fall of man" is all about. The result was, I think, not so much a change in human nature, but a change in man's environment and a loss of man's relationship with God. If you read the Genesis story with that in mind, it is clear enough right there. There is not a word about a change in the nature of man, but much about the change in man's environment—particularly his alienation from the source of life.

So, we return to the Apostle Paul to see how he develops his theme of sin, law, and reconciliation. Here again is where we started:

> Now we know that what things soever the law saith, it saith to them who are under the law: that every mouth may be stopped, and all the world may become guilty before God. Therefore by the deeds of the law there shall no flesh be justified in his sight: for by the law is the knowledge of sin (Romans 3:19-20).

Christians need to understand that this is not merely a New Testament idea. Men were not justified by works of the law in the Old Testament, and then by faith in the New Testament. Remember, Abraham was said to be righteous because he believed God. This is justification by faith. The evidence of that belief and the covenant that grew out of it is described thus: "Because that Abraham obeyed my voice, and kept my charge, my commandments, my statutes, and my laws" (Genesis 26:5). First came faith, then came obedience. Paul went on:

> But now the righteousness of God apart from the law is manifested, being witnessed by the law and the prophets; Even the righteousness of God which is by faith of Jesus Christ unto all and upon all them that believe: for there is no difference: *For all have sinned*, and come short of the glory of God (Romans 3:21-22).

There is an important distinction to be made here. We don't need Adam's sin to make us guilty. We have all sinned. But there is more:

> Being justified freely by his grace through the redemption that is in Christ Jesus: Whom God hath set forth to be a sacrifice of atonement through faith in his blood, to declare his righteousness *for the remission of sins that are past*, through the forbearance of God (Romans 3:23-25 KJV).

All die because all have sinned, and the way back is closed. What is needed now is reconciliation—a reconciliation we cannot accomplish on our own. Remember, there are two different results connected with sin: consequences and punishment. Justification, by definition the remission of sins past, occurs through the forbearance of God. Because we believe, he restores the relationship and punishment is suspended.

But that says nothing at all about the *consequences* of sin. Let's suppose you go out on the town with the guys and have too much to drink. Then you compound the error by driving your car. On the way home, you go to sleep at the wheel, veer off the road, and roll your car. In the accident, you lose your left arm and nearly lose your life. Where are you now before God? You sinned. You alienated yourself from God (no one likes to be around a drunk except perhaps another drunk). You broke man's law and will be charged with a DUI. Upon repentance, God will forgive you. But he won't give you your arm back, and he will let the courts deal with your DUI offense. Justification, then, is the forgiveness of sin and the restoration of the relationship with God that was severed by your sins. But justification has nothing whatever to do with the natural and civil consequences of sin. There is no promise from God to deliver you from the consequences of the things you we do.

Jesus said as much:

> Agree with thine adversary quickly, while thou art in the
> way with him; lest at any time the adversary deliver thee to
> the judge, and the judge deliver thee to the officer, and thou
> be cast into prison. Verily I say unto thee, Thou shalt by no
> means come out thence, till thou hast paid the uttermost
> farthing (Matthew 5:25-26 KJV).

And so, Paul summarized his argument thus:

> Therefore we conclude that a man is justified by faith
> without the deeds of the law. Is he the God of the Jews
> only? is he not also of the Gentiles? Yes, of the Gentiles
> also: Seeing it is one God, which shall justify the
> circumcision by faith, and uncircumcision through faith. Do
> we then make void the law through faith? God forbid: *yea,*
> *we establish the law* (Romans 3:28-31 KJV).

That makes a great deal of sense. Just because God forgave you
for driving drunk, does not suggest that it is now okay for you to do
it again. *No, if you believe God, then the Law of God is established*
in your eyes. This section of the letter to the Romans is a
comprehensive theology of sin and justification. To make his point,
Paul went to Abraham.

> What shall we say then that Abraham our father, as pertaining
> to the flesh, hath found? For if Abraham were justified by
> works, he hath whereof to glory; but not before God. For what
> saith the scripture? Abraham believed God, and it was counted
> unto him for righteousness (Romans 4:1-3).

At first blush, it seems strange to think of Abraham as needing
any justification, but he did. Paul said so. And how was he
justified? He believed God. There is nothing new at all in the idea
of justification by faith. There has never been any other way. Paul
continued to explain why it must be so:

Now when a man works, his wages are not credited to him as a gift, but as an obligation. However, to the man who does not work but trusts God who justifies the wicked, his faith is credited as righteousness (Romans 4:4-5 NIV).

Paul then called on David for a further explanation, but when he did, he raised yet another issue. He cited David thus: "Blessed are they whose transgressions are forgiven, whose sins are covered. Blessed is the man whose sin the LORD will never count against him (Romans 4:7-8 NIV).

I am often asked about this last statement. To some, it seems to say that sin does not matter for some men, because God doesn't impute sin to them. But sin does matter because the consequences of sin are not repealed. A man who is in a faithful covenant with God, who believes God, may sin through error or weakness. The grace of God will cover that. But it is a terrible error to presume on that grace and thus break covenant with God.

When David is brought into the story, we learn some interesting things. David is described as a man after God's own heart (1 Samuel 13:14). Yet David's sins and errors are prominent all through the story. As if that were not enough, there is this statement of God to Jeroboam: "Yet thou hast not been as my servant David, who kept my commandments, and who followed me with all his heart, to do that only which was right in mine eyes" (1 Kings 14:8 KJV). Anyone who has read the story up to this point is likely to get whiplash. David? Kept the commandments? He did a fairly thorough job of breaking the seventh commandment, and that wasn't all he did.

So, how can God say that David did only that which was right in God's eyes? There is one very important difference between David and his son, Solomon. In all of David's life, he never had any other God than Jehovah. Thus, the way back, the way to repair the breaches, was always open to him. And when one repents and turns back, God says he will never remember our sins. But God help the man who presumes on God's mercy and grace.

Now Paul had to deal with the burning question of his time, the conversion of the Gentiles. The people he was writing to in Rome were, for the most part, Jewish Christians, people who had perhaps been converted on a trip to Jerusalem. Paul knew a number of them by name and was well acquainted with the house churches in Rome. So, Paul asked these people, what about the Gentiles?

> Comes this blessedness then upon the circumcision only, or upon the uncircumcision also? for we say that faith was reckoned to Abraham for righteousness. How was it then reckoned? when he was in circumcision, or in uncircumcision? Not in circumcision, but in uncircumcision (vv. 9-10 KJV).

So justification by faith in the Old Testament did not require circumcision. Why should anyone think it does now? You would think the simple logic contained in that statement would have settled the issue at the Jerusalem conference, but for some it did not. Paul was still dealing with this issue among Roman Jews, and he had already addressed it with the Galatian Gentiles.

Circumcision, for Abraham, was a sign, a token, which followed on his justification and his covenant with God. Paul said that God did it that way to make Abraham the father of all who believed, circumcised or not. Paul went on to point out that the promise that was given to Abraham and his seed did not come through the law, but through faith.

In both Testaments, the word for "sin" is derived from a verb which means "to miss." That is to say that one misses the standard God holds up for us. But in common English usage sin means: "Actions by which humans rebel against God, miss His purpose for their life, and surrender to the power of evil rather than to God."[1] It seems to me that this goes too far, because there are sins small and sins great. There are sins mortal, and sins venial. There are sins of error and there are high-handed sins. These are dealt with in different ways.

Perhaps the classic example of this is the judgment of a man who gathered sticks on the Sabbath day. What is often overlooked is that this story does not fall in a narrative of Israel's travels. It falls within the laws dealing with sins of ignorance:

> One and the same law applies to everyone who sins *unintentionally*, whether he is a native-born Israelite or an

---

1. Holman Bible Dictionary.

alien. But anyone who sins *defiantly*, whether native-born or alien, blasphemes the LORD, and that person must be cut off from his people. Because he has despised the LORD's word and broken his commands, that person must surely be cut off; his guilt remains on him (Numbers 15:29-31 NIV).

This is followed immediately by an example: the man who gathered wood on the Sabbath day. Thus, one can conclude that this was not a sin of ignorance, weakness, or unintended. It was a defiant sin. Remember, no man could be punished without due process. Had he been gathering sticks because it had suddenly turned cold and his wife was in labor, the judgment might have been different.

There were sins that separated a man from the community, and sins that cut him off from God. The problem with sin is that it breaks covenant with God. Sins of ignorance can be covered by the grace of God as a result of simple belief. I found an online statement about sin that was interesting:

Sin is a term used mainly in a religious context to describe an act that violates a moral rule or the state of having committed such a violation. In monotheistic religions, the code of conduct is determined by God. Colloquially, any thought, word, or act considered immoral, shameful, harmful, or alienative might be termed "sinful." [1]

The word, "alienative," is important. Sin alienates man from the relationship. God's forbearance, his grace, tolerates the sin up to a point, but will not tolerate just anything.

In Judaism, sin is the violation of divine commandments. Western Christianity, much like Judaism, regards sin as a *legal* infraction. But Eastern Christianity (Orthodox) looks at sin as it affects relationships. In other words, they see it as a breach of covenant.

Sin is the transgression of the law, undifferentiated. That is to say, not this or that category of law, but law as the underlying principle of right conduct. Sin alienates man from God. Not because of God's anger, but because we are simply drawing away

---

1. Wikipedia, article, "Sin,"

from him.

In what sense is man "fallen"? Every man is fallen, as Paul put it, because "all have sinned." I don't think we are born fallen, except in the sense that we are born away from God. But then, we exercise our independence and draw further away from God. According to Paul, sin entered the world by one man, and death passed upon all men because "all have sinned." Death passing on all men is what I understand by the term "fallen."

The theologies of sin and justification are so convoluted, it is small wonder that people are confused. Is there a fundamental difference between justification and reconciliation? That long discussion of Paul's in Romans is where the answer can be found. First, Paul concluded that no one can be justified by the deeds of the law, because that is not what the law is for. The law is intended to convey the knowledge of what sin is (Romans 3:20).

Paul then proceeded to define what it means to be justified. One is justified by grace, freely, through Jesus Christ whom God set forth as a redeemer, to grant "the remission of sins that are past." Later, Paul will conclude:

> For if, when we were enemies, we were reconciled to God by the death of his Son, much more, being reconciled, we shall be saved by his life. And not only so, but we also joy in God through our LORD Jesus Christ, by whom we have now received the atonement (Romans 5:10-11).

Paul commonly made a play on words, and there is one here that the King James translators obscure. "Reconciled" is a verb. "Atonement" is the noun form of the same verb. Even without a knowledge of Greek you can see the relationship between the words: *katallasso* and *katalagge*. The NIV gets it right:

> For if, when we were God's enemies, we were reconciled to him through the death of his Son, how much more, having been *reconciled*, shall we be saved through his life! Not only is this so, but we also rejoice in God through our LORD Jesus Christ, through whom we have now received *reconciliation* (Romans 5:10-11 NIV).

13

The Meaning of Grace

But thou, O LORD, art a God full of compassion,
and gracious, longsuffering,
and plenteous in mercy and truth (Psalm 86:15).

It had been a hard three days. David and the handful of young men with him had left in a hurry and had taken no food. By the time they got to a place called Nob, they were in a bad way. They needed food and there was only one place David thought they might get something to eat. The Tabernacle at Nob.[1]

When David arrived at the Tabernacle, the priest was fearful. David was the most powerful man in the kingdom after Saul, and he usually traveled with a large retinue. He asked, "Why are you here alone?" David replied, "The king charged me with a certain matter and said to me, 'No one is to know anything about your mission and your instructions.' As for my men, I have told them to meet later at a designated place."

Now David lied to the priest. He was fleeing for his life from Saul. And if it were not enough that he lied, he went on to compound his lawbreaking. "What do you have to eat here?" he demanded. "Give me five loaves of bread, or whatever you can find."

"I don't have any ordinary bread on hand," the priest replied, "however, there is some consecrated bread here—provided the men have kept themselves from women."

---

1. The story begins in 1 Samuel 21:1.

"Indeed," said David, "women have been kept from us, as usual whenever I set out. The men's things are holy even on missions that are not holy. How much more so today!" So the priest gave David the hallowed bread (1 Samuel 21:5-6 NIV).

This is a classic example of rationalization, because it was clearly an infraction of the law. Only the priests were allowed to eat the holy bread. If you were the judge, what would you have thought about this? As it happens, we have an answer, because Jesus himself commented on the event.

His remarks came on an occasion when he and his disciples passed through a field on the Sabbath day and, being hungry, the disciples began to pluck the ears of corn and to eat. In the eyes of the Pharisees, this was harvesting and, therefore, it was working on the Sabbath. "Look!" exclaimed the Pharisees, "your disciples are doing what is unlawful on the Sabbath."

Jesus replied, "Haven't you read what David did when he and his companions were hungry? He entered the house of God, and he and his companions ate the consecrated bread—which *was not lawful for them to do*, but only for the priests" (Matthew 12:3-4 NIV).

Note first that Jesus acknowledged that what David did was unlawful. But then he seemed ready to justify David. Why would he do that, and on what basis? When it comes to matters of the law, there are those who say, "Give them an inch and they'll take a mile." This approach was characteristic of the Pharisees. They felt they had to spell things out in detail lest someone accidentally step over the line.

It is clear that Jesus and the Pharisees were on opposite sides of this fence. A Pharisee might well have objected to Jesus by quoting the law. "How can you justify David," he would want to know, "when the law is so plain?"

How would Jesus have answered that question? I am going to provide an answer and, in the process, I am going to explain one of the most important things you will ever learn about biblical law. If you can grasp what I am going to explain, it may revolutionize the way you read the Bible, the way you relate to God, and the way you relate to one another. If that sounds a little presumptuous to you, please wait and judge when I have finished.

First, lets get a few things clear:

- I am not against the law. I am a radical believer in the Law of God. I take Jesus at his word when he says that not one jot or tittle shall pass from the law till everything has come to pass (Matthew 5:18).

- The law of the showbread was not superseded or set aside by any actions of David. He did not have that kind of authority. The law of the showbread was not unimportant. It was just as important as any other Law of God. It was the law then, and it will be the law when there is a Tabernacle once again.

- All rationalizations considered, David did break the law. Jesus said he ate the bread which *it was not lawful* for him to eat.

Why, then, does Jesus use this example in reply to the accusation that his disciples were breaking the Sabbath? How can he justify David when there is not a hint of repentance on David's part, nor anything done to make up for his error?

The answer comes in one word, a familiar word, one that has been used so much that no one seems to understand what it means anymore. The word is *grace*. And along with this word comes a concept of profound importance: Grace is every bit as much in play in the Old Testament as it is in the New. David was justified, not because what he did was right, but because God is *gracious*. Everyone knows this, but do they know what it means? Let me try to explain.

There is a beautiful example of the graciousness of God right in the beginning of his relationship with man. You know it well. First, God created man in his own image, male and female. And the man and the woman were naked, and were not ashamed. God told them to be fruitful and multiply, *and then he left them alone.*

There are two kinds of people reading this: On the one hand are those who believe that God is all seeing, that he knows everything that is happening, that nothing is hidden from him. On the other hand are those who believe that the Book of Genesis suggests otherwise. I find the Genesis account totally charming, because God did what a *gracious* man would do. He created these two perfect physical specimens, put them in a gorgeous outdoor garden totally naked, and then granted them total privacy. God did not hide in the bushes and watch. Why not? Because he is *gracious,* that's why. Graciousness is that character trait which responds to awkward situations gracefully.

Does it limit God to say that he didn't watch? Hardly. It limits God if you say that he couldn't help but watch. God is not a voyeur. He is too gracious for that.

There are those who seem to believe that God is like a computer. If you press the delete button, things disappear. Automatically. Remorselessly. They believe that God enforces the law like a computer. You break the law, the law breaks you. But, you see, that is not what happened to David. God is not a computer, he is a person. Not only is he a person, he is a kind person, a gentle person, a compassionate person, a forgiving person, and above all, God is a *gracious* person.

Now it is true that God can be very strict at times, because he is also just. Without justice, you have only caprice, and there is a great gulf between a God who is gracious, and one who is capricious. Because there was justice, Adam and Eve were eventually shut out of the Garden and denied access to the Tree of Life. But that was because of a choice they had made. They could have had either of the trees in the garden, but apparently not both.[1]

Time passed and two sons were born, Cain and Abel. And in a fit of anger, Cain killed his brother, and then he lied to God. Justice would have called for the death of Cain as well. Why did God not kill Cain? Why did he merely exile him and even set a mark on him to protect him? It is obvious, isn't it? Cain was allowed to live as an act of divine grace, perhaps because he was the first man born of the flesh. God could not bring himself to kill him, so he sent Cain into exile.

More time passes, and things really deteriorate on planet Earth. The earth was filled with violence, and things got so bad, that God was sorry he ever started the project. I realize this runs counter to the idea that God knows everything in advance, but what can I say. It seems better to me that I should take God as he is, not as I think he *ought* to be. Here is what the Bible says about this time:

---

1. For a full discussion of this, see, *The Lonely God*, Ronald Dart, pp. 37ff.

Then the LORD saw that the wickedness of man was great on the earth, and that every intent of the thoughts of his heart was only evil continually. And the LORD was sorry that He had made man on the earth, and He was grieved in His heart (Genesis 6:5-6 NASB).

Somehow, it seems foolish to apologize for God and to attempt explanations that sound good to the modern mind. I am sorry if it is upsetting to learn that God does not control everything. By his own choice, he does not.

So God decided to end the whole Earth project, to just wipe it out, and except for one thing, he would have. What was that one thing? "But Noah found *grace* in the eyes of the LORD" (v. 8).

Mind you, Noah was a good man. He was righteous in his generation. But if you think that is the reason he and his family survived the flood, you have it all wrong. Noah was a good man, but he was not that good. He survived the flood because God was *gracious* to him.

More time passes, and God struck up a friendship with a man named Abraham. This friendship was remarkably personal. God wanted Abraham to have a son by Sarah and told him so. Abraham laughed. He not only laughed, he fell on the ground laughing.[1] And he was not laughing for joy, he was laughing because the idea of Sarah having a baby was, well, laughable.

Now what does this tell us about the relationship between God and Abraham? Most of us would not be able to laugh in the presence of God, no matter what he said. And God did not smite Abraham with boils for laughing at the idea as an *ungracious* God might do. He just said, "You'll see." I think he took a certain amount of pleasure in doing all this the hard way. God, it seems, also has a sense of humor, which, by the way, is a constant characteristic of the most gracious of people.

More time passed, and God called on Abraham on his way to Sodom and Gomorrah.[2] If you had been hiding nearby watching this encounter, what you would have seen would have been commonplace. You would have seen three men walking down the road. You would have seen Abraham run out and greet them in the

---

1. Genesis 17:17.

2. See Genesis 18:1 ff.

145

customary fashion. You would have seen him have water brought so the men could wash their feet—which they did. You would have seen food brought and you would have watched them eat.

All very ordinary, right? Except that two of these three "men" were angels and the third was God himself. Now does it seem out of the ordinary that they washed their feet and ate a meal? Do Spirit beings get dirty feet? Do they get hungry? When they appear in the flesh, apparently they do. On the other hand, God created food to be enjoyed, and he may simply have come by Abraham's place to enjoy a good feed.

But as he left Abraham to go on to Sodom, God paused. He said, as though speaking to himself, "Shall I hide from Abraham that thing which I do? . . . For I know him, that he will command his children and his household after him, and they shall keep the way of the LORD, to do justice and judgment; that the LORD may bring upon Abraham that which he hath spoken of him" (Genesis 18:17-19).

So, God told Abraham what he was about to do. "The outcry against Sodom and Gomorrah is so great and their sin so grievous that I will go down and see if what they have done is as bad as the outcry that has reached me. If not, I will know" (vv. 20-21 NIV).

Then followed the classic example of a man reasoning with God, an example of intercessory prayer rendered face to face. "It is not like you to destroy the righteous with the wicked," Abraham pleaded. "Shall not the Judge of all the earth do right?" Abraham's boldness is staggering. From a less gracious God, he would have been inviting a rebuke, or worse.

But God listened and allowed Abraham to talk him down from destroying the city into not destroying the city if he found ten righteous people there. Why did God let Abraham talk him down like this? Because God is gracious. God does not *like* the idea of executing judgment. He is merciful. He doesn't like killing people, even when they have it coming, and is willing to accept almost any excuse for not doing so.

There are so many examples of this in the Old Testament that it would be exhausting to review them all. But let me give you the definitive illustration of what I am driving at.

Still more time passed and a prophet named Jonah was sent to the city of Nineveh with a message. The message was simple

146

enough: "Yet forty days and Nineveh shall be overthrown." No ifs, no ands, no buts, Nineveh is finished. So Jonah started his march through the town proclaiming the message. But something truly astonishing happened. The people of Nineveh believed him. The king proclaimed a fast and all of them from the least to the greatest covered themselves with sackcloth and sat in ashes, totally humbling themselves. Even the animals had to fast. The proclamation of the king was revealing:

> Let neither man nor beast, herd nor flock, taste any thing: let them not feed, nor drink water: But let man and beast be covered with sackcloth, and cry mightily unto God: yea, let them turn every one from his evil way, and from the violence that is in their hands. Who can tell if God will turn and repent, and turn away from his fierce anger, that we perish not? (Jonah 3:7-9).

The reason God gave for the destruction of Sodom and Gomorrah was that the cities were filled with violence. The reason for the destruction of the world in the days of Noah was that the whole earth was filled with violence. Here again in Nineveh, violence has brought God's attention to a city.

But Nineveh repented, and to Jonah's everlasting surprise, so did God. He decided not to destroy the city, but to rewrite history. How could he do that? He made an outright prophecy about this city. There was nothing equivocal, there was no if/then statement, not even a call for repentance. God's word would seem to be at stake. What happened?

God felt sorry for them. They had repented, or at least acted like they were sorry. And Nineveh found grace in God's eyes. The whole thing infuriated Jonah, and here is something we need to understand. Too many times we are closer to Jonah than to God in our attitude toward sinners. Jonah was not gracious about this at all. He was frustrated. "Didn't I say this before I ever left?" he ranted. "I knew that you are a gracious God, merciful, slow to anger, great kindness and repent of the evil, that you won't even carry out what you say you will do" (see Jonah 4:2). If this had been a lesser god, Jonah might have been toast.

"Therefore take my life," he cried, "it is better for me to die than to live." Jehovah was not the kind of God that Jonah wanted him to be. Jonah was the archetype of the man who wants his religion by the numbers. He didn't want Nineveh to fall on the 39th day and he didn't want Nineveh to fall on the 41st day, he wanted Nineveh to fall on the 40th day. And he wanted blood in the streets. Why? Well they probably deserved it. And for men like Jonah, exceptions to the rules drive them crazy.

And in fact Jonah was a little bit crazy here. It is not entirely rational to display anger toward God. The irony is that if Jehovah had been the kind of God that Jonah thought he wanted, the LORD would have taken a giant fly swatter to Jonah.

So, said God, "are you doing well to be this angry?" Jonah didn't answer, but went out of the city and sat on the east side of the city and there made him a shelter and sat under the shadow that he might see what would become of the city. And the LORD prepared a plant that grew up quickly with big broad leaves, and it gave shade to Jonah to grant relief from the beating sun. It was a kind thing to do.

Mind you, I made the point above that God has a sense of humor. There are many ways to teach men things. God chose this one. He made a shadow to deliver him from his grief and Jonah was very glad because that plant was there. Then God prepared a worm when the morning came the next day. And as a result of the worm the plant died before the day was over.

The next day when the sun came up, God prepared a vehement east wind and the sun beat on the head of Jonah and he passed out. And when he came to, he wished he were dead. "It's better for me to die than to live" he moaned. And God said to Jonah, "Are you doing the right thing here? Is it good for you to be angry about this plant?" Jonah replied, "Yes! Yes I do well to be angry even to death. I want to die." Then said the LORD:

> You have had pity on the gourd, for which you have not laboured, neither made it grow; which came up in a night, and perished in a night: And should not I spare Nineveh, that great city, wherein are more than one hundred and twenty thousand persons that cannot discern between their right hand and their left hand; and also much cattle?" (Jonah 4:10-11).

You feel sorry for the plant, he said, and you can't grant me the right to feel sorry for a city, with women, children and animals? God even feels sorry for the animals. So why did God spare Nineveh? It's utterly simple. He spared the city because he is gracious.

Perhaps it is becoming clearer what I meant when I said that *grace* is an Old Testament idea. Throughout the Old Testament, we encounter grace again and again and again. Yet when we read the book, we focus on all the things a Jonah would want, and we gloss over the things that God wants. True, God is strict. He can be severe. It is certain that he is a God of justice. It is true that he incinerated Sodom. But even there, grace was found. Lot along with his wife and daughters were spared. It was not that the wife and daughters were righteous, though Lot was. It was because God is gracious. In the last moments, Lot was standing there, delaying his departure, and the angel had to take him, his wife, and his daughters by the hand and lead them out of the city. Lot was saved by the grace of God. He was saved because he was Abraham's nephew and God really cared about Abraham. God didn't want Abraham to grieve over the loss of family.

There's an odd thing about grace in the New Testament. In all four Gospels, the complete accounts of all Jesus' life ministry and works, there is not a single occasion where Jesus ever used the word grace. To me, that seems strange. One would think, given the role of grace in New Testament doctrine, that he would have said something about it. But it would be a mistake to think that grace was absent. Speaking of Jesus as a child, Luke described him this way: "And the child grew, and waxed strong in spirit, filled with wisdom: and the grace of God was upon him" (Luke 2:40).

That means the graciousness we see all the way through the Old Testament rested on one little boy. The graciousness of God who could have killed a man, but didn't. The God who healed the sick and let people off again and again, had a graciousness about him that now rested on Jesus.

John also, in speaking of the coming of the Word of God, said: "And the Word was made flesh and dwelt among us, and we beheld his glory, the glory as of the only begotten of the Father, *full of grace and truth*" (John 1:14). Jesus would later say that he was "The way, the truth, and the life" (John 14:6). He was more than that. He was also grace personified.

And it is here that we can begin to understand how the Law of God plays into the story. Certainly, no man has ever kept it perfectly, although there is no single precept of the law that a man cannot keep. What covers us when we, like David, through weakness or even hunger, break the law? John gave us the answer: "For the law was given through Moses, grace and truth came through Jesus Christ" (John 1:17 NIV).

The Law of God is glorious, but *the law is not God*. God is gracious. The law does not have that capacity. Without grace, the law can become a tyrant. With grace, it can become a way of life. God is not like a computer. God is personal, and kind, and merciful, and forgiving.

If you should ask what is wrong with the Christian churches right now, the answer is simple enough. Great grace was upon Jesus Christ. Great grace is *not* upon us. When we condemn our brothers over some doctrinal lapse, this is not grace. When we are unforgiving of one another, when we take offense easily, this is not grace. When we make ourselves, personally or collectively, out to be better than others, this is not grace. Envy and suspicion are a lapse of grace.

The truth is, we may not have received in ourselves enough of God's grace to be able to share it with others. If we had received it, we would be more gracious. In order for us to be gracious with others, we have to receive grace in ourselves.

Jesus was gracious to sinners far and wide. One day when teaching in a remote location, he fed five thousand people by means of a miracle. What character trait led him to do that? Obviously, it was grace.

On another occasion, John tried to get Jesus to stop a man who was *successfully* casting out demons. Why? Because the man wasn't one of the "in group." Mind you, the man wasn't merely trying to do it, he was actually getting it done. I can't think where John's head was, but Jesus told him to let the man alone. And what character trait was exemplified on that occasion? Grace, of course.

When Jesus' disciples wanted to call down fire on a village in Samaria because the villagers refused to receive Jesus on his way from Jerusalem, Jesus flatly refused. He said, "You don't know what spirit you are of." What character trait led Jesus to refuse that option and correct the attitude of his disciples? It was grace, of course.

There was one occasion when Jesus at first seemed to respond ungraciously. He flatly refused to heal a woman's daughter because she was a Canaanite:

> And behold, a Canaanite woman came out from that region, and began to cry out, saying, "Have mercy on me, O Lord, Son of David; my daughter is cruelly demon-possessed." But He did not answer her a word. And His disciples came to Him and kept asking Him, saying, "Send her away, for she is shouting out after us." But He answered and said, "I was sent only to the lost sheep of the house of Israel." But she came and began to bow down before Him, saying, "Lord, help me!" And He answered and said, "It is not good to take the children's bread and throw it to the dogs" (Matthew 15:22-26 NASB).

If ever there was a remark that could cause offense, this was it. It seems a terribly ungracious thing to say. The event illustrates well the importance of persistence and of not taking offense. The woman's reply is classic: "Yes, Lord; but even the dogs feed on the crumbs which fall from their masters' table" (v. 27 NASB). It was at this point that nothing but grace would suffice.

"O woman, your faith is great," Jesus replied, "be it done for you as you wish." And her daughter was healed from that very hour. And his reply is suggestive that faith plays a major role on the road to grace.

Then there was the touching occasion when Jesus was having dinner with a Pharisee and a woman came behind him[1] and began to wash his feet with her tears and wipe them dry with her hair. As the Pharisee watched this, he thought to himself, "This man, if he were a prophet, would have known who and what manner of woman this is that toucheth him: for she is a sinner" (Luke 7:39). Apparently the woman had a reputation that preceded her. Jesus, knowing what the man was thinking, offered a parable and then explained:

---

1. It was the custom to recline on one side at meals so that one's feet were behind him.

And he turned to the woman, and said to Simon, See this woman? I entered into thine house, you gave me no water for my feet: but she hath washed my feet with tears, and wiped them with the hairs of her head. You gave me no kiss: but this woman since the time I came in hath not ceased to kiss my feet. My head with oil you did not anoint: but this woman has anointed my feet with ointment. Wherefore I say unto thee, Her sins, which are many, are forgiven; for she loved much: but to whom little is forgiven, the same loves little (vv. 44-47).

Forgiveness is one of the greatest of graces. The humility and obvious repentance of the woman could bring only one response from a gracious man. And it is of more than passing interest that love enters the picture alongside grace.

We know that the disciples of Jesus were different men after the empowering on the Day of Pentecost. Something very important happened to them on that day that is easy to overlook. We know they had power, but they had something more: "And with great power gave the apostles witness of the resurrection of the LORD Jesus: *and great grace was upon them all*" (Acts 4:33).

As I noted earlier, if there is one thing missing among Christians these days, it is that great grace is *not* with us. Oh, we know that we are under God's grace. We have experienced his grace toward us and we are grateful for it. Now if we can just learn to show the same grace to one another, we will be on the way to greater things.

Sometimes I wonder if we understand grace at all. Take the example Jesus offered to the Pharisee when the woman had washed his feet with her tears:

There was a certain creditor which had two debtors: the one owed five hundred pence, and the other fifty. And when they had nothing to pay, he frankly forgave them both. Tell me therefore, which of them will love him most? (Luke 7:41-42).

Obviously, even the Pharisee could see the answer. And it would seem that each man who knows how much he has been forgiven would find it easy to forgive. The one who has received grace should bestow grace freely.

Finally the words of Paul, "Wherefore we, receiving a kingdom which cannot be moved, *let us have grace*" (Hebrews 12:28). This is not mere verbiage. Sad to say, the word "grace" has been abused and much of the meaning is lost. When Paul calls on us to have grace it means something. There should be something in us that enables us to serve God with grace, a grace manifested by our graciousness to our fellow man.

And it is in the truth about grace that our dilemma begins to resolve. There are three possible results when a man sins. Punishment, chastisement, and consequences. Grace covers the first two, but the consequences can remain. Forgiveness is simply the grace of God withholding his chastisement. But to reverse the consequences of sin takes a miracle.

14

On Being Perfect

Be ye therefore perfect,
even as your Father which is in heaven is perfect
(Matthew 5:48).

The call for perfection that Jesus included in the Sermon on the Mount seems to ask the impossible of us. How on earth can any man ever achieve perfection? One explanation is that perfection is the goal, and we will reach it only in the resurrection. We strive for perfection in this life, but there is no way we can achieve it in the flesh. But if that is what Jesus meant, there were many ways he could have said precisely that.

There is an odd thing about this passage. Jesus did not actually say, "Be you perfect." Jesus, of course, spoke these words in Aramaic and Matthew rendered them in Greek. What has come down to us is this statement: "Be ye therefore *teleios*, even as your Father which is in heaven is *teleios*." With all the wonderful Bible study programs now available, anyone can consult a Greek lexicon and do his own word search. The definition of *telios* in the lexicon is "complete." You can do a word study through the New Testament to see how the word is used, and you will find that "complete" works in every instance. Jesus said, "Be you therefore complete." And there is a world of difference between "complete" and "perfect." The word "perfect" is defined as "being entirely without fault or defect." I am sure that is an accurate description of God. I am equally sure that it is an utterly inaccurate description of any man or woman alive.

154

"Complete" is a different idea entirely. I am a private pilot with instrument, glider, and multi-engine ratings. When I completed my instruction for the last rating, my instructor signed me off, shook my hand, and said, "Congratulations. Now you are a complete pilot." I didn't know exactly what he meant, because no one knew better than I how far I was from perfect. I think he meant that I now had a full set of the ratings available for a private pilot. Of course, the fact is that there is no such thing as a perfect pilot. There are simply too many variables that can arise in that complicated pursuit for anyone ever to claim perfection. In a way, it is a nice analogy with life.

One of the biggest problems we face when tackling a subject like this is getting our semantics right. What do we mean by the words we use? For most of us, the definition of "perfect" I offered above is perfectly accurate. Now I have to explain where "perfect" misses the sense of what Jesus intended to say.

Imagine a pianist in recital, performing a difficult Chopin etude. It is possible for him to do a flawless performance, getting all the notes right, using the pedal as indicated on the page, following the instructions for loudness and softness. I have heard people, listening to such a performance in recital, comment on its perfection saying that he "didn't miss a single note," (a high compliment for a novice). They were defining the performance in terms of what did not happen. There were no errors.

Can we agree that it is possible to do a perfect, flawless performance, and yet have a performance that is mediocre and uninspired? You can have a flawless piano solo by one pianist, and a performance of the same piece by a genius, and even the untrained ear can hear the difference. Perfection and excellence are two entirely different things. Once again, we fall back on the meaning of words. Excellent means "eminently good, first-class." Perfection means "being entirely without fault or defect."

It dawned on me out of the blue one day that the idea of perfection is a *negative* idea. It is negative in that it defines a thing in negative terms. The thing does not have fault. It does not have a defect or blemish. All perfection describes is what is *not* there. It says little about what is there.

Once the idea had taken root, I had to find out more, so I headed off to the Internet where you can find out anything about everything (or is it everything about anything?). The word I chose to search for was "perfectionism." I found two starkly opposing views on the subject. One held that perfectionism is a good thing if it's managed properly. That view acknowledges that the perfectionist can be neurotic, but by and large, it's a good thing.

The other held that perfectionism is entirely a neurotic condition and is harmful. The difference between these views is superficial and arises from semantics, but it is instructive, nonetheless. I found a helpful paper on the Web by Dr. Carol Peters which outlines the various ways of approaching the subject. It seems that scholars in the field describe two types of perfectionist—the normal and the neurotic. Normal perfectionists are people who derive real pleasure from painstaking work. Neurotic perfectionists are those who are unable to find any satisfaction because, in their own eyes, nothing they do is ever good enough.[1]

So Carol Peters is persuaded that perfectionism can be good or bad, it all depends. But she also notes that, "A number of researchers . . . have linked perfectionism with depression, anorexia nervosa, bulimia, migraine, personality and psychosomatic disorders, Type A coronary-prone behaviour and suicide." Is it a good thing? Or is it harmful?

Peters cites another author who lists five characteristics of perfectionist teachers and students:

1. Procrastination.
2. Fear of failure.
3. The all-or-nothing mindset.
4. Paralysed perfectionism.
5. Workaholism.[2]

These characteristics are said to contribute to underachievement. Procrastination affects all of us from time to time. The fear of being less than perfect, of not living up to one's own expectations, can produce overwhelming feelings that lead us to put things off. I don't think many of us consciously go through this line

1. Carol C. Peters, "Perfectionism," *Excellence in Education*, Perth, 1996.

2. Adderholt-Elliot, M. "Perfectionism and underachievement," *Gifted Child Today*, 12 (1), 19-21.

of thought, but the fear of making a mistake, of having a fault, can prevent us from starting a project in the first place. This probably lies near the root of what we call "writer's block." Successful writers have come to understand that the blank page has to be assaulted with words, so they just start writing. They can always come back and rewrite. It is a curious thing that most drafts of papers, books, or novels, can be improved merely by cutting off the first few paragraphs. Once the block is passed, the work gets better.

Putting things off until the last minute, when a deadline is bearing down, is called procrastination. It makes life harder on everyone connected with a project. But some people cannot bring themselves to start until they absolutely must.

Apathy also keeps the writer from starting, but that may be merely another manifestation of perfectionism. He knows his work will never measure up, so he just never starts. And thus, never has to face the lack of perfection.

I recall a sermon I gave years ago in England. It was one of those fire and brimstone sermons that people strangely seem to enjoy (mostly, I think, because they are sure I am talking about someone else). After the sermon, and after the usual round of congratulations, which I always take with a grain of salt, a gentleman came to me and said something that shook me to my roots.

"My, Mr. Dart," he said, "when you preach like that, I just feel like I am never going to make it." He meant it as a compliment, but it woke me up to one of the major errors of young preachers. The last thing I wanted was to make people feel like they could never make it.

I have thought about this encounter a great deal, and I have come to see it in an entirely new light. When you hold up unrealistically high standards for people, the end result is likely to be apathy. When a man comes to feel that he "can't make it," the natural response is "Why try? I can never measure up to this standard. I can never do this without making a mistake. I can never reach the faultless plateau, I am too flawed, I just can't reach this level. I might as well give up."

Those perfectionists who can't live with apathy tend to become workaholic. According to Peters, they are "dependent on performance since self-esteem is tied to external rewards." Too often, it is tied to how we think others look at us. We can't find satisfaction inside ourselves.

Workaholics don't delegate well, because no one can achieve their high expectations—not even themselves. They also have a hard time saying "no" and get over-committed, losing any sense of balance in their lives. Sometimes people don't like letting go of something because they are afraid of failure on the part of the person to whom they have delegated the job. Perfectionists have a hard time allowing someone else do the job and then accepting the job when it is finished. Sometimes the person performing the job simply cannot do the job as well as the perfectionist would like.

So we are left with a person who either cannot delegate, or having delegated cannot let go. A person who can't say no, because, "If I don't do it, who will?" or "Nobody can do it the way I think it ought to be done." This hardly seems to be what Jesus was advocating in the Sermon on the Mount. But there is another side to the story.

At the end of our Internet search, we find one theorist telling us that perfectionism is a neurosis and another telling us that it is not. Now how can this be? The answer? Semantics. Read this paragraph carefully:

> Students can be helped to cope with *perfectionism* by accepting it as a basic part of their giftedness, by emphasizing its positive aspects, and by acknowledging the anxiety and frustration it provokes (Silverman, 1995, p. 4). Difficult challenges generate anxieties which require inner strength and a great deal of persistence to overcome. Gifted learners need support to persist despite constant awareness of failure. *Excellence* takes more time and hard work than mediocrity. [Emphasis mine.][1]

Did you catch it? The author switched words on us in mid stride. What is he talking about, excellence or perfectionism? The author uses these words interchangeably, but they don't mean the same thing. Excellence transcends perfection. Excellence can be imperfect, even flawed. Excellence may not be exactly what is written in the score of a piece of music. It is possible, after all, to

---

1. Ibid.

improve on Bach.

A story is told of an organist in a German cathedral who, one day, encountered a stranger who was examining his organ. Learning that the visitor was also an organist, he proposed that they play together. The cathedral had two organs, so there began a kind of contest, dueling organs, if you will. Each would propose a theme which would be answered by the other. Step by step, they ascended into ever more complex themes and variations. Finally, the visitor proposed a theme that the other could not answer. The organist walked over to the stranger and said, "Either you are an angel from heaven, or you are Johann Sebastian Bach." Bach was a genius at the organ, they say, a greater performer than he was a composer. Genius transcends perfectionism, it goes beyond the music that is on the page. Yet genius may be flawed. So we have to be sure we know what is at issue here. Is it excellence, or perfection?

And it is here that a major issue can be addressed in Christian theology and Christian conduct. *Excellence can be flawed.* One can be complete without being perfect. This is true even when it comes to the Law of God.

Peters had this good advice: "Maintain high standards for yourself but don't impose them on others—they will run the other way fast!" Then she adds this admonition: "Maintain high standards for yourself, but don't impose them on others *lest you become a tyrant.*"

That last sentence underscores what too many Christians have had to endure. I recall preaching sermons when I was younger in which I held up a standard so high, that no one could hope to measure up to it—certainly I could not. I was asking the congregation to be, well, perfect. I think not a few preachers become tyrants because they are perfectionists and they are demanding things of the people that they themselves cannot measure up to. Not only that, their standards and God's standards may not be the same. Imagine how terrible this can become if the preacher creates an organization that thinks it must *enforce* his standards. This is the stuff that cults are made of.

God's standards (and you can always count on this) are administered with grace. Men's standards, unfortunately, are too often not. And that is precisely where the divide came between the disciples of Jesus and those of the Pharisees.

In my research, I happened on a publication of the University of Illinois counseling center. I presume it was a kind of pamphlet for incoming students and was attempting to help them adjust to university life. They offered this warning about perfectionism.

> Perfectionism refers to a set of self-defeating thoughts and behaviors aimed at reaching excessively high unrealistic goals. Perfectionism is often mistakenly seen in our society as desirable or even necessary for success. However, recent studies have shown that perfectionistic attitudes actually interfere with success. The desire to be perfect can both rob you of a sense of personal satisfaction and cause you to fail to achieve as much as people who have more realistic strivings.[1]

I can see a Christian reading that and balking. After all, Jesus said we should be perfect, and they are telling us that perfectionistic attitudes can actually interfere with success. But that *wasn't* what Jesus was saying. He was calling on man to be complete, to strive for excellence. And the person who is striving for excellence will almost always surpass the one who is striving for mere perfection.

Many years ago, I was teaching public speaking at a small college in England. All speeches were evaluated and given a critique. It was my custom to allow the students to evaluate one another which, at times, got downright brutal. But the student evaluators focused on eradicating faults, errors, and mistakes. Unfortunately the poor rascal who had given the speech was often bombarded with a barrage of trivial imperfections. It took some work to get the students to give attention to the really important things. Did you understand what the speaker was saying? Were you persuaded by his arguments? Did he move you to do something about his issue?

It is a point often overlooked, but if you spend your lifetime working on your weaknesses, your faults, your mistakes, the best you can ever hope for is mediocrity. How do you transcend that? You work on your strong points. You work on making your gifts and talents stronger. If you are a teacher, you look at what a student

---

1. http://www.couns.uiuc.edu/brochures/perfecti.htm.

does well, and you try to lift it to the point of excellence. In that way, you have a chance to take a young person far beyond what he thought he could do. He has a chance of excellence that the pursuit of mere perfection would deny him.

There is an unexpected benefit of this approach. A person's faults and weaknesses get drawn up into the striving for excellence, and they often as not take care of themselves. I am talking in the context of teaching speech, but it applies in every aspect of life. If, when working with your children, all you do is work on faults, weaknesses and mistakes, your kids are likely to grow up to be, at best, mediocre performers. At the worst, they may end up neurotic perfectionists.

But, when working with anyone, children, employees, students, wife, husband, your question should be, "What does he do well?" What are the strengths? How do you make them better and stronger so that the strengths, the things a person is really good at, sweep up and carry along the mistakes and faults?

The University of Illinois pamphlet continued:

> If you are a perfectionist, it is likely that you learned early in life that other people valued you because of how much you accomplished or achieved. As a result you may have learned to value yourself only on the basis of other people's approval. Thus your self-esteem may have come to be based primarily on external standards. This can leave you vulnerable and excessively sensitive to the opinions and criticism of others. In attempting to protect yourself from such criticism, you may decide that being perfect is your only defense.[1]

As a counselor, I encounter people in that situation. They value themselves entirely on the basis of the approval of others, never realizing that being perfect will only get them more criticism. You will not avoid criticism by being perfect. You will only get more of it.

> Perfectionists tend to anticipate or fear disapproval and rejection from those around them. Given such fear,

---

1. Ibid.

perfectionists may react defensively to criticism and in doing so frustrate and alienate others.[1]

Sooner or later in life you must learn to avoid being defensive about criticism. The more successful you are, the more criticism you will receive. I have a wastebasket under my desk, and whenever I read a letter that is harshly critical and lacking in constructive ideas, I rarely get beyond the first two paragraphs. From long experience, I can recognize hostility quickly, and the letter goes to the waste basket. I once had a friend who, when he got one of those letters, would systematically tear it up. I don't even give the letter that much attention. Critical emails should get the same treatment. It is even how we should handle destructive conversations. If all a person can do is find fault, they are telling you that you aren't perfect. But you already know that, so listening is a waste of time.

> Without realizing it, perfectionists may also apply their unrealistically high standards to others, becoming critical and demanding of them. Furthermore, perfectionists may avoid letting others see their mistakes, not realizing that self-disclosure allows others to perceive them as more human and thus more likeable. Because of this vicious cycle perfectionists often have difficulty being close to people and therefore have less than satisfactory interpersonal relationships.[2]

I told you all this to explain what Jesus meant when he told us to be "perfect as our Father in heaven is perfect." Perfectionism can be defined as an excessive striving to be without fault or defect. This is not to say that we shouldn't try to overcome our faults or defects. But there is an obsessive striving that is unhealthy. Perfectionism, then, is negative because it defines what is not there rather than what is. And when it comes to the Law of God, that is not good enough, as Jesus explained in the Sermon on the Mount.

I have often heard it said that no one can keep the law perfectly. The statement is entirely true, and completely irrelevant. The law is

---

1. Ibid.

2. Ibid.

not given to define perfection. It is given as a guide to life. The purpose of the law is stated quite simply by the psalmist: "Your word is a lamp to my feet And a light to my path" (Psalm 119:105). It is there so we won't fall down and hurt ourselves.

15

Covenant, First Steps

*And I will establish my covenant between you and me
and your seed after you in their generations
for an everlasting covenant, to be a God to you,
and to your seed after you (Genesis 17:7).*

Three things create difficulties for us when reading the Bible: Language, culture, and dogma. Language is always a problem because any time you translate from one language to another, there is the possibility of losing meaning. Culture is a problem, because we have limited understanding of how things were done in ancient times. For example, we have only the vaguest notion of what marriage was like. Was there a ceremony? Was there someone like a rabbi who stood in front of people officiating, and did they break a glass under foot? Did they make oaths and swear vows? Did they sign a marriage contract, or did they just move in together? The Bible doesn't tell us very much. Archaeology attempts to describe ancient cultures, but frequently has to guess. There is still disagreement among scholars over whether the settlement at Qumran[1] was a kind of monastery, or a pottery factory. For all we know, it could have been both.

As if these peculiarities were not enough, we have problems with dogma. This is a tricky item because when you attempt to examine what happened in Old Testament times, you are influenced far more than you think by the doctrinal structure of

---

1. Qumran is the settlement near which the Dead Sea Scrolls were found.

your church or denomination. Nowhere is this more evident than in the study of the covenants.

While we wrestle with issues of language, culture, and dogma, what we are really looking for is *meaning*. What did God mean when he used the word "covenant," and how did men like Abraham understand it? It is tempting, when you do a word study, to try to find a single word that will fit all contexts. That doesn't work in English, and there is no reason we should think it works in Hebrew. In any case, it's not a *word* we're looking for, it's *meaning*.

The word "covenant" has a broad application in the Bible. A covenant can be an agreement, a compact, a contract, a promise, a commitment, a relationship, even a real estate transaction. So when we encounter the word, we have to think about the circumstances where it is used. Take for example the first occurrence of the word in the Bible. God was speaking:

And, behold, I, even I, do bring a flood of waters upon the earth, to destroy all flesh, wherein is the breath of life, from under heaven; and every thing that is in the earth shall die. *But with you will I establish my covenant*; and you shall come into the ark, you, and your sons, and your wife, and your sons' wives with you (Genesis 6:17-18).

This does not read like an "agreement" between two parties. Rather it reads like instructions on how to save your life. The usage is also different from some later covenants in that it is "established." In later usage, a covenant is "cut," presumably because literal cutting was involved in creating the covenant. In some cases, a covenant created a new relationship where one did not exist before, but that doesn't work well here.

After the flood was over, God described the covenant further:

And God spoke to Noah, and to his sons with him, saying, "Behold, I establish my covenant with you, and with your seed after you; And with every living creature that is with you, of the fowl, of the cattle, and of every beast of the earth with you; from all that go out of the ark, to every beast of the earth. And I will establish my covenant with you; neither shall all flesh be cut off any more by the waters of a flood; neither shall there any more be a flood to destroy the earth" (Genesis 9:8-11).

God does not "establish a relationship" with cows, so we are still looking for the meaning of covenant. "Well," one might say, "it is a promise." True, but it is more than that. This covenant is a *commitment*. What is the difference? Take a real estate transaction as an illustration. If we are dickering over the price of a piece of land, I may say, "I will take 75,000 dollars for the land." You reply, "It's a deal." That is a verbal agreement. But when we sign a dated contract and earnest money is accepted, I am *committed* to sell the land to you. Up to that point, I could change my mind without legal obligation. There is a moment when a promise is formalized, and when a consideration is accepted as a token of the agreement. After that, I can be compelled by law to follow through with the sale.[1]

This one chapter has no less than seven occurrences of the word, "covenant," and in all cases, the idea of commitment is central. But there is one thing more—a token of the covenant that formalizes the commitment.

And God said, This is the *token* of the covenant which I make between me and you and every living creature that is with you, for perpetual generations: I do set my bow in the cloud, and it shall be for a token of a covenant between me and the earth (vv. 12-13).

There is a constant in law which has survived through the ages. It is one thing to give your word. It is another thing to *formally* give your word. In court, for example, a witness is asked to raise his right hand and swear to tell the truth, the whole truth, and nothing but the truth. It is this oath that formally binds a man under the law. In a way, it is the moment of covenant. The witness is formally committed to tell the truth and there are consequences if he does not. The raising of the right hand and the oath are tokens of a covenant to tell the truth. In the same way, the rainbow is the token of God's covenant with man that he will never send a flood like that again. It is a promise, but it is more than that. It is a formal commitment.

---

1. The action is called a suit for specific performance.

The next time we encounter a formal covenant in the Bible is with the man Abraham, and the covenant that arose on this occasion is a landmark. The conversation between God and Abraham began:

> After these things the word of the LORD came unto Abram in a vision, saying, Fear not, Abram: I am your shield, and your exceeding great reward. And Abram said, LORD GOD, what wilt thou give me, seeing I go childless, and the steward of my house is this Eliezer of Damascus? (Genesis 15:1-2).

Inheritance was a very big deal in those days because of the enormous responsibility it entailed. Abram was a wealthy and powerful man. He had a wife and a household to oversee. He owned vast flocks and herds, and had so many servants that he was able to field a private army of 318 trained fighting men. I suspect this translated into close to a thousand men, women and children for whom he was responsible. Thus, Abram's concern. What was to happen to these people once he was gone? The only one capable of keeping it together was Eliezer, a man who had been born into Abram's household. Abraham had known him since he was a child, and no doubt had trained him well.

> And, behold, the word of the LORD came unto him, saying, This shall not be your heir; but he that shall come forth out of your own bowels shall be your heir. And he brought him forth abroad, and said, Look now toward heaven, and tell the stars, if thou be able to number them: and he said unto him, So shall your seed be. And he believed in the LORD; and he counted it to him for righteousness (vv. 4-6).

This is the first formal statement of what it takes to be counted righteous before God. You have to believe God, which in this case, required a great deal of trust. Abram was an old man, his wife, Sarah, was far past the change of life, and that sky full of stars was awesome. Paul cited this passage in his classic defense of justification by faith.[1] Jehovah continued speaking to Abraham:

---

1. See Romans 4:1-3.

And he said unto him, I am the LORD that brought you out of Ur of the Chaldees, to give you this land to inherit it. And he said, LORD GOD, whereby shall I know that I shall inherit it? (vv. 7-8).

It turns out that my earlier analogy of a real estate contract is apt. First, God gave Abram a verbal, then Abram asks for a contract—in this case a covenant. The steps necessary to formalize the covenant follow:

And he said unto him, Take me an heifer of three years old, and a she goat of three years old, and a ram of three years old, and a turtledove, and a young pigeon. And he took unto him all these, and divided them in the midst, and laid each piece one against another: but the birds divided he not. And when the fowls came down upon the carcases, Abram drove them away (vv. 9-11).

There is nothing in the account which explains this, but we know a little bit about the ancient rites of covenant. In this case, the animals had to be cut in two, hence the expression, "to cut a covenant."[1] Now God speaks further:

And when the sun was going down, a deep sleep fell upon Abram; and, lo, an horror of great darkness fell upon him. And he said unto Abram, Know of a surety that your seed shall be a stranger in a land that is not theirs, and shall serve them; and they shall afflict them four hundred years; And also that nation, whom they shall serve, will I judge: and afterward shall they come out with great substance. And thou shalt go to your fathers in peace; thou shalt be buried in a good old age. But in the fourth generation they shall come hither again: for the iniquity of the Amorites is not yet full (vv. 12-16).

In real estate contracts, there is usually a date of possession, so the delay in this covenant has to be explained. Full possession is delayed for 400 years, and what is to happen to his descendants is

---

1. Which survives to this day in our expression: "to cut a deal."

outlined. The last sentence in that statement is of some interest. It seems to be saying that the corruption of the Amorite people was not sufficient to warrant eviction from the land at that time, but that would come. By the time Israel's sojourn was complete, they would be fully justified in dispossessing the Amorites.

> And it came to pass, that, when the sun went down, and it was dark, behold a smoking furnace, and a burning lamp that passed between those pieces. In the same day the LORD made a covenant with Abram, saying, Unto your seed have I given this land, from the river of Egypt unto the great river, the river Euphrates (vv. 17-18).

Following the real estate contract analogy, we must include a property description. This one is stunning. All the land from the Nile to the Euphrates would belong to Abram's descendants.

This is the first time in the Bible the word "cut" is used in connection with a covenant and the first time the cutting of animals is involved. Thus, we have the first *blood covenant*. Among Semitic peoples, the blood covenant involved cutting, often cutting themselves and drinking one another's blood.[1] It seems gruesome to the modern mind, but it was symbolic. It meant that the men were now blood brothers. A new relationship existed where one had not existed before—a new relationship with all the obligations, rights, privileges, and burdens that go with family. The men had formally *bonded*.

In later generations, the blood of an animal was substituted for human blood, but God put a stop to that practice.[2] Animal sacrifice remained a part of the making of a covenant, but men ate the flesh of the sacrifice instead of drinking the blood.

If you are familiar with the Bible, you are already hearing echoes of the New Testament, especially with something Jesus said to the Jews on one occasion:

---

1. *The Jewish Encyclopedia*, article, *Covenant*: "The old, primitive way of concluding a covenant ('to cut a covenant') was for the covenanters to cut into each other's arm and suck the blood, the mixing of the blood rendering them 'brothers of the covenant' (see Trumbull, 'The Blood Covenant,' pp. 5 et seq., 322; W. R. Smith, 'Religion of the Semites,' pp. 296 et seq., 460 et seq.)."

2. See Genesis 9:4 and Leviticus 3:17.

Then Jesus said unto them, Verily, verily, I say unto you, Except ye eat the flesh of the Son of man, and drink his blood, ye have no life in you. Whoso eats my flesh, and drinks my blood, has eternal life; and I will raise him up at the last day (John 6:53-54).

This passage makes no sense unless you understand the concept of blood covenant. Jesus' audience on this occasion did not seem to grasp what he was driving at. Even his disciples would not understand it until the last Passover with Jesus. But we mustn't get ahead of ourselves. The cutting of the covenant with Abram is only the first step in an ongoing relationship. Later:

When Abram was ninety-nine years old, the LORD appeared to him and said, "I am God Almighty; walk before me and be blameless. I will *confirm* my covenant between me and you and will greatly increase your numbers." Abram fell face down, and God said to him, "As for me, this is my covenant with you: You will be the father of many nations. No longer will you be called Abram; your name will be Abraham, for I have made you a father of many nations. I will make you very fruitful; I will make nations of you, and kings will come from you" (Genesis 17:1-6 NIV).

The rendering, "I will confirm my covenant," is correct. The covenant was already cut. Now it was confirmed and advanced. Abram would have only one son and two grandsons, but one of those grandsons, Jacob by name, would have 12 sons. Once his name was changed to Israel, a history was begun that would indeed result in nations and kings. And this was the point where Abram's name was changed to Abraham.[1]

The original covenant with Abram appeared to be an unconditional grant. Now a condition is added, something of an addendum. "Walk before me, and be blameless." The word here rendered "blameless" is the Hebrew *tamiym*, which means "entire" or "complete."[2] I take God to be saying, "I am El Shaddai. Go all the way with me and I will *confirm* my covenant with you."

---

1. In Hebrew, Abraham means "father of a multitude."
2. In Greek, this would be *teleios*, also meaning whole or complete. See Matthew 5:48.

Moreover, this covenant would be perpetual:

> I will establish my covenant as an everlasting covenant between me and you and your descendants after you for the generations to come, to be your God and the God of your descendants after you. The whole land of Canaan, where you are now an alien, I will give as an everlasting possession to you and your descendants after you; and I will be their God." Then God said to Abraham, "As for you, you must *keep*[1] my covenant, you and your descendants after you for the generations to come" (vv. 7-9).

We have moved somewhat beyond the mere covenant grant to the establishing of a relationship that must be "kept"—i.e., hedged about, guarded. The relationship of Abraham and his children with God was not passive. They were expected to keep covenant with God—to be faithful to the covenant. Moreover, this covenant was not merely personal. It involved all of Abraham's family, *and his household*:

> This is My covenant, which you shall keep, between Me and you and your descendants after you: every male among you shall be circumcised. And you shall be circumcised in the flesh of your foreskin; and it shall be the sign of the covenant between Me and you. And every male among you who is eight days old shall be circumcised throughout your generations, a servant who is born in the house or who is bought with money from any foreigner, who is not of your descendants. A servant who is born in your house or who is bought with your money shall surely be circumcised; thus shall My covenant be in your flesh for an everlasting covenant. But an uncircumcised male who is not circumcised in the flesh of his foreskin, that person shall be cut off from his people; he has broken My covenant" (Genesis 17:10-14 NASB).

Even though a given servant was not a descendant of Abraham, if he was to be a part of the community that formed around

---

1. Hebrew *shamar*, "to hedge about," i.e., to guard.

Abraham's leadership, he was to be circumcised. This may be the earliest example of what is today called a "social contract." It also sheds light on the expression, "cut off from his people." If a man rejects the obligations of the covenant, he has left the social contract, the community, and loses all the rights and privileges that contract provides.

> Then God said to Abraham, "As for Sarai your wife, you shall not call her name Sarai, but Sarah shall be her name. And I will bless her, and indeed I will give you a son by her. Then I will bless her, and she shall be a mother of nations; kings of peoples shall come from her." Then Abraham fell on his face and laughed, and said in his heart, "Will a child be born to a man one hundred years old? And will Sarah, who is ninety years old, bear a child?" And Abraham said to God, "Oh that Ishmael might live before Thee!" (Genesis 17:15-18 NASB).

For Abraham to doubt God on any issue is unusual, to say the least. But there is a part of me that understands. I am merely 73, and I feel rather old to be chasing a child around. Abraham was 99. And, I think he was truly fond of Ishmael and wished the birthright for him. It was not to be:

> But God said, "No, but Sarah your wife shall bear you a son, and you shall call his name Isaac; and I will establish My covenant with him for an everlasting covenant for his descendants after him. And as for Ishmael, I have heard you; behold, I will bless him, and will make him fruitful, and will multiply him exceedingly. He shall become the father of twelve princes, and I will make him a great nation. But My covenant I will establish[1] with Isaac, whom Sarah will bear to you at this season next year." And when He finished talking with him, God went up from Abraham (vv. 19-22 NASB).

While God did not reject Ishmael or his people, *he did not establish a relationship with them*. Ishmael would be blessed, but

---

1. i.e., confirm.

the covenant would rest on Isaac.[1] God would give Ishmael and his sheiks the Arabian Peninsula, But the original land covenant would remain with the descendants of Isaac. I call this the *Abrahamic Covenant* and it forms the basis of the later *Sinai Covenant* with Israel.

Circumcision was the token of this covenant, and this sheds light on the decision of the Jerusalem conference that Gentiles need not be circumcised.[2] Not being descendants of Isaac, they were not heirs of the land anyway, and circumcision was a token "in the flesh." Not being fleshly descendants of Abraham, it was pointless for Gentiles to be circumcised. It's my impression that in the early Christian church, Jewish Christians continued to circumcise their children while Gentile Christians did not.

Later, we come to a different kind of covenant altogether—a "covenant treaty." Abraham was becoming increasingly powerful in the region, and was coming up against his neighbors, one of whom was a king named Abimelech. Sharing a border, they needed an understanding of the relationship between the two houses:

> Now it came about at that time, that Abimelech and Phicol, the commander of his army, spoke to Abraham, saying, "God is with you in all that you do; now therefore, swear to me here by God that you will not deal falsely with me, or with my offspring, or with my posterity; but according to the kindness that I have shown to you, you shall show to me, and to the land in which you have sojourned." And Abraham said, "I swear it." (Genesis 21:22-24 NASB).

But there remained an issue. Water rights were very important in that dry land, and there had been a dispute over a well between Abraham's servants and those of Abimelech. Abraham registered a complaint, and the king assured him that he had known nothing of the dispute.

> And Abraham took sheep and oxen, and gave them to Abimelech; and the two of them made a covenant. Then

---

1. "Isaac" means "laughter" in Hebrew. It seems to be a reminder that Abraham laughed when God told him he would have a son. I presume he would have been a happy child.

2. See Acts 15:1 ff.

Abraham set seven ewe lambs of the flock by themselves. And Abimelech said to Abraham, "What do these seven ewe lambs mean, which you have set by themselves?" And he said, "You shall take these seven ewe lambs from my hand in order that it may be a witness to me, that I dug this well." Therefore he called that place Beersheba; because there the two of them took an oath. So they made a covenant at Beersheba; and Abimelech and Phicol, the commander of his army, arose and returned to the land of the Philistines (vv. 27-32 NASB).

The comparison to a real estate contract suggests itself again. First, Abraham swore, which was a verbal agreement as to their border. Then consideration is given in the form of sheep and cattle. Abraham then included a token of the deal that assured ownership of the well. Thus a permanent relationship between two nations, tribes, was established by a covenant.

Yet another conflict arose between these two families, and it involved a well again. A famine had come to the region of Palestine, and Isaac had to pull up stakes and move. He went, as his father had done, to Abimelech, because God had told him not to go to Egypt:

And the LORD appeared unto him, and said, Go not down into Egypt; dwell in the land which I shall tell you of: Sojourn in this land, and I will be with you, and will bless you; for unto you, and unto your seed, I will give all these countries, and I will perform the oath which I swore unto Abraham your father (Genesis 26:2-3).

The old saying is that possession is nine tenths of the law. If Isaac abandoned the land, he might have lost title to it. But there was more in this statement:

And I will make your seed to multiply as the stars of heaven, and will give unto your seed all these countries; and in your seed shall all the nations of the earth be blessed; Because that Abraham obeyed my voice, and kept my charge, my commandments, my statutes, and my laws

174

(Genesis 26:4-5).

This last is of special interest in that there existed a *known system* of God's Law at this time. Not only that, but the covenant of Abraham was made possible by his obedience. That is not to say that his obedience gave him the land or created the covenant. His obedience made the relationship with God possible.

But there is one kind of covenant we have not yet considered, and it is older than all these. It is the marriage covenant.

16

The Oldest Covenant

*Therefore shall a man leave his father and his mother,
and shall cleave unto his wife:
and they shall be one flesh (Genesis 2:24).*

While I was wrestling with the idea of covenant, an email appeared in my inbox with an attachment. I usually don't open attachments (viruses, you know), but this one seemed safe enough. It was a long discussion of "godly government" produced by the doctrinal committee of a church that had gone through a major reorganization in recent years. They were attempting to develop a biblically-based explanation of how they were governed. As I read along, I came across a paragraph that brought several of the questions I had been wrestling with into sharp relief. Here's what the paper said about government in marriage:

> When God created Eve, a new level of government came into existence. Prior to her creation God led Adam to realize he was incomplete and needed a partner (Genesis 2:18, 20). That Eve was to be his helper indicates Adam was to be the leader (confirmed by Paul in 1 Corinthians 11:3, ". . . the head of every man is Christ, the head of woman is man, and the head of Christ is God"), not because of any inferiority on her part—she was "comparable" to him—but rather as a difference in family function. Governmental authority within the family structure was thus established by God with the creation of the first

family, prior to sin entering their world.[1]

The opening sentence seemed wrong to me. As I read through the paper, I found much emphasis on authority, both in the church and in marriage. What I didn't find was an adequate explanation of the relationship within which that authority is exercised—the marriage *covenant*. If there's one thing that's clear in the Bible, it is that marriage is a covenant; there is leadership in marriage to be sure, but that leadership is defined by the covenant.

It seemed obvious to me that what came into existence with Eve was not a new level of government, but a new covenant—that is to say, a new relationship. And if that is true, then it is worth our time to consider what God said about this relationship from the start.

The story began with a statement from God: Having concluded that it was not good for the man to be alone, he decided to make for Adam a help that was comparable to him (Genesis 2:18). God then proceeded to put Adam to sleep, removed a rib from him and used it to make a woman and he brought her to Adam.

Adam said, This is now bone of my bones, and flesh of my flesh: she shall be called Woman, because she was taken out of Man. Therefore shall a man leave his father and his mother, and shall cleave unto his wife: and they shall be one flesh. And they were both naked, the man and his wife, and were not ashamed (Genesis 2:23-25).

The paper in question argued that, since Eve was made as a helper to Adam, the man was to be the leader. The problem with this idea is that elsewhere, *God* is said to be our helper and that hardly means that man is the leader of God.[2] The rendering, "a help comparable to him," suggests rather that the woman was to be a helper to the husband comparable to the way the husband was a helper to the wife. Looking again to the Hebrew, the word for "comparable" is *neged*, literally, "a part opposite," or counterpart. The woman was to be the counterpart for man—a duplicate,

1. http://www.ucg.org/papers/governance.pdf

2. "Our soul waits for the LORD; He is our help [Heb. *Ezer*] and our shield" (Psalm 33:20 NASB).

something that fit him perfectly.

When Adam looked at the woman, he said, "This is now bone of my bones and flesh of my flesh." Nothing could have been closer. She was actually taken from his body, as every man from then on would be taken from the body of his mother. They were made of the same substance, bone and flesh. They will be called, "one flesh," even though they are two persons.

And upon the basis of Adam's statement (the word "Therefore" is operative), God concludes that a man would leave his father and mother and be joined to his wife. The old family relationship is superseded, and a new family is created. The two of them are now, in law, to be one flesh.[1]

Of more than passing interest at this point is the fact that man, male and female, was made in God's image. This is strongly suggestive of the long standing dogma that God, Father and Son, are one substance. As Adam and Eve were one flesh, so Father and Son are one Spirit. Everyone easily understands how Adam and Eve could be one, so where is the mystery in saying that God, Father and Son, are one?

The story of the first family concludes with the observation that the man and his wife were naked and "were not ashamed." It wasn't immediately clear why they might have been ashamed, so I looked up the word. The Hebrew *buwsh* literally means, "to pale," the opposite of blushing, one would think. But a secondary meaning is, "to disappoint." I dare say Adam and Eve were not disappointed in what they saw of one another.

This joining of man and woman as one flesh is the oldest and highest expression of human covenant. And out of this covenant will come children who will leave the family and form new covenants, new families.

Now I had long understood that the word "covenant" is synonymous with "contract," but I had never made the connection with the Jewish marriage contract. In Judaism, marriage is not a sacrament; it is a civil contract.[2] Marriage contracts customarily

---

1. The law treats a corporation as "a body formed and authorized by law to act as a single person although constituted by one or more persons and legally endowed with various rights and duties including the capacity of succession."

2. For a explanation of ancient Jewish marriage custom, including the oldest known marriage contract, see http://www.myjewishlearning.com/lifecycle/Marriage/-AboutMarriage.

specified what the father of the groom pays for the bride, what the groom is providing to the marriage, what he will have to give the bride upon a divorce, what is to happen to the children in such an event, what property rights are involved, and anything else deemed germane to the contract. Often, the parents of the bride and groom are signatories to the contract in addition to the bride and groom.

Some Jewish sages insisted upon a marriage contract and said that to maintain a wife without a contract, or without specification of fair conditions, should be regarded as prostitution (ouch!). Others seem to say that keeping a woman without a contract makes her a concubine—perhaps the equivalent of a common-law wife.[1] The essence of the contract is an enumeration of the conditions that the husband guarantees to fulfill regarding his wife, and of financial and other guarantees. It includes payment in the event of divorce and inheritance provisions. Actually, it's not dissimilar to the prenuptial agreement frequently used in second marriages to determine inheritance, the rights of children, and the distribution of property. It's all contractual and covered by law so that any problems that might arise are forestalled.

If you enter marriage without a contract, all these situations are governed by the laws of the state. In effect, when you sign the marriage license, you agree to the implicit contract created by state law. In fact, you have a marriage contract whether you want one or not. It is a civil contract in our society that is governed by laws. Those laws determine what happens, for example, in the case of divorce. They state what is community property and how it is to be distributed, and even how custody of the children will be decided. You weren't thinking about any of these thing as you planned your wedding, so the state thought of them for you. What business is it of the state? The state carries an obligation to your children. After all, someone has to think about them.

So in signing your marriage license and ratifying it in the presence of witnesses, you actually enter a contract with provisions described by state law that affect inheritance, divorce and many other considerations. Much of state law covers the same issues found in many Jewish marriage contracts.

---

1. Concubine: a woman with whom a man cohabits without being married: as a: one having a recognized social status in a household below that of a wife. b: mistress.

It's a shame that so much of the contract is merely oral. As a minister, I stand before the bride, the groom, and a collection of witnesses and I ask: "Do you solemnly promise in the presence of God and these witnesses to faithfully. . ." and then I continue with a set of promises that they probably won't remember after the marriage ceremony is over. Most wedding couples never hear any of that; they are just waiting until they get to say "I do" and kiss one another. I never expect them to remember, so I often give them a copy of the service. It's understandable that they don't remember. They are the center of everybody's attention and they're nervous.

It is sad that so many people treat their marriage vows as words spoken in the air. They are promptly forgotten and they have little or no effect on the performance of either party in the marriage after that time. The Jewish marriage contract was written down and signed before witnesses. You have to wonder how that might change relationships if we had to do that before we got married. What if your wife was able to whip out a contract and say, "See, before we got married, you promised that you would put your dirty socks in the clothes hamper"?

Now to those who are living together without a signed marriage contract, prepared either by a lawyer or the state, there are a few things we can say. From a biblical point of view, ladies, you are at best a concubine, at worst, a prostitute.[1] Unless your state law makes you a common-law wife (i.e., a concubine) and thus grants you certain rights, you have none and you have little or no protection under the law. Neither would any children, intentional or otherwise.

Marriage, then, is a contractual arrangement; there is government within the relationship, but the relationship comes first and determines the nature of the authority in the relationship. Some marriages get in trouble because the nature of the authority in the relationship was not clear and accepted by both parties going into the covenant. Falling in love is wonderful and love is essential in a marriage, but it doesn't make a marriage without a *covenant*.

It has been argued in some quarters that the Bible doesn't specify any marriage ceremony so the marriage ceremony isn't important. It is true that there is no marriage ceremony in the Bible,

---

1. The difference lies with your intent. If the relationship is temporary, it may be fornication. If it is permanent, it is concubinage—biblically speaking.

but that is entirely irrelevant. There is a marriage *covenant* in the Bible, and it defines the difference between a wife on the one hand, and a concubine, mistress, or harlot on the other. The wedding ceremony is merely part of the covenant. It is the covenant that rules, not the ceremony.

Now what does all this have to do with "godly government"? Well, quite a lot actually, because the government of God seems always to be based on covenant. Which is to say, it is always *relational*. And the government is always determined by the covenant.

Marriage is the oldest covenant known to man. And there is a strong analogy between marriage and the covenant God made with Israel, an analogy the prophets borrowed on heavily. But remember, it is only and always an *analogy*. God was not literally "married to Israel." But he was in covenant with her which is very similar. Malachi developed this theme in his rebuke to the priests: "Have we not all one father?" he asked, "has not one God created us? why do we deal treacherously every man against his brother, by profaning the covenant of our fathers?" (Malachi 2:10). Here, we are talking about abject betrayal, and a dissolving of the covenant. Judah, God said, had broken faith with God, committed detestable things, and "has married the daughter of a strange god" (v. 11).

This seems to have been the pattern ever since Solomon introduced the practice by marrying the daughters of foreign kings and even building temples for their gods. It also becomes treachery in the family. Malachi, speaking for God cries out to the priests:

> Another thing you do: You flood the LORD's altar with tears. You weep and wail because he no longer pays attention to your offerings or accepts them with pleasure from your hands. You ask, "Why?" It is because the LORD is acting as the witness between you and the wife of your youth, because you have broken faith with her, though she is your partner, the wife of your marriage covenant. Has not the LORD made them one? In flesh and spirit they are his. And why one? Because he was seeking godly offspring. So guard yourself in your spirit, and do not break faith with the wife of your youth. "I hate divorce," says the LORD God of Israel, "and I hate a man's covering himself with violence

as well as with his garment," says the LORD Almighty. So guard yourself in your spirit, and do not break faith (Malachi 2:13-16 NIV).

This is fascinating, because it underlines the reason God hates divorce. It is because he wanted godly children brought up in godly families. Breaking covenant, whether with God, with your wife, with your husband, is treachery. Preachers are fond of comparing the Israelite covenant as a marriage to God. But we should remember that this is only a metaphor. The reason the analogy works so well is because *both relationships are covenants*.

We mustn't overlook one very important statement in this passage. "The LORD is acting as the witness between you and the wife of your youth." When we make vows in a wedding ceremony, we make promises *in the presence of God* and all those assembled. Then, we sign our marriage license, which for most is their marriage contract. Then, the witnesses to the marriage also sign. Consider the implications. We call on God as a witness to our covenant. Shall we then betray our mate and violate the covenant?

Let's be sure we understand what God was saying. It is not merely that God hates divorce because it hurts society. The problem with divorce in God's mind is that it involves the breaking of a covenant. He expects his people to be people of their word, to make vows and keep them, to be the kind of person who, having sworn even to his own hurt, stands by his word.[1]

Note the repeated use of the idea of "breaking faith" throughout. The term implies not merely making a mistake, but the violation of a sacred covenant. Treachery is not merely shooting yourself in the foot, it is the breaking apart of a contracted relationship.

Some have wondered why, in the Law of Moses, that premarital sex is not dealt with in the same way as adultery. A young couple, unmarried, get too close and have sex together. The Bible does not require that you stone them and put them to death. Rather the young man is required to marry the girl if the father permits.[2] But if a woman who is married to a man commits adultery, she may be stoned to death, along with the man.

---

1. See Psalm 15:1-4.

2. Exodus 22:16-17.

What is it that makes the difference? The act is the same. The difference is that the married woman is in covenant. Adultery is treachery, while premarital sex betrays no existing human covenant. Premarital sex is a sin, it's harmful, it is dangerous, neither the woman nor any children from the union have any protection under the law, but it does not involve the betrayal of a covenant with one's mate for life.

There are other laws that deal with the same idea, and they are deeply rooted in a culture very different from our own. It has been a custom in many societies for the family of the bride to give a sum of money or other valuables to the family of the groom as a dowry. Generally, it is a contribution to help the happy pair get off to a good start. Because of the inability of poor families to pay a dowry, the custom tended to prevent the marriage of a poor girl into a wealthy family. The opposite of this practice, which made its way from Rome to British Common Law is the "dower" where the family of the groom pays money to the family of the bride. Presumably, it would improve the lot of the girl to be married off into a better family. It appears that the custom of dower was regulated by Israelite law.

> And if a man sell his daughter to be a maidservant,[1] she shall not go out as the menservants do. If she please not her master, who has betrothed her to himself, then shall he let her be redeemed: to sell her unto a strange nation he shall have no power, seeing he has dealt deceitfully with her (Exodus 21:7-8).

In this case, the girl was being contracted as an *amah*. It is fascinating how widespread the usage of this word is. The word is found in Chinese, Portugese, Latin, Hindi, and other languages and cultures, and is commonly used even by English speaking people residing in the East. General Douglas MacArthur carried his *amah*, along with his family when he fled the Philippines during WWII. An *amah* is a maidservant, perhaps a nanny.

The context of this law in the Bible, though, suggests that although she enters the new family as an *amah*, the purpose is marriage in that he has betrothed her to be his wife or the wife of

---

1. Hebrew: *amah*.

his son. He has paid a dower for her. And even though the custom of the time might allow an indentured servant to be sold off (contracted out, as it were), that could not be done with female servants. The object of the law, then, turns out to be exactly the opposite of what it might first appear. The object is to protect the rights and safety of women in that culture at that time. He must, if the family desires, allow her to be redeemed. But the law goes further.

> And if he have betrothed her unto his son, he shall deal with her after the manner of daughters. If he take him another wife; her food, her raiment, and her duty of marriage, shall he not diminish. And if he do not these three unto her, then shall she go out free without money (vv. 9-11).

That last sentence implies that he paid a considerable sum of money to bring her into his household. If he does not fulfill his obligations to her, she can simply go home. The contract is void and the money forfeit. Note that I use the word contract here synonymously with covenant. Marriages have commonly been contracts or covenants in most societies. In this case the contract is broken because "he has dealt deceitfully with her" (v. 8). The expression for "dealt deceitfully" is *bagad*, the word we saw earlier rendered, "treacherously."

Marriage is the oldest covenant of man, and it serves to introduce us to some important ideas about governance and relationships.

17

The Social Contract

Now therefore, if you will obey my voice indeed,
and keep my covenant, then you shall be a peculiar treasure
unto me above all people (Exodus 19:5).

Scholars recognize two main categories of covenant: the covenant grant, and the covenant treaty.[1] The covenant grant is usually irrevocable. In a previous chapter, we saw two crucial examples of the covenant grant: the covenant with man after the great flood, and the covenant with Abraham. We also saw examples of covenant treaties between powerful men.

What we call "the Old Covenant" is a kind of covenant treaty, but it differs in one important aspect from those seen earlier. It applies to the relationship between God and a society. It is a *social covenant*. Even though it has been called the Old Covenant and the Mosaic Covenant, it is neither. It is the Israelite Covenant, and it only became "old" when God spoke of a future New Covenant.

The Israelite covenant resembles what today would be called a "social contract," and that resemblance may prove instructive. In the 17th and 18th centuries, philosophers were beginning to develop "social contract theory." These ideas were destined to become very important in both the American and French revolutions. A social contract was understood to be an implicit agreement within a state regarding the rights and responsibilities of the state and its citizens. All members within a society are assumed to agree to the terms of

---

1. Avery Cardinal Dulles, "The Covenant with Israel," First Things, November, 2005.

the social contract by their choice to stay within the society without violating the contract; according to the theory, such a violation would signify a problematic attempt to return to "the state of nature." [1]

The expression, "state of nature" was a synonym for anarchy. I think a true state of nature rarely existed. Man, desiring the society of other men found it easy to find at least an implicit social contract with others, especially with family. It was a kind of informal covenant. If you didn't like the terms of the deal, you could leave the society.[2]

All this calls to mind an important document in American history, the Mayflower Compact. When the Pilgrims arrived in the new world, they realized that many earlier attempts at colonization had failed because of a lack of government. The Mayflower Compact was in essence a social contract in which the settlers consented to follow the rules and regulations of the government for the sake of survival. The government, in return, would derive its power from the consent of the governed.[3]

Think about the narrow means of survival for members of the Plymouth Colony and consider what it would mean to be cut off from the social contract. Then the seriousness for any Israelite in the wilderness becomes clear. Being cut off from his people could be a matter of survival. Still more, it would mean being disinherited, cut off from inheriting the land promised to Abraham. Keep this in mind, and the various issues that arise from circumcision will become clearer.

The Mayflower Compact is a fascinating document. In case you didn't encounter it in school, here it is for your consideration:

In the name of God, Amen. We whose names are underwriten, the loyall subjects of our dread soveraigne Lord King James by the grace of God, of Great Britaine, Franc, & Ireland king, defender of the faith, &c. Haveing undertaken, for the glorie of God, and advancemente of the Christian faith and honour of our king & countrie, a voyage

1. http://en.wikipedia.org/wiki/Social_contract.

2. As did the prodigal son in Jesus' parable: Luke 15:11 ff.

3. http://en.wikipedia.org/wiki/Mayflower_compact.

to plant the first colonie in the Northerne parts of Virginia, doe by these presents solemnly & mutualy in the presence of God, and one of another, covenant & combine our selves togeather into a civill body politick, for our better ordering & preservation & furtherance of the ends aforesaid; and by vertue hearof to enacte, constitute, and frame such just & equall lawes, ordinances, Acts, constitutions, & offices, from time to time, as shall be thought most meete & convenient for the generall good of the Colonie, unto which we promise all due submission and obedience. In witnes wherof we have hereunder subscribed our names at Cap-Codd ye .11. of November, in the year of the raigne of our soveraigne Lord King James, of England, France, & Ireland ye eighteenth, and of Scotland the fiftie fourth. Ano: Dom. 1620.[1]

Notice that these gentlemen all "covenanted and combined" themselves, with a purpose in mind, into a "civil body politic." They signed a simple, one paragraph agreement for the establishing of majoritarian governance for their little group. By virtue of this, all the signatories to this covenant promised to enact laws as necessary, and to submit and obey all such laws once they were enacted by the majority.

From Cape Cod, let's take ourselves back in time, to the foot of Mount Sinai where a different sort of covenant was enacted, one that also amounted to a social contract. Some three months after leaving Egypt, the Israelites arrived at the foot of Mount Sinai, and Moses went up the mountain to speak with God. Here, God spoke to Moses and laid out the covenant and its objective:

Now therefore, if you will obey my voice indeed, and keep my covenant, then you shall be a peculiar treasure unto me above all people: for all the earth is mine: And you shall be unto me a kingdom of priests, and an holy nation (Exodus 19:5-6).

---

1. Bradford, William (1898). "Book 2, Anno 1620", Hildebrandt, Ted Bradford's History "Of Plimoth Plantation" (PDF), Boston: Wright & Potter. Retrieved from Wikipedia, November 23, 2006.

So, there is the deal.[1] It is a classic if/then statement which makes it more a covenant treaty than a covenant grant. Both sides must agree.

> And Moses came and called for the elders of the people, and laid before their faces all these words which the LORD commanded him. And all the people answered together, and said, *"All that the LORD has spoken we will do."* And Moses returned the words of the people unto the LORD (vv. 7-8).

So the contract is proposed and accepted. It is even simpler than the Mayflower Compact. But just as contracts must be signed, or at least confirmed by a handshake, this covenant also had to be formally ratified. So the next step in the process followed:

> And the LORD said unto Moses, Lo, I come unto you in a thick cloud, that the people may hear when I speak with you, and believe you for ever. And Moses told the words of the people unto the LORD. And the LORD said unto Moses, Go unto the people, and sanctify them to day and to morrow, and let them wash their clothes, And be ready against the third day: for the third day the LORD will come down in the sight of all the people upon mount Sinai (vv. 9-11).

Just as in a real estate transaction, the parties to the contract must be physically present, so it was necessary for the people to meet God. To begin to enter this covenant, God came down on the mountain in front of the people, covered by a thick cloud. The people had prepared, washing all their clothes and avoiding ceremonial uncleanness in the three days before this. What happened next was terrifying to behold:

> And Moses brought forth the people out of the camp *to meet with God*; and they stood at the lower part of the mount. And mount Sinai was altogether on a smoke,

---

1. It is surprising how easily the word, "deal," substitutes for "covenant." We even speak of "cutting a deal," which is entirely consonant with the biblical idea of cutting a covenant.

because the LORD descended upon it in fire: and the smoke thereof ascended as the smoke of a furnace, and the whole mount quaked greatly. And when the voice of the trumpet sounded long, and waxed louder and louder, Moses spake, and God answered him by a voice. And the LORD came down upon mount Sinai, on the top of the mount: and the LORD called Moses up to the top of the mount; and Moses went up (vv. 17-20).[1]

Steps were taken to ensure that neither the people nor the priests came too near. There was danger from the enormous power of the place. Only Moses and Aaron were allowed to come up the mountain. Then, God spoke the Ten Commandments, the foundation of all the laws to follow. There is every indication that all the people heard him speak the Ten Commandments. But the power and emotion of the moment were, understandably, too much for them.

And all the people saw the thunderings, and the lightnings, and the noise of the trumpet, and the mountain smoking: and when the people saw it, they removed, and stood afar off. And they said unto Moses, Speak you with us, and we will hear: but let not God speak with us, lest we die. And Moses said unto the people, Fear not: for God is come to prove you, and that his fear may be before your faces, that you sin not. And the people stood afar off, and Moses drew near unto the thick darkness where God was. And the LORD said unto Moses, Thus you shalt say unto the children of Israel, You have seen that I have talked with you from heaven (Exodus 20:18-22).

This was crucial. It would not have been the same if Moses had gone up the mountain and come back and told the people what God had said. In the future, he would do that, but this is the moment of covenant, and the people had a right to have God present and to hear his voice. One can only imagine how shaken they were by this

1. As you read through this section, notice the repetition of the divine name. Every time you see the small caps "LORD" it is the name of God: Yahweh or Jehovah, in the Hebrew. It is not a covenant with a nameless God. It is a covenant with a real person.

powerful experience.

What follows is also important. They had heard *words* from God. They were not given this revelation in pictures or images, thus a strenuous prohibition against any form of image. God would speak through his Word,[1] not through images. Then God handed down judgments on issues that were current (Exodus 21, 22, 23). These have been called, "The Book of the Covenant." Maybe, but they are called *judgments*, which is suggestive that they deal with specific issues of the day, which is obvious in the content. After Moses got all this from God, he took it to the people:

> And Moses came and told the people all the words of the LORD, and all the judgments: and all the people answered with one voice, and said, All the words which the LORD has said will we do. And Moses wrote all the words of the LORD, and rose up early in the morning, and built an altar under the hill, and twelve pillars, according to the twelve tribes of Israel (Exodus 24:3-4).

Here we have a verbal agreement to a social contract. Note also that there is no oral law here. Moses wrote down *all the words* of God, and we have them right there in the book. But we must go beyond a verbal agreement. The contract must be formalized:

> And he sent young men of the children of Israel, which offered burnt offerings, and sacrificed peace offerings of oxen unto the LORD. And Moses took half of the blood, and put it in basins; and half of the blood he sprinkled on the altar. And he took the book of the covenant, and read in the audience of the people: and they said, All that the LORD has said will we do, and be obedient. And Moses took the blood, and sprinkled it on the people, and said, *Behold the blood of the covenant*, which the LORD has made with you concerning all these words (Exodus 24:5-8).

This was the moment of formalizing the covenant between God and Israel. Note that there was not only the presence of the parties, but there was a consideration in the form of the sacrifices offered to

---

1. John 1:1 ff.

God as part of the compact. Mind you, on this day, this was not the "Old Covenant," It was brand new. It wasn't the Mosaic Covenant. It was the Israelite Covenant with God—their social contract.

What was this contract? It is true that the Ten Commandments were included. It is also true that the judgments of Exodus 21-23 were included. *But these are not the covenant.* The covenant, the contract that Israel made with God was a covenant treaty. It had two parties. Here is the contract by each of the parties:

God: "Now therefore, if you will obey my voice indeed, and keep my covenant, then you shall be a peculiar treasure unto me above all people."

Israel: "All the words which the LORD has said we will do."

That is the contract, the whole contract, and nothing but the contract. And it is not to say that the contract is limited to the words between Exodus 19 and 24. God said, "if you will indeed obey my voice." That included all that he had said, and all that he ever would say.

There is one side issue that needs to be clarified before going on. There is nothing in this passage about the covenant being a marriage. Marriage is used as an *analogy* to this covenant by the prophets, but the idea is not found in Exodus. The Israelite covenant is *metaphorically* a marriage covenant, it is not a literal marriage.

Since this is not called "the Old Covenant" anywhere in this context, it is worth asking how that terminology came to be so widely accepted. It was Jeremiah who laid the groundwork, and the author of Hebrews who underlined it. Here is how Jeremiah set it up:

Behold, the days come, says the LORD, that I will make a new covenant with the house of Israel, and with the house of Judah: Not according to the covenant that I made with their fathers in the day that I took them by the hand to bring them out of the land of Egypt; which my covenant they broke, although I was an husband unto them, saith the LORD (Jeremiah 31:31-32).

Two things are introduced here. One is the marriage analogy, and the other is a future New Covenant. The author of Hebrews picks that up and takes it forward:

> For this is the covenant that I will make with the house of Israel after those days, says the LORD; I will put my laws into their mind, and write them in their hearts: and I will be to them a God, and they shall be to me a people: And they shall not teach every man his neighbor, and every man his brother, saying, Know the LORD: for all shall know me, from the least to the greatest. For I will be merciful to their unrighteousness, and their sins and their iniquities will I remember no more. In that he says, A new covenant, he has made the first old. Now that which decays and waxes old is ready to vanish away (Hebrews 8:10-13).

Only when he spoke of a new covenant, did he make the first old. Two questions often arise at this point. One, aren't the Ten Commandments the Old Covenant? Two, didn't they pass away when the Old Covenant passed? The answers to the questions are no, and no. We have already seen that the covenant was not the law, although it included laws. What we then see in Hebrews, some 30 years after the ascension of Christ, is that the Old Covenant is *ready* to pass away, not that it has already passed away. Then, there is Jesus' word on the issue which we have already reviewed at length:

> Do not think that I have come to abolish the Law or the Prophets; I have not come to abolish them but to fulfill them. I tell you the truth, until heaven and earth disappear, not the smallest letter, not the least stroke of a pen, will by any means disappear from the Law until everything is accomplished (Matthew 5:17-18 NIV).

If you are reading this, we can safely assume that heaven and earth have not disappeared and therefore no stroke of the pen, nor even a letter has passed from the Law. But what about those judgments? Aren't some of them outdated? Yes and no. Judgments do not require literal obedience. They may be dated, but they still serve as precedents in law. Judgments are obeyed in the spirit of the law. They are there to inform us in making future judgments. We are supposed to think about them, or in the words of the psalmist, to meditate on them, for they are the will of God applied to a given time and place. Technology may change, but the will of God remains.

18

Covenant and Government

*Ye know that the princes of the Gentiles exercise
dominion over them, and they that are great
exercise authority upon them. But it shall not be so
among you: but whosoever will be great among
you, let him be your minister (Matthew 20:25-26).*

Once we grasp the idea of covenant, we can understand much
better some of the things we read in the Bible about government.
Jesus didn't have a lot to say about the governance of the church.
You would have expected, given the importance that churches
came to place on governance, that he would have said more. But
what he did say is unequivocal and extremely important.

The definitive Scripture, the only time he ever really addresses
the subject, arises from an encounter with the mother of two of his
disciples. She came, asking a favor of Jesus. "Grant that these two
sons of mine may sit, one on Your right hand and the other on the
left, in Your kingdom." Apparently her sons were right there,
consenting to her request, because Jesus' answer is directed to
them:

> "You don't know what you are asking," Jesus said to them.
> "Can you drink the cup I am going to drink?" "We can,"
> they answered. Jesus said to them, "You will indeed drink
> from my cup, but to sit at my right or left is not for me to
> grant. These places belong to those for whom they have
> been prepared by my Father" (Matthew 20:22-23 NIV).

It is a startling idea that these positions in Christ's kingdom were not his to give. One has to think for a while about the implications of this statement. Those places have been prepared for someone—apparently for neither of these young men. The other disciples were unhappy about what amounted to a power play, so Jesus' felt it was time to get a couple of things straight. He gathered the men around him and explained:

You know that the rulers of the Gentiles lord it over them, and their high officials exercise authority over them. Not so with you. Instead, whoever wants to become great among you must be your servant (vv. 25-26).

Those words are Jesus' only instructions regarding governance to the disciples. Apparently, he left the details to them, but he explicitly forbade two forms of governance, those that exercised (1) lordship over and (2) authority over. Thus, hierarchy and authoritarian governance are forbidden—explicitly.

Having ruled out what is sometimes called "rule from the top down," what did Jesus allow? Rule from the bottom up? Well, hardly. That's not likely to be any better. What is left is *government by covenant*.

It is interesting how often teachers appeal to the marriage covenant to explain Christ and the Church. The comparison is valid; you run into it again and again in the pages of Scripture. Some have drawn analogies with the Jewish wedding ceremony, but there is doubt as to whether the Jewish wedding, as we know it, goes back more than a few centuries from today. There are similarities, of course, between the idea of marriage and the church, because both involve covenants.

Paul leans heavily on this analogy in his letter to the Ephesians. After several exhortations to the church, Paul comes to a key statement regarding their relationship with one another: "Submit to one another out of reverence for Christ (Ephesians 5:21 NIV). This idea of mutual submission is impossible in an authoritarian, top down, administration; and this is true of marriage or church. *Mutual submission is not possible in the absence of a covenant.* Without it, the only governance possible is master/servant. There has to be an agreement, a contract, a covenant, and then all can submit to the terms of the covenant. Paul goes on to illustrate mutual submission by an analogy between marriage and the church. Remember as you read this that Paul's object is the relationship of the church to Christ. The analogy:

> Wives, submit yourselves unto your own husbands, as unto the LORD. For the husband is the head of the wife, even as Christ is the head of the church: and he is the saviour of the body. Therefore as the church is subject unto Christ, so let the wives be to their own husbands in every thing (Ephesians 5:22-24).

If this were all there were to the covenant, it would have been a one sided deal with master and servant. But Paul was driving at something altogether different. He continued:

> Husbands, love your wives, *even as Christ also loved the church, and gave himself for it. . .* So ought men to love their wives as their own bodies. He that loveth his wife loveth himself. For no man ever yet hated his own flesh; but nourisheth and cherisheth it, even as the LORD the church: For we are members of his body, of his flesh, and of his bones. For this cause shall a man leave his father and mother, and shall be joined unto his wife, and they two shall be one flesh (Ephesians 5:25-31 KJV).

In the absence of love, submission is mere servitude. It is not even a governmental relationship, for one governs a free people. Masters dominate servants. That is not to be true of either marriage or church.

Understand that this is not being presented to us in governmental terms. It is being presented to us in the terms of a covenant. The reason I can say that is because when Paul first says "Wives submit yourselves to your husband" that is one paragraph. The next paragraph starts in verse 25 "Husbands love your wives." This is an acceptance of mutual obligations by man and wife as they go into a marriage covenant. "Love your wives like Christ loved the church and gave himself for it."

That's a mighty high standard for a man. This should be the Christian marriage contract, and it's a pity that all of us men, when we got married, didn't have to sign our names at the bottom of a contract that said, "I will love my wife as Christ loved the church."

This hearkens back to the statement Jesus made citing Genesis where it says a man shall leave his father and his mother and be joined to his wife and they two shall become one flesh. And Paul asked, "How can a man hate his own body?" Because his wife is indeed his own body, a part of who he is and what he is.

Then, by comparison, Paul said this: "For we are members of his body, of his flesh, and of his bones." We who are in covenant with Christ and his church are members of Jesus' body, his flesh, his bones. Once again the comparison is drawn between a husband and a wife, Adam and Eve, and a man and Christ. A husband and a wife are one flesh. The church is Christ's body—in the sense that Eve was Adam's body, and we are members of his body and one with him. It is the oneness of *covenant* that is described here. "For this cause shall a man leave his father and mother and shall be joined to his wife and they two shall be one flesh."

Then, Paul says something truly astonishing. "This is a great mystery: but I speak concerning Christ and the church." The whole purpose in developing this analogy is the relationship we have, as individuals and as the church, with Jesus Christ.

Perhaps the most important lesson for us to take from this is that of the relationship described. Christ is the head of the church and we are all brethren. Our administration in the church should be based on covenant, and the authority structures that exist in the church should be described *and limited* by the obligations that covenant imposes.

Now as I studied this matter, I came to the firm conclusion that the model for church government in the New Testament is the model of the covenant. Church members should not be merely consumers, they should be full participants in the covenant.

Too many marriages try to run on implicit covenants, but words spoken in the air too often don't hold. In most states, verbal agreements in contracts are not enforceable. That's why the state issues a marriage license to protect foolish women from men who want a no-obligation relationship. They want to have all the benefits and none of the responsibilities so the state requires a marriage license. But you can't do that with a church, can you?

I wouldn't have thought so, but then I read Rick Warren's book, *The Purpose Driven Church*. Saddleback Church in Orange County, California, *has a written covenant*. Now you can freely attend that church and I suspect you can be baptized there, but you cannot *join* the church without first attending a membership class. The class only takes about four hours and has to do with what the church is, what the church stands for, what their mission is, what they are trying to do in the community, what they are trying to do in the world, what their doctrinal beliefs are, and what the new member's personal relationship with the church ought to be.

At the end of the four hour class, in order to become a member of that church, you must sign a membership covenant. In the covenant, you make promises: to support the church leadership, to support the church financially, to partake of ministry in the church, to find your place in the ministry of the church by examining your own spiritual gifts and you promise to serve in whatever way you can. You make lots of promises in this covenant as you enter into a written, signed covenant with your church. [1]

I expect it is shocking to a few people that this is a requirement for membership in a church. Now you should also know that every item that they have in their covenant lists all the Scriptures that support that particular item. All this may sound somewhat demanding, but I think the premise is that it's better to have a small, tight church that really hangs together and is really sincere about what they're doing. This church started in 1978 in the pastor's living room. Fifteen years later they were considering their very first church building, just as they passed 10,000 in membership. Up to that time, they had migrated through 79 different facilities and when they finally built a church, they were meeting in a tent— holding four services a day.

Small church? Not really. At the time the book was published, they were 12,000 strong and growing. By the way, in their history, they had also spun off dozens of other churches. They planted churches in other outlying communities throughout Southern California.

So would you conclude, then, that setting high standards for membership would harm a church? Would you consider that it's too

---

1. Rick Warren, *The Purpose Driven Church*, Zondervan, 1995, 321.

much to ask people to attend a membership class? To sign a covenant with their church? To actually formalize their relationship with the Church of Jesus Christ? I wouldn't think so.

One of the things I think we have to learn, and this is crucial in understanding the governance of a church, is that *we are not called to be consumers of God's Grace*. We are not mere customers. We are called to be *full partners in covenant* and it's within that covenant and only within that covenant that we can even begin to talk about governance, how we administer our affairs, how we're going to work together, and who is going to submit to whom. We are called to be full partners in covenant with all the privileges, responsibilities, and obligations that that implies. Government does not come first. First comes covenant, then comes leadership. Covenant rules.

19

Israel and the Covenants

Behold, the days come, saith the LORD,
that I will make a new covenant
with the house of Israel,
and with the house of Judah
(Jeremiah 31:31).

Jews and Christians have been conflicted about one another for a very long time. After all, we worship the same God, and the Jewish Bible, what we call the Old Testament, forms the largest part of the Christian Bible. One would think having the same God would lead to resolution, but it seems to make things more difficult, not unlike two women claiming the same man as husband.

A dialogue has been opened in more recent years, and it seems to run deeper between Roman Catholics and Jews, probably because they have a longer history of tension between them. Centuries past, Catholics engaged in outright persecution of the Jews, and they have perhaps had further to come than some.

Since World War II, a lot of progress has been made in relations between the two religions, progress that could never happen between Judaism and Islam. The emergence of the truth about the Holocaust, and the establishment of the State of Israel, presented the Jews before the Christian world in a light that Christians could no longer ignore.[1]

For some time now, Catholic theologians have been rethinking

---

1. It posed a very different problem for the Islamic world, and the response there has been to deny the Holocaust and reject the state of Israel.

historic positions of the church. As Avery Cardinal Dulles[1] wrote: "The question of the present status of God's covenant with Israel has been extensively discussed in Jewish-Christian dialogues since the *Shoah*."[2]

Shoah is the Hebrew word for "catastrophe," and it denotes the catastrophic destruction of European Jewry during World War II. It seems strange that it took something like the Holocaust to create a turning point in Christian-Jewish dialogue. Historically, the Catholic church has never been as benign toward Jews as it has been since the mid 20th century. I suppose, when one sees the far outcome of antipathy toward a people, it has a way of focusing the mind.

The Catholics, though, have their historic doctrines to cope with, and these were still to be considered in the Second Vatican Council. The council held with Scripture that "there is one God and one Mediator between God and men, the man Christ Jesus" (1 Timothy 2:5). The council could not possibly conclude that there is salvation in any name other than that of Jesus. Cardinal Dulles continues:

> In Christ, the incarnate Son of God, revelation reaches its unsurpassable fullness. Everyone is in principle required to believe in Christ as the way, the truth, and the life, and in the Church he has established as an instrument for the salvation of all. Anyone who, being aware of this, refuses to enter the Church or remain in her cannot be saved. On the other hand, persons who "through no fault of their own do not know the gospel of Christ or His Church, yet sincerely seek God, and moved by grace, strive by their deeds to do His will as it is known to them" may attain to everlasting salvation in some manner known to God.[3]

---

1. Cardinal Dulles is an interesting fellow. Born in 1918, son of John Foster Dulles. Harvard educated, including Harvard Law, he was a naval officer during WWII serving in the Atlantic and Mediterranean theaters with the rank of Lieutenant. He entered Novitiate of the Society of Jesus (Jesuit) on August 14, 1946 and was ordained as a priest ten years later, and as Cardinal in 2001.

2. Avery Cardinal Dulles, "The Covenant with Israel," *First Things*, November, 2005.

3. Ibid.

This is a statement of more than passing interest. Up to a point, it is the fundamental belief of every Christian church. The point where things begin to diverge is the requirement of belief in the church. When Catholics speak of "the Church," they mean the Catholic church. Only the last sentence of the paragraph keeps the door open for non-Catholics, including Jews.

I might also quibble with the council's statement that the church is established by Christ as an instrument for the salvation of all. If, by that, the council means "as an instrument of preaching the Gospel," then well, but if they mean that the church is somehow a savior, I have a problem. There is only one Savior, the LORD Jesus Christ.

Still, Cardinal Dulles steps up and addresses one of the long-standing issues of the church.

> In seeking to spread the faith, Christians should remember that faith is by its very nature a free response to the word of God. Moral or physical coercion must therefore be avoided. While teaching this, the council regretfully admits that at certain times and places the faith has been propagated in ways that were not in accord with—or were even opposed to—the spirit of the gospel.

This has to be said, especially in aftermath of Islamic terrorism at the beginning of the 21st century. Some Islamists are apt to throw the Crusades in the face of Christians who condemn the practice of conversion by the sword. Cardinal Dulles continues:

> . . . as the council's dogmatic constitution on divine revelation, *Dei Verbum*, declares, God "entered into a covenant with Abraham (cf. Gen 15:18) and, through Moses, with the people of Israel." The principal purpose to which the plan of the Old Covenant was directed was to prepare for the coming both of Christ, the universal Redeemer, and of the messianic kingdom. One and the same God is the inspirer and author of both the Old and the New Testaments. He "wisely arranged that the New Testament be hidden in the Old and that the Old be made manifest by the New."

That is well said. Some Christian churches do themselves mortal harm when they decide that they no longer need (or want) the Old Testament. The Catholic church correctly concludes that the Bible is one book, not two, and that there is an overarching unity between the two. But Cardinal Dulles doesn't shy away from a central issue:

> The Second Vatican Council, while providing a solid and traditional framework for discussing Jewish-Christian relations, did not attempt to settle all questions. In particular, it left open the question whether the Old Covenant remains in force today. Are there two covenants, one for Jews and one for Christians? If so, are the two related as phases of a single developing covenant, a single saving plan of God? May Jews who embrace Christianity continue to adhere to Jewish covenantal practices?

This is a major point of discussion, particularly among Roman Catholic theologians. Cardinal Dulles thought that a place to start was with the term "Old Covenant." As he notes, the term is solidly in place, but I don't think it is well understood. How can a term be so commonly and solidly in use when it is found only once in the Bible?[1]

Mind you, a word search of the entire Bible for "Old Covenant" yields only one reference, which seems odd. That said, when you speak of "New Covenant," you imply the old, and that usage started with the Prophet Jeremiah. "The time is coming, declares the LORD, when I will make a new covenant with the house of Israel and with the house of Judah" (Jeremiah 31:31 NIV).

By speaking of a New Covenant, the LORD implies that the first covenant had become old. Thus, the term "Old Covenant" is meaningful. But an important item for understanding this broad subject lies here. The New Covenant spoken of in this place is not made with all people. It is made with the House of Israel and the House of Judah. This is where it is helpful to know the story told in the Books of Samuel and Kings.

When Israel ended their 40 years of wandering in the desert with the conquest of Canaan, for many years they lived in a true

---

1. See 2 Corinthians 3:13-16.

theocracy. God, it seems, governed with a very light hand in those years, and the government was decentralized. But the people had their ups and downs. They were told to drive out the previous inhabitants of the land because they could not be assimilated. They were also told what would ensue if they didn't. Any people they allowed to stay would become "pricks in your eyes, and thorns in your sides, and shall vex you in the land wherein ye dwell (Numbers 33:55).

This came to pass in spades. It was not unlike the situation that Israel faces today with the Palestinians. The years of the judges were years of wars and insurgencies. When they remembered God and carried on their lives in accord with the covenant, they prospered. When they forgot God, which they did regularly, they had war.

At long last they came to Samuel, perhaps the greatest of all the judges, and demanded that he give them a king like all the nations around them. It was a turning point in history. What God told Samuel at that moment bears heavily on the rest of their history. "Listen to the voice of the people in all that they say to you" God said, "for they have not rejected you, but they have rejected me, that I should not reign over them" (1 Samuel 8:6-7).

Israel would no longer be a theocracy. Now the people moved into monarchy with all the negatives that went with it—taxes, a military draft, forfeiture of land, and a host of familiar ills that go with heavily centralized government. The monarchy continued through three kings, Saul, David, and Solomon.

Solomon, wise man that he was, had a weakness when it came to women. With 700 concubines and 300 wives, he couldn't see clearly what was happening to him. Some of the wives were thoroughgoing pagans, and he yielded to the point of building temples to their gods and allowed the resultant corruption.

Because of this, God allowed the kingdom to be divided into two houses, the House of Israel under Jeroboam, with its capital ultimately in Samaria, and the House of Judah, under Rehoboam, Solomon's son ruling from Jerusalem.[1]

---

1. The expression, "house of," is used in a broad variety of applications. Here it is used to designate two political (not ethnic) entities. As in the case of Abraham, they included not only the physical descendants of this or that tribe, but everyone living within that social contract. Thus, a Benjamite living under the king of Judah was considered a part of the house of Judah—a Benjamite Jew, as it were.

The two kingdoms existed alongside one another, sometimes cooperating, sometimes at war, for some 250 years. Then Israel was carried captive into Assyria, and Judah continued alone until Nebuchadnezzar carried them away to Babylon.

With this in mind, we can return to Jeremiah's prophecy:

> "The time is coming," declares the LORD, "when I will make a new covenant *with the house of Israel and with the house of Judah.* It will not be like the covenant I made with their forefathers when I took them by the hand to lead them out of Egypt, because they broke my covenant, though I was a husband to them" declares the LORD (Jeremiah 31:31-32 NIV).

Thus is identified what is meant by "the Old Covenant." What we call the Old Covenant was itself new at one time. It was a covenant made with the forefathers of Israel at the time of the Exodus. It might have been clearer had we identified it as the Covenant of Sinai. To be accurate, it is not the Mosaic covenant, because it was made with God, not Moses.

> "This is the covenant I will make with the house of Israel after that time," declares the LORD. "I will put my law in their minds and write it on their hearts. I will be their God, and they will be my people. No longer will a man teach his neighbor, or a man his brother, saying, 'Know the LORD,' because they will all know me, from the least of them to the greatest," declares the LORD. "For I will forgive their wickedness and will remember their sins no more (vv. 33-34).

Obviously, Jeremiah was looking far into the future, to a time when the whole earth is full of the knowledge of the LORD.[1] Moreover, the *Houses* of Israel and Judah were never reunited at any time in history. That will only be possible at some future time. Thus Jeremiah's prophecy is looking at the last days of man.

Also note that the law was not to be discarded. It was now to be written, not in tables of stone, but in the hearts and minds of the

1. See also Isaiah 11:9 and context.

people—it would be internalized. Moreover, God had most assuredly not walked away from Israel permanently:

> This is what the LORD says, he who appoints the sun to shine by day, who decrees the moon and stars to shine by night, who stirs up the sea so that its waves roar—the LORD Almighty is his name: "Only if these decrees vanish from my sight," declares the LORD, "will the descendants of Israel ever cease to be a nation before me." This is what the LORD says: "Only if the heavens above can be measured and the foundations of the earth below be searched out will I reject all the descendants of Israel because of all they have done," declares the LORD (Jeremiah 31:35-37 NIV).

Fascinating. What he was saying here is that as long as the sun, moon, and stars continue, he will not be finished with the descendants of Israel, as a people. Thus, the House of Israel, alongside the House of Judah, will be a recipient of a New Covenant. Ezekiel also looks forward to a time when the House of Israel and the House of Judah will be one again.[1] Statements like these lead some to believe that the lost ten tribes of the House of Israel still exist somewhere. The British Israel movement attempts to explain far too much, but we ought to keep an open mind to the existence of an Israel that is not Judah.

The Book of Hebrews reached back to this prophecy and offered a new interpretation of it. The first point to be made was that this was no longer a matter of Moses and Aaron. We have a new Moses, a new leader, and a new High Priest—Jesus Christ.[2] If Jesus were on earth, the author noted, he would not be a priest, seeing that there were priests at that time carrying on the service in the Temple.[3] That said, something new had happened.

> But now hath he obtained a more excellent ministry, by how much also he is the mediator of a better covenant, which was established upon better promises. For if that first

---

1. See Ezekiel 37:15 ff.

2. See Hebrews 8:1 ff.

3. This is taken by many to indicate that Hebrews was written prior to 70 A.D.

covenant had been faultless, then should no place have been sought for the second. (Hebrews 8:6-7).

Moses was a mediator of the first covenant. If that covenant could have stood up over time, there would have been no need for a second covenant. But it was broken.

For finding fault with them, he saith, Behold, the days come, saith the LORD, when I will make a new covenant with the house of Israel and with the house of Judah: Not according to the covenant that I made with their fathers in the day when I took them by the hand to lead them out of the land of Egypt; because they continued not in my covenant, and I regarded them not, saith the LORD. For this is the covenant that I will make with the house of Israel after those days, saith the LORD; I will put my laws into their mind, and write them in their hearts: and I will be to them a God, and they shall be to me a people: And they shall not teach every man his neighbour, and every man his brother, saying, Know the LORD: for all shall know me, from the least to the greatest. For I will be merciful to their unrighteousness, and their sins and their iniquities will I remember no more (vv. 8-12).

It is important to remember that what we call the Old Covenant is a *national* covenant, a covenant with a people, not a person. That is a very big difference. What Christians tend to mean when they speak of the New Covenant is the personal covenant each of us has with Christ, symbolized by the bread and wine of the Last Supper. What may be surprising to many is that the New Covenant spoken of by Jeremiah and cited in Hebrews is, like the Sinai Covenant, also national, as opposed to personal.

By calling this covenant "new," he has made the first one obsolete; and what is obsolete and aging will soon disappear (Hebrews 8:13 NIV).

The structure of this passage leads me to think that he is not saying that the Old Covenant has passed away, but that it is ready to pass away. But this was written late in the first century. If it had been nailed to the cross, as some think, I would have expected the author of Hebrews to say so right there. Instead, he says the first covenant is growing old, becoming geriatric (Greek, *gerasko*). Cardinal Dulles recognizes the same thing:

> The term "covenant" is the usual translation of the Hebrew *b'rith* and the Greek *diatheke*. Scholars commonly distinguish between two types of covenant, the covenant grant and the covenant treaty. The covenant grant, modeled on the free royal decree, is an unconditional divine gift and is usually understood to be irrevocable.[1]

As an example, consider the covenant with Noah after the flood. However, Dulles thinks the Sinai Covenant is an example of a *conditional* covenant. I can see why he said that, but the passage just read from Jeremiah would not seem to agree. It is conditional and bilateral in some aspects, and Israel certainly broke covenant, but prophet after prophet had God feeling sorry for Israel in the latter days and visiting them again.

The very making of a New Covenant is suggestive that the Old Covenant actually passes when the New Covenant is made, and not before. All this is necessary in discussing the relationship between the Jews and Christians. Dulles continues:

> In Second Corinthians Paul refers to the "old covenant" as the "dispensation of death," which has "faded away." In Romans he speaks of Christ as "the end of the Law," apparently meaning its termination, its goal, or both. The Mosaic Law ceases to bind once its objective has been attained.[2]

Before we jump to any conclusions about what the Cardinal was saying here, we should bear in mind that he was presenting a discussion of what is on the one hand as opposed to the other.

---

1. Avery Cardinal Dulles, "The Covenant with Israel," *First Things*, November, 2005

2. Ibid.

All these texts, which the Church accepts as teachings of canonical scripture, have to be reconciled with others, which seem to point in a different direction. Jesus, in the Sermon on the Mount, teaches that he has come, not to abolish the Law and the prophets but to fulfill them, even though he is here embarking on a series of antitheses, in which he both supplements and corrects certain provisions in the law of Moses.[1]

I have to comment that this is only true if as part of "the law of Moses," Cardinal Dulles includes the Oral Law. This is the Jewish view, but most Christians have not seen it that way. They take "the Law of Moses" and "the Torah" to be limited to the written law. Jesus himself made that distinction when he said that not one stroke of the pen would pass from the law. Not a few biblical interpreters have stumbled over this.

In a passage of great importance, Paul asserts in Romans that the Jews have only stumbled. They are branches broken off from the good olive tree, but are capable of being grafted on again, since they are still beloved by God for the sake of their forefathers, whose gifts and call are irrevocable. This seems to imply that the Jewish people, notwithstanding their failure as a group to accept Christ as the Messiah, still remain in some sort of covenant relationship with God.[2]

I think this is true. Their very survival would seem to suggest that. Against all odds, and against great opposition, the nation of Israel was established *in the land* after World War II. It seems the most unlikely of events given the opposition of the entire Arab world, along with the indifference of nearly everyone else.[3] Continuing to examine Cardinal Dulles' article:

---

1. Ibid.

2. Ibid.

3. If you have never seen the movie *Exodus*, you owe it to yourself. It is a relatively painless way of experiencing what those days were like. Better yet, read the novel by Leon Uris on which the movie was based.

Such is the Church's respect for Holy Scripture that Catholic interpreters are not free to reject any of these New Testament passages as if one contradicted another. Systematic theology has to seek a way of reconciling and synthesizing them. The task, I believe, is feasible if we make certain necessary distinctions. Thomas Aquinas, gathering up a host of patristic and medieval authorities, distinguished the moral, ceremonial, and judicial precepts of the Old Law. Inspired in part by his reflections, I find it useful to distinguish three aspects of the Old Covenant: as law, as promise, and as interpersonal relation with God. The law, in turn, may be subdivided into the moral and the ceremonial.

Any subdivision of the law into compartments is subjective and may be misleading. The law is too often subdivided for the purpose of disposing of one part or another. Jesus, however, does set forward a distinction between written law and oral tradition.

There is a distinction between the basic law (often called the moral law) as applied to the individual on the one hand, and the administrative law applied to the community on the other. Moses' administration was still in effect when Jesus came on the scene.

If you are a Christian, and a thoughtful person, somewhere along the way, you have probably wondered about the relationship of the Jewish people to God. You know that there is no salvation in any other name than Jesus, and yet you also know that God made a covenant with Israel, and that he is not through with them yet. At least Paul certainly thought he was not. It seems the Catholic church sees it the same way.

Jesus acknowledged that Moses' administration was still in effect at the time he spoke:

Then Jesus said to the crowds and to his disciples: "The teachers of the law and the Pharisees sit in Moses' seat. So you must obey them and do everything they tell you. But do not do what they do, for they do not practice what they preach. They tie up heavy loads and put them on men's shoulders, but they themselves are not willing to lift a finger to move them. "Everything they do is done for men to see: They make their phylacteries wide and the tassels on their garments long; they love the place of honor at banquets and the most important seats in the synagogues; they love to be greeted in the marketplaces and to have men call them 'Rabbi.' But you are not to be called 'Rabbi,' for you have only one Master and you are all brothers. And do not call anyone on earth 'father,' for you have one Father, and he is in heaven. Nor are you to be called 'teacher,' for you have one Teacher, the Christ" (Matthew 23:1-10 NIV).

This is a challenging passage. Hardly anyone objects to a Christian calling his dad his Father. Nor do we mind very much referring to our seventh grade Algebra teacher as a teacher. And this leaves me wondering what Christ was talking about here. If we take it in the culture of the time, the Sages, the Scribes, the Rabbis and the Masters, had taken on themselves the mantle of Moses, the lawgiver. Their decisions, in their view, were on a par with the written law, with Moses himself. Consequently, these titles, Rabbi, Teacher, and Father, implied far more authority than God had ever given to man. It was only in that sense that Jesus was forbidding the use of the terms. Cardinal Dulles continued to make his case:

The moral law of the Old Testament is in its essentials permanent. The Decalogue, given on Sinai, is at its core a republication of the law of nature, written on all human hearts even prior to any positive divine legislation. The commandments reflecting the natural law, reaffirmed in the New Testament, are binding on Christians. But, as St. Thomas explains in the Summa (I-II.98.5), the Mosaic Law contains additions in view of the special vocation and situation of the Jewish people. The Decalogue itself, as given in Exodus and Deuteronomy, contains some ceremonial prescriptions together with the moral.

It has been said that the devil is in the details and that is certainly true of this statement: "The commandments reflecting the *natural* law, reaffirmed in the New Testament, are binding on Christians." We are left to ponder what constitutes natural law, and which commandments contain some ceremonial prescriptions.

First, it is clear that something cannot be deemed abolished merely because it is ceremonial. The Christian Passover, also called Holy Communion or the LORD's Supper by some churches, is totally ceremonial. The Cardinal explains:

> Injunctions that were over and above the natural law could be modified. The Church, adapting the law to a new stage in salvation history, was able to transfer the Sabbath observance from the last day of the week to the first and to cancel the Mosaic prohibition against images. The New Law, in its moral prescriptions, is much more than a republication of the Old. The law is broadened insofar as it is extended to all peoples and all ages, inviting them to enter into a covenant relationship with God. It is deepened insofar as Christ interiorizes and radicalizes it, enjoining attitudes and intentions that were not previously matters of legislation.

On this point, the Cardinal and I disagree. Why is it necessary for the New Testament to reaffirm the commandments? Even a cursory reading of the New Testament should make it clear that it is built on and assumes the authority of the Old Testament. It takes the written law of the Old Testament as its own statement of law. That said, there are two ways of reaffirming something. One is by stating the reaffirmation. The other is by living it.

There is this simple incontrovertible fact: Throughout the entire period when the New Testament was being written, from the mid 50s A. D. to, say, the late 70s, the entire Christian church, worldwide, in every nation and every place, continued to observe the Sabbath on the last day of the week, not the first. And they all continued in the observance of the Passover, the Days of Unleavened Bread, Pentecost, The Feast of Tabernacles, and even the Day of Atonement. All this is easily demonstrated if one just remembers when reading the New Testament, you are reading someone else's mail.[1] That said, the Cardinal's article is about the Covenant God made with Israel:

---

1. See *The Thread, God's Appointments with History*, Ronald L. Dart, (Wasteland Press, 2006).

The Pontifical Biblical Commission draws the correct conclusion: "The early Christians were conscious of being in profound continuity with the covenant plan manifested and realized by the God of Israel in the Old Testament. Israel continues to be in a covenant relationship with God, because the covenant-promise is definitive and cannot be abolished. But the early Christians were also conscious of living in a new phase of that plan, announced by the prophets and inaugurated by the blood of Jesus, 'blood of the covenant,' because it was shed out of love."

Cardinal Dulles is working his way around to the conclusion that the Jews are still in a covenant relationship with God. And, I think the author of Hebrews would agree.

For this is the covenant that I will make with the house of Israel after those days, says the LORD; I will put my laws into their mind, and write them in their hearts: and I will be to them a God, and they shall be to me a people: And they shall not teach every man his neighbour, and every man his brother, saying, Know the LORD: for all shall know me, from the least to the greatest. For I will be merciful to their unrighteousness, and their sins and their iniquities will I remember no more. In that he says, A new covenant, he hath made the first old. Now that which decayeth and waxeth old is ready to vanish away (Hebrews 8:10-13).

There is rather a large gap between vanishing, and being ready to vanish, but there is something more that is commonly overlooked. This covenant is not the same as the one Jesus made with his disciples at the Last Supper. We now find ourselves with two "New Covenants" on the table. Jesus said frankly at the Last Supper, "For this is My blood of the new covenant, which is shed for many for the remission of sins" (Matthew 26:28). This covenant is personal, as Jesus' blood was shed for each of us. But the covenant cited above is different. It was a national covenant, made with a people, not merely a person. An Israelite, cut off from the community, was cut off from the covenant as well. Abraham's covenant was personal and had to do with his descendants. The

Israelite Covenant, called here the Old Covenant, was made with and for a people living in the land of Israel and conducting their affairs as a community.

The Apostle Paul wrestled with this question in his letter to the Romans.[1] Cardinal Dulles writes of this:

> Without any pretense of giving a final solution I shall try to indicate some elements of a tenable Catholic position. Paul in this passage clearly teaches that God has not rejected His People, for His gifts and call are irrevocable. As regards election, they are unceasingly beloved for the sake of their forefathers. "If they do not persist in their unbelief," he says, the children of Israel "will be grafted in" to the olive tree from which they have been cut off. He predicts that in the end "all Israel will be saved" and that their reconciliation and full inclusion will mean life from the dead. God's continuing love and fidelity to his promises indicate that the Old Covenant is still in force in one of its most important aspects—God's gracious predilection for His Chosen People.

He notes, as I have, that the persistence of the Jews as a people in spite of all attempts to destroy them, stands as a witness that God has not finally washed his hands of them. The incredible hatred of the Jews by forces of evil in the world is also a witness. Finally, from Cardinal Dulles:

> The last word should perhaps be left to Pope Benedict XVI. In a set of interviews from the late 1990s, published under the title *God and the World,* he recognizes that there is "an enormous variety of theories" about the extent to which Judaism remains a valid way of life since the coming of Christ. As Christians, he says, we are convinced that the Old Testament is directed toward Christ, and that Christianity, instead of being a new religion, is simply the Old Testament read anew in Christ. We can be certain that Israel has a special place in God's plans and a special mission to accomplish today. The Jews "still stand within

---

1. See Romans, chapters 9-11.

the faithful covenant of God," and, we believe, "they will in the end be together with us in Christ. We are waiting for the moment when Israel, too, will say Yes to Christ," but until that moment comes all of us, Jews and Christians, "stand within the patience of God," of whose faithfulness we can rest assured.

I am not a Catholic, but I find what the Pope says on this topic quite reasonable and even reassuring. And the statement that Christianity, instead of being a new religion, is "simply the Old Testament read anew in Christ," is profound, for that is precisely what Christ was doing in the Sermon on the Mount. What he did on that occasion was a typical rabbinic interpretation of the law with one major exception. The scribes would have quoted other scribes. Jesus said, "But I say unto you." He was not abolishing the law. He was reinterpreting the law upon his own authority.

20

The Newest Covenant

*Then he took the cup, gave thanks and offered it to them, saying,
"Drink from it, all of you. This is my blood of the covenant,
which is poured out for many for the forgiveness of sins
(Matthew 26:27-28 NIV).*

Years ago, when personal computers first became available, all
you had to work with was a black screen and green letters.
Everything a person could do was limited to what could be done
with a standard keyboard that had a few extra symbols and some
function keys. That was it. If you were a person who liked games,
that posed problems—what kind of games can you play with
nothing but a keyboard, a black screen, and green text?

Some ingenious fellows created text games. In these, the
computer describes a scene, say a room with various objects in it.
You then had to type in what you wanted to do, but what you could
do was limited. You could look right, look left, move left or right,
and perhaps pick up or drop objects. Then, you could move through
this puzzle, picking up bits of information, objects that could be
used later, and creating in your mind a mental image of this
labyrinth, this maze, and achieve some objective.

I played one of these games once, and learned an important
lesson. I had solved the maze. I had been in every room, seen all
the information that was there and there was no way out. So I did
something different. I looked up. Sure enough, in one of the rooms,
there was a hole in the ceiling and I could go up. Problem was,
when I went up I entered yet another maze.

I think I must have died in that maze, but I did learn something: Two dimensional thinking is not good enough in a three dimensional world. And it occurs to me that three dimensional thinking may not be good enough to grasp all that is real.

I often encounter this same problem when studying the Bible. I go into a scene, I look around, and I think I have seen everything there, but I haven't. And just like a text game, it has been necessary to go back over it, room by room, verse by verse, and to ask myself, "What is here that, for one reason or another, I have not seen?"

All too often, our presuppositions, our preferences, influence what we see and what we don't see when we look at a passage of Scripture. For the most part, we see what we expect to see, and our expectations are all different and they are shaped by many influences. You can play a scene in front of a handful of people and you'll find almost as many different descriptions of that scene as there are people who watched it. Each observer brings himself to the scene, along with all of his experiences and prejudices.

Thus, it can be useful to go back and approach a subject with fresh eyes, to ask "What have I missed? What is here that I have not seen? What is here that I laid aside because it didn't fit with my worldview?" It may even be useful to ask, "What is not here that *ought* to be if my worldview is right?" because the "ought to" may arise from your preconceptions. You have seen what you expected to see.

I said all that to suggest that we take yet another look at the Last Supper of Jesus with his disciples. It is the first appearance in the New Testament of the word, "covenant." If you are reading the King James Version, as fewer and fewer people seem to be, you may miss it altogether. Here's the way it reads in the New International Version:

Then he took the cup, gave thanks and offered it to them, saying, "Drink from it, all of you. This is my blood of the covenant, which is poured out *for many* for the forgiveness of sins" (Matthew 26:27-28 NIV).

At this moment, Jesus offered his disciples a new covenant with him. And it was not merely offered to those present. It was for many. To enter that covenant, you must drink. You may not demur, because in drinking the wine, you are literally entering a blood covenant with Jesus Christ. We noted previously that, among the Hebrews, the drinking of blood was prohibited, so the practice shifted to eating a sacrificial meal.[1] An example is the original Passover where the blood was not drunk, but was placed on the door post and lintel, and the lamb was eaten. In the New Testament Passover, the symbolic blood *and body* of Jesus is seen in the wine and the bread. Matthew describes what happened first: "And as they were eating, Jesus took bread, and blessed it, and brake it, and gave it to the disciples, and said, Take, eat; this is my body" (Matthew 26:26).

For some reason, the idea of the body of Christ has not had the emphasis that is placed on the blood. The importance of this is discussed elsewhere,[2] but when we recall that, in ancient times, the entry into covenant took place in connection with a feast that featured the body of a sacrificial animal, we can begin to understand how Jesus' blood *and flesh* were a part of this covenant.

When we come to Luke's account of the Last Supper, we find a little more detail. For a long time this event has been at the center of what is called the "synoptic problem." There have been discussions about whether this was a pre-Passover meal, whether Jesus was using a different calendar from the Jews, and even whether the Jews had gotten the timing all wrong. Whatever the case, Luke is clear about one thing; the Last Supper was a Passover:

> And He sent Peter and John, saying, "Go and *prepare the Passover* for us, that we may eat it." And they said to Him, "Where do You want us to prepare it? . . ." And they departed and found everything just as He had told them; and they *prepared the Passover.* And when the hour had come He reclined at the table, and the apostles with Him. And He said to them, "I have earnestly desired *to eat this Passover* with you before I suffer; for I say to you, I shall never again eat it until it is fulfilled in the kingdom of God" (Luke 22:8-16 NASB).

1. See Leviticus 17:10 ff.

2. See *The Thread, God's Appointments with History,* Ronald Dart, 2006.

The expression, "earnestly desired," is very strong. The added, "before I suffer" speaks to the fact that this was an exceptional Passover. The phrase suggests that this Passover was eaten early, because Jesus would die the following day.

On every occasion where this supper is described, it is said that "this is the covenant in my blood," and the disciples took it and drank it. To any Hebrew this would have been seen as the moment when a covenant is formalized. So Jesus' disciples, then and now, are in a New Covenant with Jesus Christ. We are, in a very real sense, his blood brothers.

This is markedly different from the conventional view of the "New Covenant." On the one side, we seem to think in terms of Jesus' blood being shed for the remission of our sins and we *passively* receive the remission of our sins. In other words, he died, he shed his blood, our sins are remitted and we are the recipients of a free gift from God, all of which is true. There's only one problem and that's the word "covenant." When people start talking about being "under the New Covenant" they start going astray. Christians are supposed to be *in* the New Covenant, but the new covenant is a contract and it has obligations that go along with the receiving of the gifts that come our way.

There is another account of this outside of the Gospels. Because the Corinthian church had abused the Passover, Paul felt it necessary to set them straight:

> For I received from the LORD what I also passed on to you: The LORD Jesus, on the night he was betrayed, took bread, and when he had given thanks, he broke it and said, "This is my body, which is for you; do this in remembrance of me." In the same way, after supper he took the cup, saying, "This cup is the new covenant in my blood; do this, whenever you drink it, in remembrance of me." For whenever you eat this bread and drink this cup, you proclaim the LORD's death until he comes (1 Corinthians 11:23-26 NIV).

Paul went on to caution his readers: "A man ought to examine himself before he eats of the bread and drinks of the cup" (v. 28). Why this self examination? The answer is because a covenant must be freely and voluntarily entered into. This is not something that you may take lightly; it's not something that is merely handed to you off the shelf. You are entering into a relationship and self examination becomes very important. Why? Because a covenant is not so much about gifts or authority; it's about relationships *and obligations*.

What obligations? Well, obligations of leadership, obligations of service, obligations of submission. These are all parts of the relationship. The marriage covenant was all about promises made by the groom to the bride and the bride's father. Written promises. Signed, ratified as a contract. It was about obligations he was undertaking on her behalf. And she also had obligations— obligations to be faithful. It was a contract freely entered, but you had to consider the obligations of the contract going in.

Too many people approach the Christian faith not as members of a covenant, but as consumers or receivers of gifts. I think that's a fair statement about the way many Christian people look at their faith. They consider themselves the recipients of gifts and promises. They do not think of themselves as partners in covenant. It is only when we understand this that Jesus' caution to his disciples that they must count the cost becomes clear.

But why is it important to underline the fact that this was a "New Covenant" being entered into on that last Passover? Well, we learn from Luke that there was a bloc of men in the fledgling church who were still insisting on the Israelite Covenant, even for Gentiles. Luke calls them "certain of the sect of the Pharisees which believed" (Acts 15:5). We have already seen that they intended to impose a version of Christian Judaism on the church. If one reads Acts 15 with this in mind, it becomes much clearer. They could not have thought this way if they had not thought the Old Covenant still controlled. In the face of Jesus' words at the Last Supper, it seems inconceivable that anyone could have missed this, but they did.

There's more. In his second letter to the Corinthians, Paul addresses the stormy relationship he had with that church, and in the process, helps resolve the issue:

> You show that you are a letter from Christ, the result of our
> ministry, written not with ink but with the Spirit of the

living God, not on tablets of stone but on tablets of human hearts (2 Corinthians 3:3 NIV).

This is an allusion to the New Covenant as described in his first letter and also in the letter to the Hebrews. The law is no longer written in tables of stone, but in the fleshly tables of the heart.[1] He continues.

> Such confidence as this is ours through Christ before God. Not that we are competent in ourselves to claim anything for ourselves, but our competence comes from God. He has made us competent as *ministers of a new covenant*—not of the letter but of the Spirit; for the letter kills, but the Spirit gives life (vv. 4-6).

Paul was speaking to a major transition that had taken place. He was emphatically *not* a minister of the Sinai Covenant. Paul was not a Levite nor a son of Aaron. He was a Benjamite and had no ministerial role to play in the Sinai covenant. Nevertheless, he was a minister of the *Christian* Covenant, which he introduced wherever he went among the Gentiles. That New Covenant, therefore, was then in place.

Some of the problem arises from the Book of Hebrews which, if read with all your assumptions intact, can be confusing. This may be a good time to take another look. The author speaks of Jesus, saying, "The LORD sware and will not repent, Thou art a priest for ever after the order of Melchisedec: By so much was Jesus made a surety of a *better Covenant*" (Hebrews 7:21-22).

King James readers may stumble over the word "testament" again, but there is no ambiguity in the Greek. This is a better *covenant* we are reading about. Jesus himself could not be a priest in the Levitical system because he was not born of a Levite. When I think about that, it becomes obvious. Everything would have looked different to a Jew if Jesus had been a descendant of Aaron. He was not. He was, humanly speaking, a Jew.[2] Paul makes a point of this fact noting that the Levitical priesthood had to be a series of

---

1. Hebrews 8:10.

2. "For it is evident that our Lord sprang out of Juda; of which tribe Moses spake nothing concerning priesthood" (Hebrews 7:14).

men, because they grew old and died. But in Jesus, we have an unchanging priesthood because he lives.

In chapter eight of Hebrews, Paul begins to summarize his argument. This was not just another priest he was writing about. This one is the Son of God.

> Now of the things which we have spoken this is the sum: We have such an high priest, who is set on the right hand of the throne of the Majesty in the heavens; A minister of the sanctuary, and of the true tabernacle, which the LORD pitched, and not man. For every high priest is ordained to offer gifts and sacrifices: wherefore it is of necessity that this man have somewhat also to offer. For if he were on earth, he should not be a priest, seeing that there are priests[1] that offer gifts according to the law (Hebrews 8:1-4).

Paul had to drive this point home. Among Hebrews of this period, the priests, sons of Aaron, were the spiritual leaders of the people. Many would not have understood how a man who was not even a Levite could serve. So Paul was making the point: this is not just another priest; this is the son of God. Continuing: "But now hath he obtained a more excellent ministry, by how much also he is the mediator of a better covenant, which was established upon better promises" (v. 6).

Now, if you read this in a straightforward fashion, you can't miss it. The author says that Jesus is the mediator of a better covenant. Not that he will be, he is. Continuing:

> For if that first covenant had been faultless, then should no place have been sought for the second. For finding fault with them, he saith, Behold, the days come, saith the LORD, when I will make a new covenant with the house of Israel and with the house of Judah (vv. 7-8).

It is from this verse, a citation from Jeremiah,[2] that the idea of a New Covenant arises. But there's a problem here and the astute

---

1. Most commentators assume from this statement that this letter was written before the destruction of the temple because it speaks of priests in the present tense.

2. Jeremiah 31:31 ff.

222

reader will pick it up. This covenant says nothing about Gentiles. This covenant is made with the house of Israel and with the house of Judah. It is a New Covenant to be made with those people—a promise that, to this day, has not been fulfilled.

> Not according to the covenant that I made with their fathers in the day when I took them by the hand to lead them out of the land of Egypt; because they continued not in my covenant, and I regarded them not, saith the LORD. For this is the covenant that I will make with the house of Israel after those days, saith the LORD; I will put my laws into their mind, and write them in their hearts: and I will be to them a God, and they shall be to me a people (vv. 9-10).

Plainly, this covenant still lay in the future when Paul made this citation. Consequently, the days will come when Israel will be reconciled with Judah, both of them will be reconciled to God, and God will enter into a New Covenant with them—a new social contract. This is utterly apart from the *personal* Christian Covenant as we know it.

But then there is this: "In that he says, a new covenant, he has made the first old. Now that which decays and waxes old is ready to vanish away" (v. 13). I can hear a believing Pharisee argue, "See there, the old covenant has not passed away." And they are absolutely correct. It has not. It is still there. It is still the social contract between God and Israel, which also, by the way, requires circumcision for any son of Israel. But that's an ethnic covenant, a covenant with a people, not a covenant with individuals.

When Christians use the term "New Covenant," they usually are not talking about this new Israelite covenant. We are talking about the Christian Covenant, the one Jesus made with his disciples in the night in which he was betrayed and which we confirm in the Christian Passover—the bread and wine that symbolize the body and blood of Christ.

There are two singular moments in a Christian's life when he must make a positive response to Christ. The first is baptism, and the second is in the moment when he accepts the bread and wine.

With the emphasis placed so strongly on faith alone, I get the feeling that some people accept salvation *passively*. It is true enough that we cannot accomplish our own justification before God. No one can say it better than Paul did: "For by grace are ye saved through faith; and that not of yourselves: it is the gift of God: Not of works, lest any man should boast" (Ephesians 2:8-9).

This is also evident in the ceremony of the Day of Atonement when the entire ceremony of reconciliation is carried out by the High Priest, while the people stand doing nothing.[1] Nothing at all. Yes, they are fasting, but that is also doing nothing, not even eating.

But from the moment of reconciliation, the ongoing relationship with God is far from passive. It is not merely forgiveness of sin and opening the gates to heaven, it is a covenant one enters with the Son of God. Baptism and justification only open the door to that relationship. They do not create it nor do they sustain it.

The question is, have you personally made a covenant with God? And that's a different matter all together. It may be here that we can find an answer to a troubling paradox which keeps bothering people.

At the hour of justification, there is nothing you can do for yourself. Justification is by faith alone. There is not one law you can keep, there is not one thing you can do, to accomplish your own justification. That's all done for you by Jesus Christ. All you've got to do is, well, nothing.

But then you start reading the Bible and you find in the New Testament obligation after obligation. There are demands that God makes of us. Yes, justification is by grace, but the process doesn't stop there. It only begins there. It is very clear that there is another side to this equation that all too often has not been addressed. Jesus has offered us a covenant with him, but we have to take the step of agreeing to and accepting that covenant with all its responsibilities and obligations.

When I conduct a service of the Christian Passover, I always include a reading of selections from Jesus' discussion with the disciples on that fateful night. It is an unusually long discourse, but it is rich with meaning. Every year, we revisit this talk and reflect on what it means to us. Each time, we can discover what might be there that we have not quite grasped before. In recent years, I have

---

1. The complete ceremony is described in Leviticus 16.

personally begun to feel the increasing weight of obligations. On that night, in the room where they had gathered to share a last supper together, Jesus said:

> Verily, verily, I say unto you, He that believeth on me, the works that I do shall he do also; and greater works than these shall he do; because I go unto my Father. And whatsoever ye shall ask in my name, that will I do, that the Father may be glorified in the Son. If ye shall ask any thing in my name, I will do it (John 14:12-14).

This Scripture is the reason most Christians close their prayers with the formula, "In Jesus' name." But this is much more than a formula for prayer. It is an acknowledgment that we are in covenant with Jesus, and we bear his name. It is not entirely different from a wife who bears her husband's name, and whatever she does, she does in his name. Jesus seems to be saying that whatever you ask the Father as one who is in covenant with his Son, he will do. The comparison with marriage is apt, because marriage also is a covenant. Just as a husband has to pick up responsibilities for his wife, and the wife for the husband, so the church has to pick up responsibilities for our LORD. Each of us and all of us have obligations to Christ and for Christ. We must never allow those things to get away from us.

Let's make this clear. My wife can enter into contracts and agreements in my name because she carries my name. We can do things for one another, on behalf of one another. In other words, we are able to act together because we have a covenant relationship.

Thus, "in my name" means more than "by my authority." My wife carries my name. Even so, as one in covenant with Christ, I bear his name. I have heard prayers ended, "We ask this by the authority of your son Jesus Christ." Here's the problem. Just because you claim that authority doesn't mean you have it. And just because you pray "In Jesus' name," doesn't mean a thing if you are not *in covenant with him*. If you are in covenant, there is another side to the equation. It is unfortunate that Bibles have a break between verses 14 and 15. Here is how it should read: "If ye shall ask any thing in my name, I will do it. If ye love me, keep my commandments." It is a classic statement of two sides of a covenant. Jesus continued:

> I am the true vine, and my Father is the husbandman. Every branch in me that bears not fruit he takes away: and every branch that bears fruit, he purges it, that it may bring forth more fruit. Now ye are clean through the word which I have spoken unto you. Abide in me, and I in you. As the branch cannot bear fruit of itself, except it abide in the vine; no more can ye, except ye abide in me. I am the vine, ye are the branches: He that abides in me, and I in him, the same brings forth much fruit: for without me ye can do nothing (John 15:1-5).

These, too, are the words of blood covenant. The more we know about covenants, the more we understand this remarkable conversation. It is not a marriage, but it is so like marriage that the analogy works. "I am the vine, you are the branches" is an analogy. So it was when Adam said of Eve, "This is now bone of my bones, and flesh of my flesh: she shall be called Woman, because she was taken out of Man. Therefore shall a man leave his father and his mother, and shall cleave unto his wife: and they shall be one flesh." The imagery that Jesus develops on this fateful night is the same sort of oneness, not so much a oneness of flesh as of spirit.

Perhaps you can hear the overtones of the marriage contract in this. The old ties must all be laid aside. Jesus' teaching about this is firm. Challenged on the question of divorce, he said:

> Have ye not read, that he which made them at the beginning made them male and female, And said, For this cause shall a man leave father and mother, and shall cleave to his wife: and they twain shall be one flesh? Wherefore they are no more twain, but one flesh. What therefore God hath joined together, let not man put asunder (Matthew 19:4-6).

In other words, the man and his wife, when they come into this marriage relationship, are no longer two, they are one flesh and therefore *cannot be joined to someone else*. The old ties with your family must be severed. You must move out of your dad's house.[1] You establish your own place of residence. You've got to be separate from your old family because you are creating a new family, a new covenant, and a new relationship. You still have the responsibility for honoring your father and your mother, but the covenant that you had with them is not the same as the one you are entering into now with a new wife. So Jesus says you can't come to me unless you're willing to sever the ties with your mother, your father, your sisters, and your brothers. You are entering into a new family. And when speaking of counting the cost, Jesus went on to say: "So likewise, whosoever he be of you that forsaketh not all that he hath, he cannot be my disciple" (Luke 14:33 KJV).

C.S. Lewis has a chapter in *Mere Christianity* that helps a beginner understand all this. It is titled, "Counting the Cost." When I was baptized, the minister took me to Luke 14 and went through these very severe statements of Jesus about counting the cost of following him. At the time, I wondered why we were wasting our time. Cost? What cost? I have found the treasure hidden in a field. It is worth everything, forget about the cost, get me under the water. Nevertheless, the bottom line remained:

If any man come to me, and hate not his father, and mother, and wife, and children, and brethren, and sisters, yea, and his own life also, he cannot be my disciple. . . So likewise, whosoever he be of you that forsaketh not all that he hath, he cannot be my disciple (Luke 14:26, 33).

It is almost startling when one compares it to what was said at the marriage of Adam and Eve. "For this cause shall a man leave his father and mother and be joined to his wife." In a very real sense, we are leaving our old family and joining a new one. I didn't take this seriously enough when I was baptized, because the rationale was all wrong. It involved being willing to die for Christ, if necessary, at some time in the distant future. Actually, it is easier to say yes to facing death someday than it is to say yes when your church asks you to spend a day painting a widow's home *this week*.

---

1. And it goes without saying that, if you cannot afford to set up a separate household, you should postpone marriage until you can. Bringing a new wife into your parent's home is a recipe for trouble.

But my understanding was limited. I didn't think I had any choice. "It's God's law. I have to obey God." My attitude was, "Count the cost? There's nothing to count because there's no choice. The Kingdom of God is out here, the Pearl of Great Price, all these things, they are the treasure hidden in the field. No, no, no, I don't need to count the cost; I'll do it." And under the water I went.

The problem is that this decision is going to start costing me tonight and tomorrow, not someday. Because at the point of time when you say before God, in the presence of witnesses, "I repent of my sins, I accept Jesus Christ as my personal Savior, and as my LORD and Master" that means, "Whatever he says, I do tonight, tomorrow, the day after tomorrow, and forever."

So, are we in the New Covenant right now, or is it a someday thing? We can be, but we shouldn't answer too quickly. It is not enough to merely be a recipient of the grace of God. One has to consciously and freely make a decision to accept his covenant. This we confirm when we partake of bread and wine as symbols of Christ's body and blood. Happily, we have a chance to confirm that covenant every year at the Christian Passover. But it is a serious matter. Having entered covenant with Christ, we now must take up our cross and follow him.

Epilogue

A pair of good friends used to chide me over my messages saying that, while I answered some questions, I raised still more. I am reasonably sure that I have done that in this book. I say that without apology, because it is in the nature of things that the more you know, the more you become aware of things you don't know. Getting the questions right is always half the battle.

There came a time in my life when I ran aground on the law and had to deal with it. It was a landmark moment to realize the truth of what Jesus said, that he had not come to destroy the law, but to fulfill it. In the years that followed, I learned that literal, legalistic observance of the law was fruitless and frustrating. It just didn't work, and most of the people who tried it found themselves compromising on all manner of issues. I have noticed that those who argue against the observance of biblical law are actually arguing against the literal, legalistic approach to the law.

One of the most important things I learned was that, if a law is written in the Bible, it hasn't gone away. It is still there for our admonition and instruction. To be sure, we don't even understand some of the laws, and there are others that we can find no immediate way to apply. But if that is true, then we are probably trying to apply them too literally. We need to look for meaning, not mere words.

But I still had to deal with what Jesus said, and so I looked for a different way of understanding the Law. No passage of Scripture was more influential in this pursuit than the 119th Psalm. It tells plainly what the Law is for: it is a lamp to my feet and a light to my path. That's a far cry from shackles and chains, or even a yoke of bondage. I began to see that the Law is a description of how to live and how to love.

But a real surprise came when it dawned on me that the Law, like prophecy, is often symbolic and aphoristic. I hadn't expected that. It was only a short step from that idea to the realization that we need to be looking for the spirit and *meaning* of the law. Even the civil law, the law that depends on a civil government, has not been abolished, but the enforcement provisions are vested, not in the individual or the church, but in the civil government of the time. Adultery is still a sin, but the church does not have the authority to stone an adulterer.

I went on to learn that, while a covenant may include the provisions of a law, it is not itself the Law. When a covenant is superseded by another covenant, it is the relationship that changes, not the law. This follows naturally when one realizes he is not *under* a covenant, he is *in* a covenant. It is a lot like marriage. It carries obligations.

This last may be the most important lesson of all. I am in covenant with Christ and with everyone else who is in covenant with Christ. We have a personal covenant and an implicit social contract. John, in his first epistle declared that our fellowship with Christ implies a fellowship with one another (1 John 1:3-7). Thus, we are in covenant with our church and with all other faithful churches. Moreover, the covenant is not only with our generation:

> But you have come to Mount Zion, to the heavenly Jerusalem, the city of the living God. You have come to thousands upon thousands of angels in joyful assembly, to the church of the firstborn, whose names are written in heaven. You have come to God, the judge of all men, to the spirits of righteous men made perfect, to Jesus the mediator of a new covenant, and to the sprinkled blood that speaks a better word than the blood of Abel (Hebrews 12:22-24 NIV).

I take this to mean that we are in covenant with every Christian who has ever lived. Let us not break faith with the generations that have gone before—many of whom shed their blood for the faith. Tradition is important. True, it doesn't have the force of law, but the accumulated judgments of the saints should be treated with all the respect it deserves. Oddly, the pursuit of the letter of the Law is destructive of the covenant. The pursuit of the spirit of the Law confirms it.

These are some of the ideas I have tried to convey in this book. It is my fervent hope that the book will generate discussion and lead us a little further down the road to understanding.

Get wisdom, get understanding;
do not forget my words or swerve from them.
Do not forsake wisdom, and she will protect you;
love her, and she will watch over you.
Wisdom is supreme; therefore get wisdom.
Though it cost all you have, get understanding
(Proverbs 4:5-7 NIV).

Printed in the United States
82479LV00001BA/10-33/A